EMILY EDISON

writing by **DAVID HOPKINS**

action and artwork by **BROCK RIZY**

Published by Viper Comics
9400 N. MacArthur Blvd., Ste #124-215
Irving, TX 75063
USA

First edition: June 2006
ISBN: 0-9777883-2-6

Printed in China.

Jessie Garza president & publisher
Jim Resnowski editor-in-chief & creative director
P.J. Kryfko assistant editor
Jason M. Burns assistant publisher

VIPER COMICS   WWW.VIPERCOMICS.COM   EST. 2001

Not too long ago, tucked away in a cold corner of the Rust Belt, Saturday mornings were my Sabbath. My communion was a massive bowl of cereal. The angels who guided me through years of blissful worship were the characters on the eye candy potpourri that anyone from my generation can lovingly sum up as "Saturday Morning Cartoons."

Precious hours spent in front of the television were anything but mind-numbing. Instead, those shows served as rocket fuel for my 1400-horsepower imagination. From Mighty Mouse and Montgomery Moose to Rescue Rangers and Robotix, I got to travel from one end of the universe to the other, a stowaway on the flagships of these 30-minute-adventurers. The Bionic Six saved me from Scarab on a weekly basis. I was there when Jem and The Holograms recorded their first music video in France. Race Bannon asked me to dogsit Bandit while he went undercover in Laos. And I can't tell you how many times I helped the heroic Autobots vanquish the evil Decepticons.

Every week, by 11:55am, Pee-Wee's scooter would be blasting off from The Playhouse. And with a final look back and a goofy wave, he'd bring about the end of my Saturday morning. As my father settled in to take over the living room with bowling or football, I'd always feel a little bit sad. Not just because my cartoons were over, but also because in my introverted, childish manner, I was saying goodbye to friends. I'd seen my comrades through their battles, helped them vanquish or reconcile with their foes, and now it was time for us to part ways. And even though we were bound to reunite in just seven days, an hour can seem like a lifetime when you're a kid. 168 hours might as well be an eternity..

Looking back on those days, there's no denying that I had fallen in love with cartoons. Not in the "Jessica Rabbit is hot" way, either. More like the love a child finds when they first read The Adventures of Huckleberry Finn or 20,000 Leagues Under The Sea. I was sucked in and had become a part of all these alien worlds where everyone wore the same outfit each day. Good prevailed over the ultimate evil. And no one batted an eye when animals, plants, and kitchen appliances spoke in perfect English. Simply put, I'd fallen in love with storytelling.

At such an early age, I'd found an undying admiration for the borderless worlds within worlds that these Saturday Morning Cartoons created. It was on these tiny planets where things that didn't really exist became all too real. Somehow, a collection of unseen gods had breathed enough life into these imaginary dimensions to make them as tangible as the rocks and trees and snow in my backyard. Those shows were my childhood mythology. The forces that brought them to me were magical.

And it's that same stream of magic that David Hopkins and Brock Rizy have tapped into to bring us Emily Edison. The minute we peek into the keyhole of this young girl's life, we're hooked. A veritable Wonder Woman with a Herculean family lineage, Emily still manages to be as hopelessly teenaged as Lizzie McGuire. Yet, despite the easy comparisons, Brock and David inoculate her world with a stunningly fresh dose of imagination. And the end result is something more than unique. Emily Edison is a part of the mythology of now. She's a direct descendent of those 30-minute-adventurers that I fell in league with as a little boy. And if you've spent some time in front of a TV on a Saturday morning , then you know exactly what I'm talking about.

So pour yourself a bowl of cereal and turn the page.

It's time to fall in love with storytelling all over again.

Dave Crosland

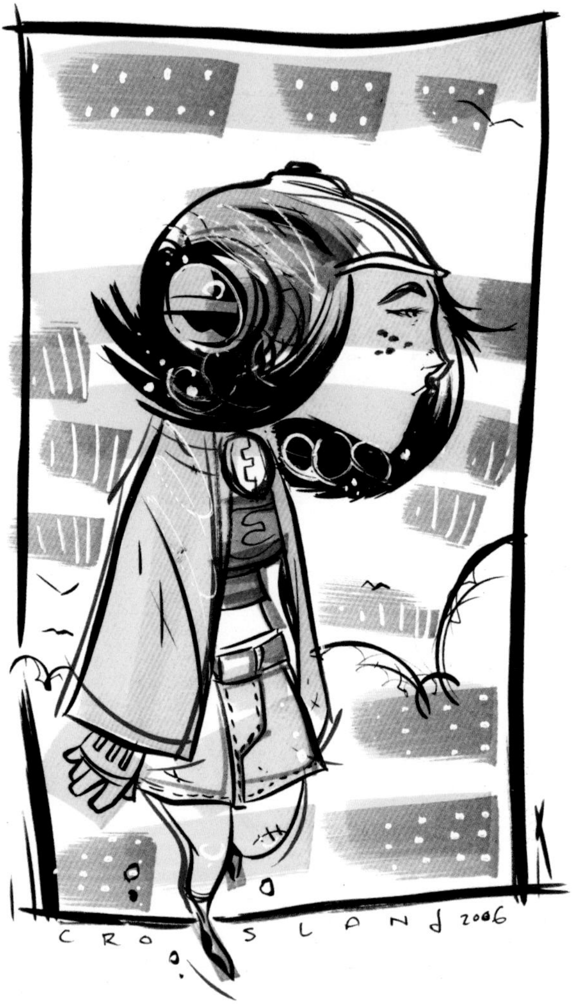
CROSLAND 2006

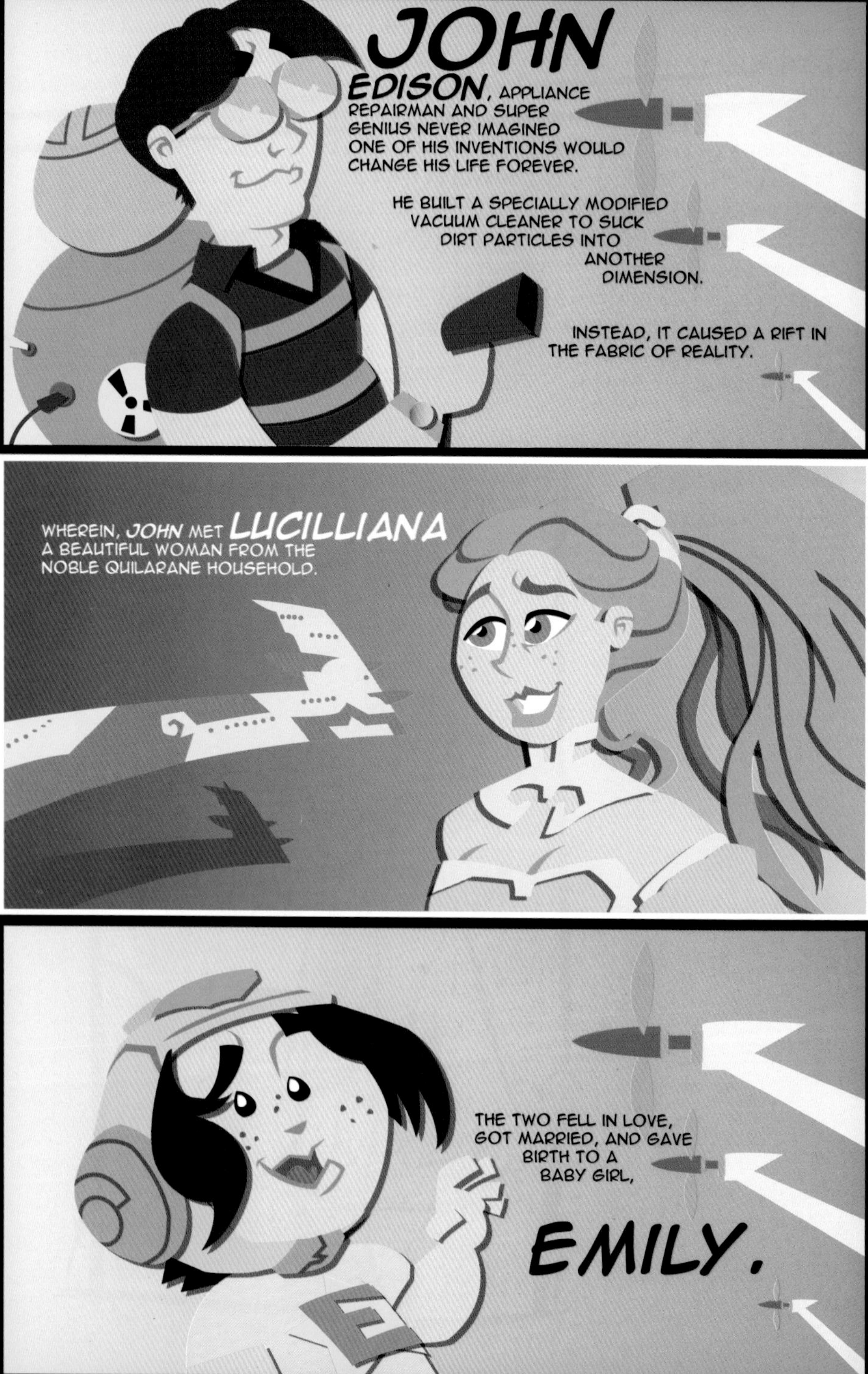
JOHN
EDISON, APPLIANCE REPAIRMAN AND SUPER GENIUS NEVER IMAGINED ONE OF HIS INVENTIONS WOULD CHANGE HIS LIFE FOREVER.
HE BUILT A SPECIALLY MODIFIED VACUUM CLEANER TO SUCK DIRT PARTICLES INTO ANOTHER DIMENSION.
INSTEAD, IT CAUSED A RIFT IN THE FABRIC OF REALITY.
WHEREIN, JOHN MET LUCILLIANA A BEAUTIFUL WOMAN FROM THE NOBLE QUILARANE HOUSEHOLD.
THE TWO FELL IN LOVE, GOT MARRIED, AND GAVE BIRTH TO A BABY GIRL,
EMILY.

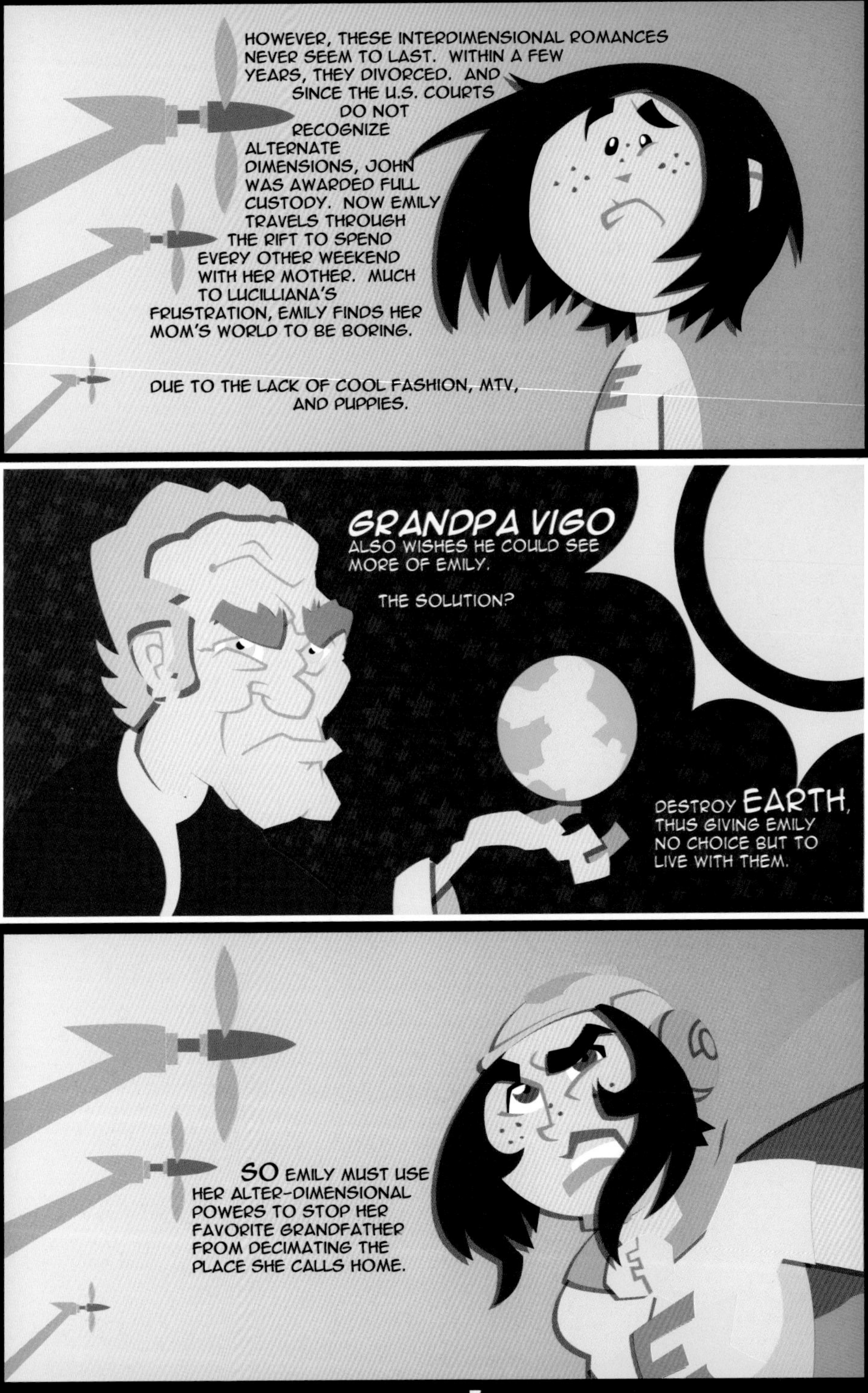
HOWEVER, THESE INTERDIMENSIONAL ROMANCES NEVER SEEM TO LAST. WITHIN A FEW YEARS, THEY DIVORCED. AND SINCE THE U.S. COURTS DO NOT RECOGNIZE ALTERNATE DIMENSIONS, JOHN WAS AWARDED FULL CUSTODY. NOW EMILY TRAVELS THROUGH THE RIFT TO SPEND EVERY OTHER WEEKEND WITH HER MOTHER. MUCH TO LUCILLIANA'S FRUSTRATION, EMILY FINDS HER MOM'S WORLD TO BE BORING.
DUE TO THE LACK OF COOL FASHION, MTV, AND PUPPIES.
GRANDPA VIGO ALSO WISHES HE COULD SEE MORE OF EMILY.
THE SOLUTION?
DESTROY EARTH, THUS GIVING EMILY NO CHOICE BUT TO LIVE WITH THEM.
SO EMILY MUST USE HER ALTER-DIMENSIONAL POWERS TO STOP HER FAVORITE GRANDFATHER FROM DECIMATING THE PLACE SHE CALLS HOME.

To Kennedy.

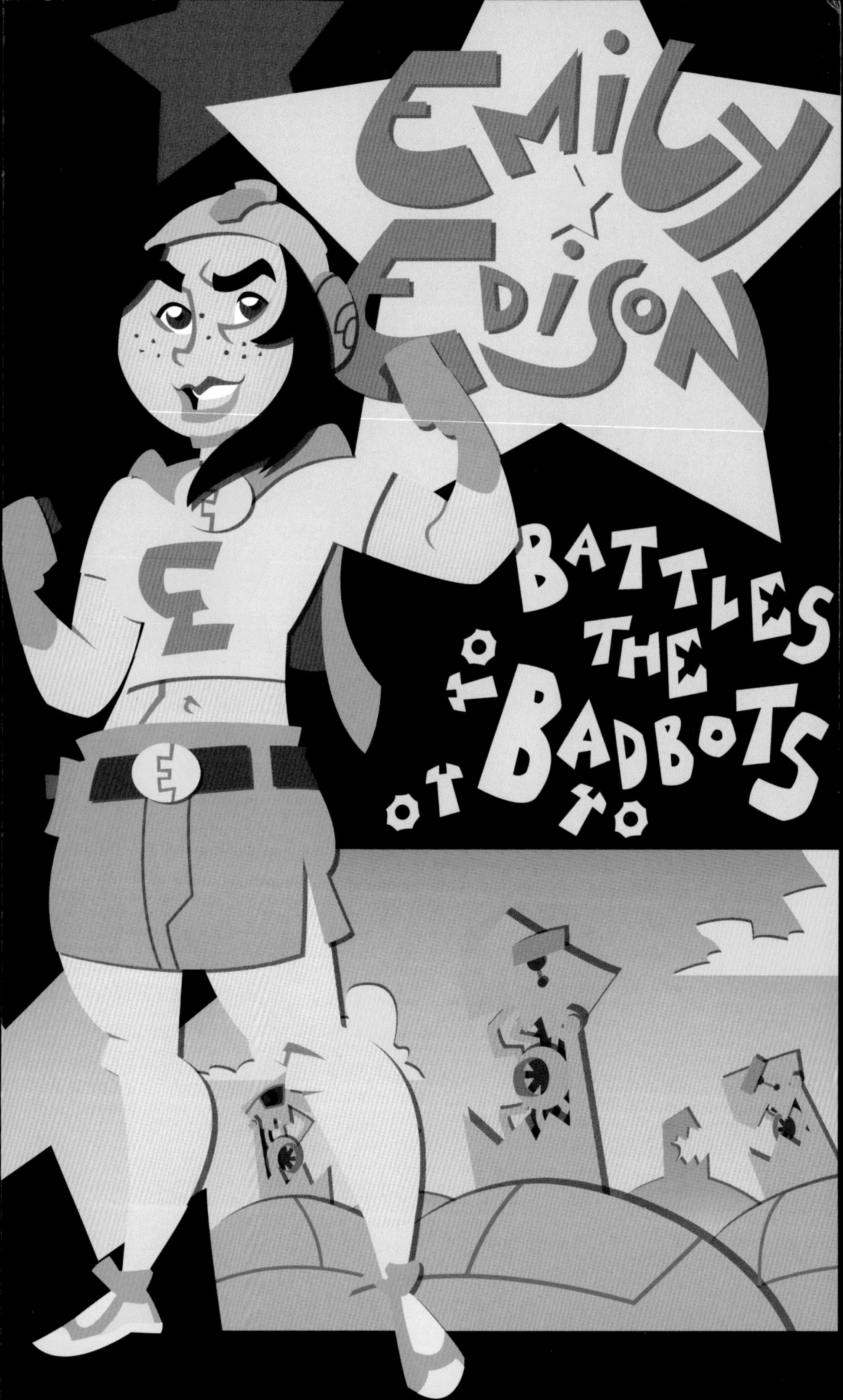
EMILY EDISON
BATTLES THE BADBOTS

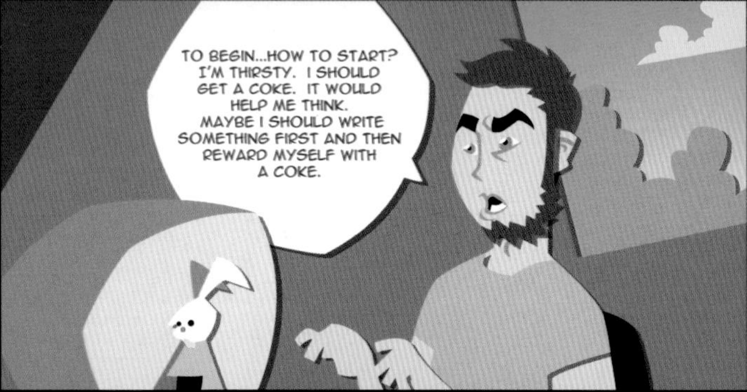
TO BEGIN...HOW TO START? I'M THIRSTY. I SHOULD GET A COKE. IT WOULD HELP ME THINK. MAYBE I SHOULD WRITE SOMETHING FIRST AND THEN REWARD MYSELF WITH A COKE.

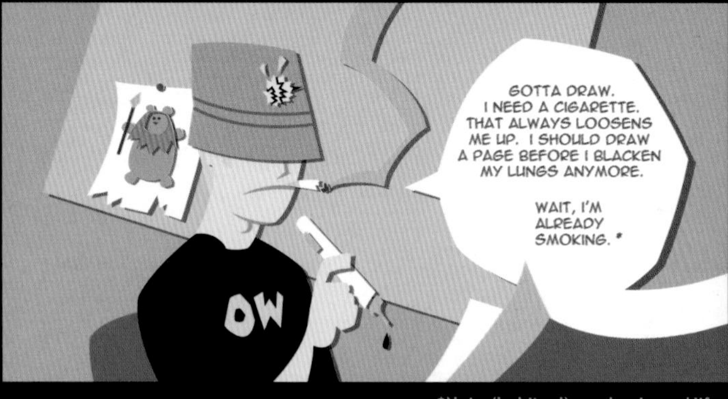
GOTTA DRAW. I NEED A CIGARETTE. THAT ALWAYS LOOSENS ME UP. I SHOULD DRAW A PAGE BEFORE I BLACKEN MY LUNGS ANYMORE.
WAIT, I'M ALREADY SMOKING. *
OW

*Not a (habitual) smoker in real life. Also, I don't really wear that hat much

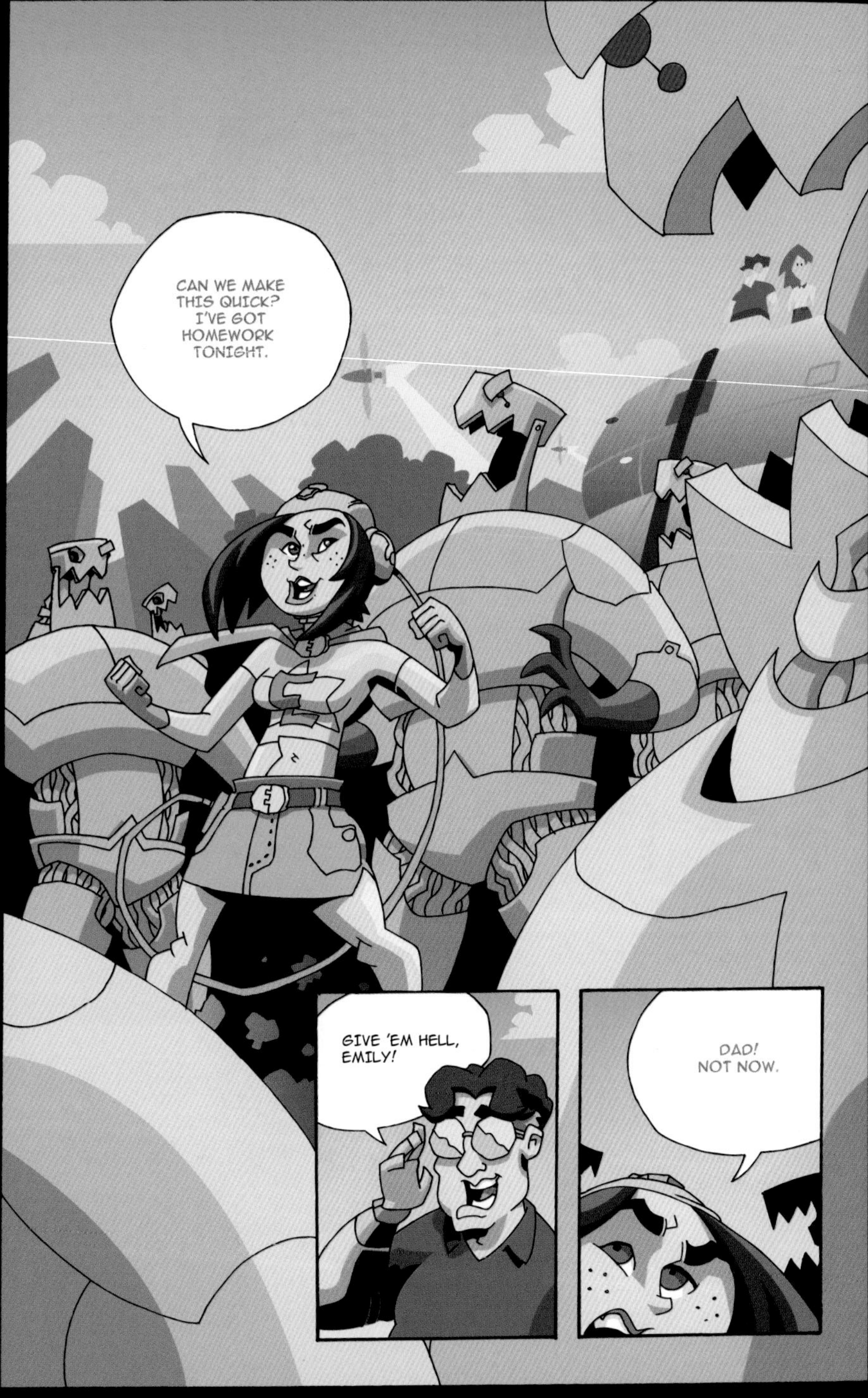
CAN WE MAKE THIS QUICK? I'VE GOT HOMEWORK TONIGHT.
GIVE 'EM HELL, EMILY!
DAD! NOT NOW.

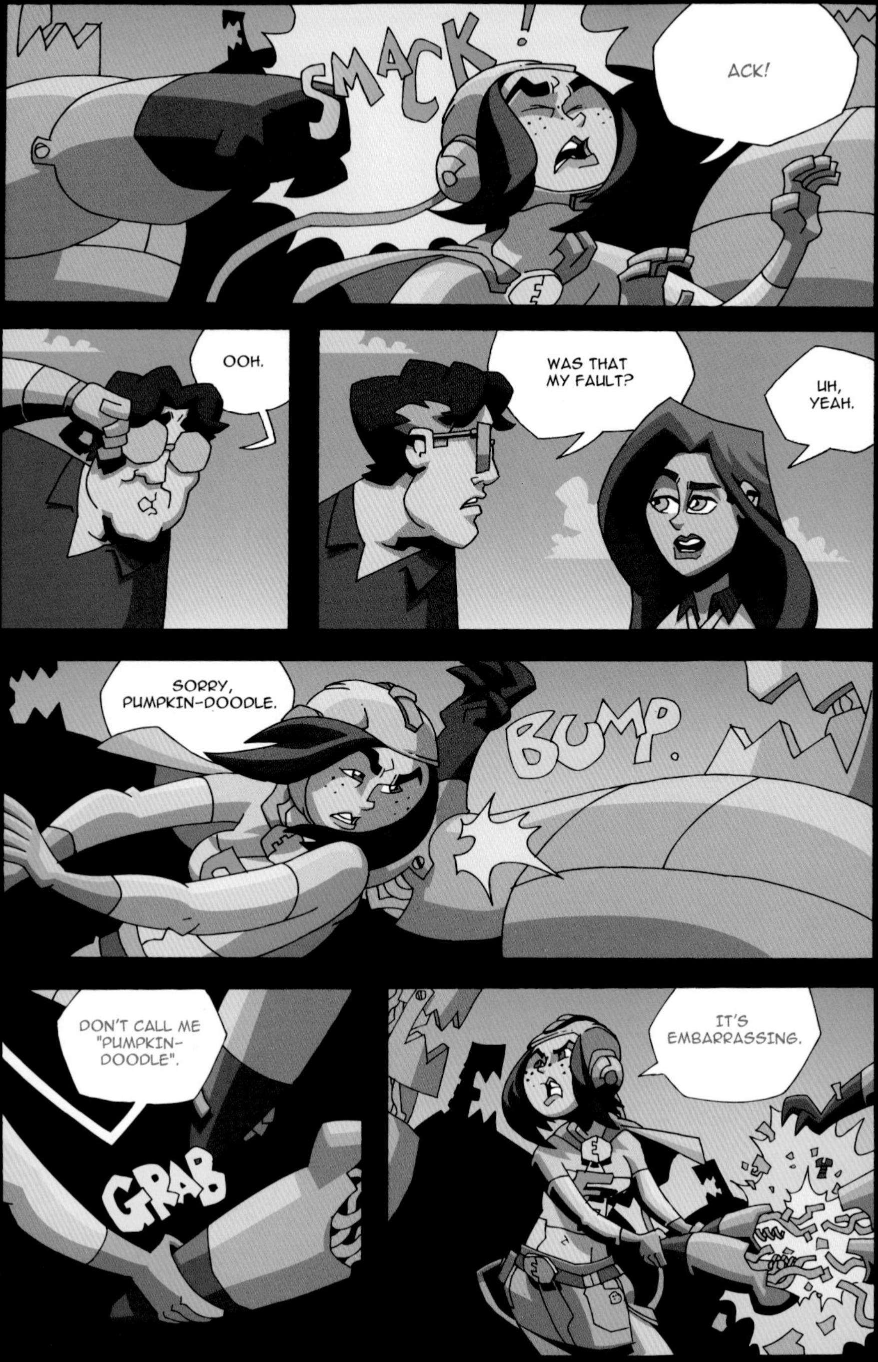
SMACK!
ACK!
OOH.
WAS THAT MY FAULT?
UH, YEAH.
SORRY, PUMPKIN-DOODLE.
BUMP.
DON'T CALL ME "PUMPKIN-DOODLE".
GRAB
IT'S EMBARRASSING.

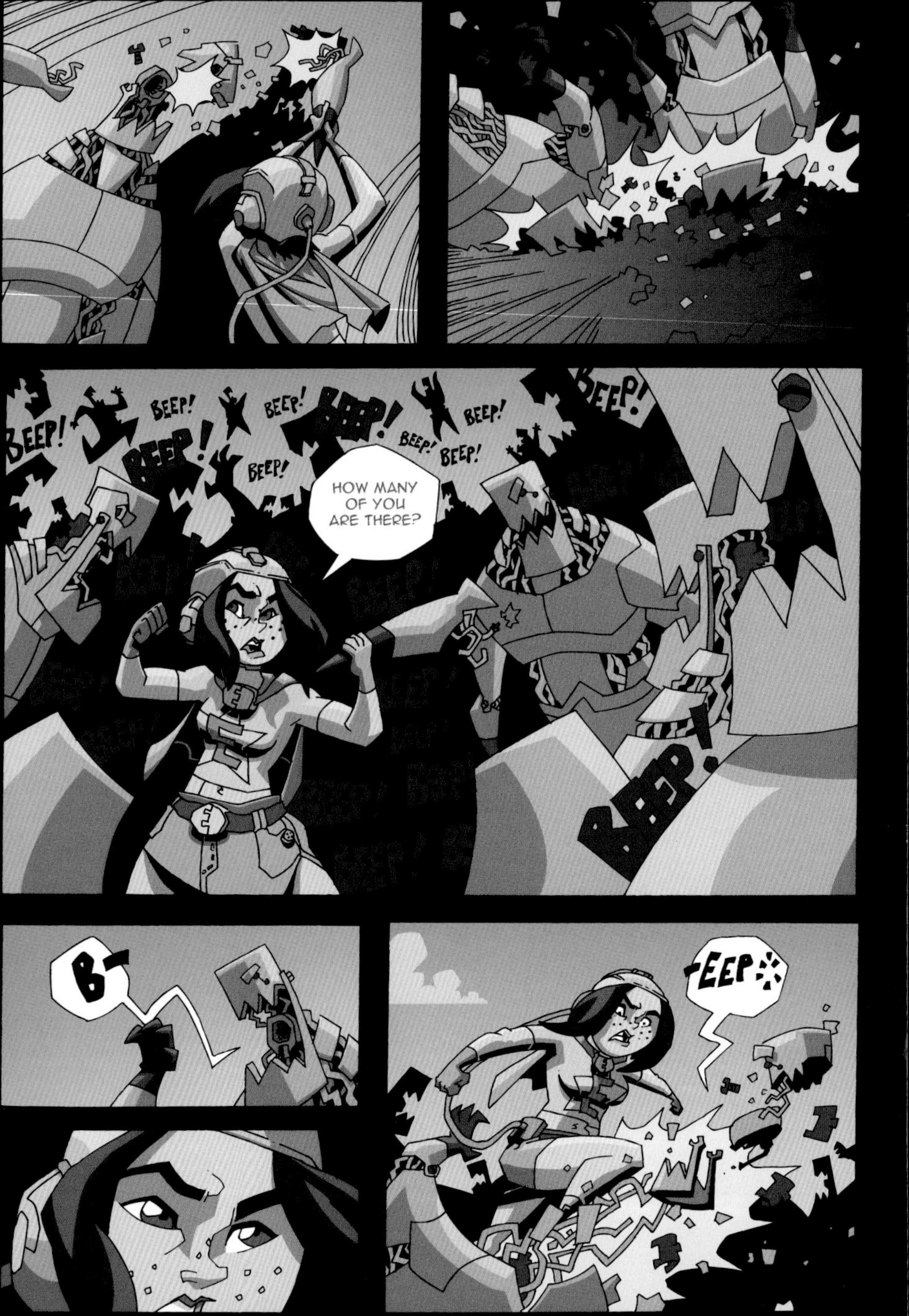
BEEP!
BEEP!
BEEP!
BEEP!
BEEP!
BEEP!
BEEP!
BEEP!
BEEP!
BEEP!
HOW MANY OF YOU ARE THERE?
BEEP!
B-
-EEP

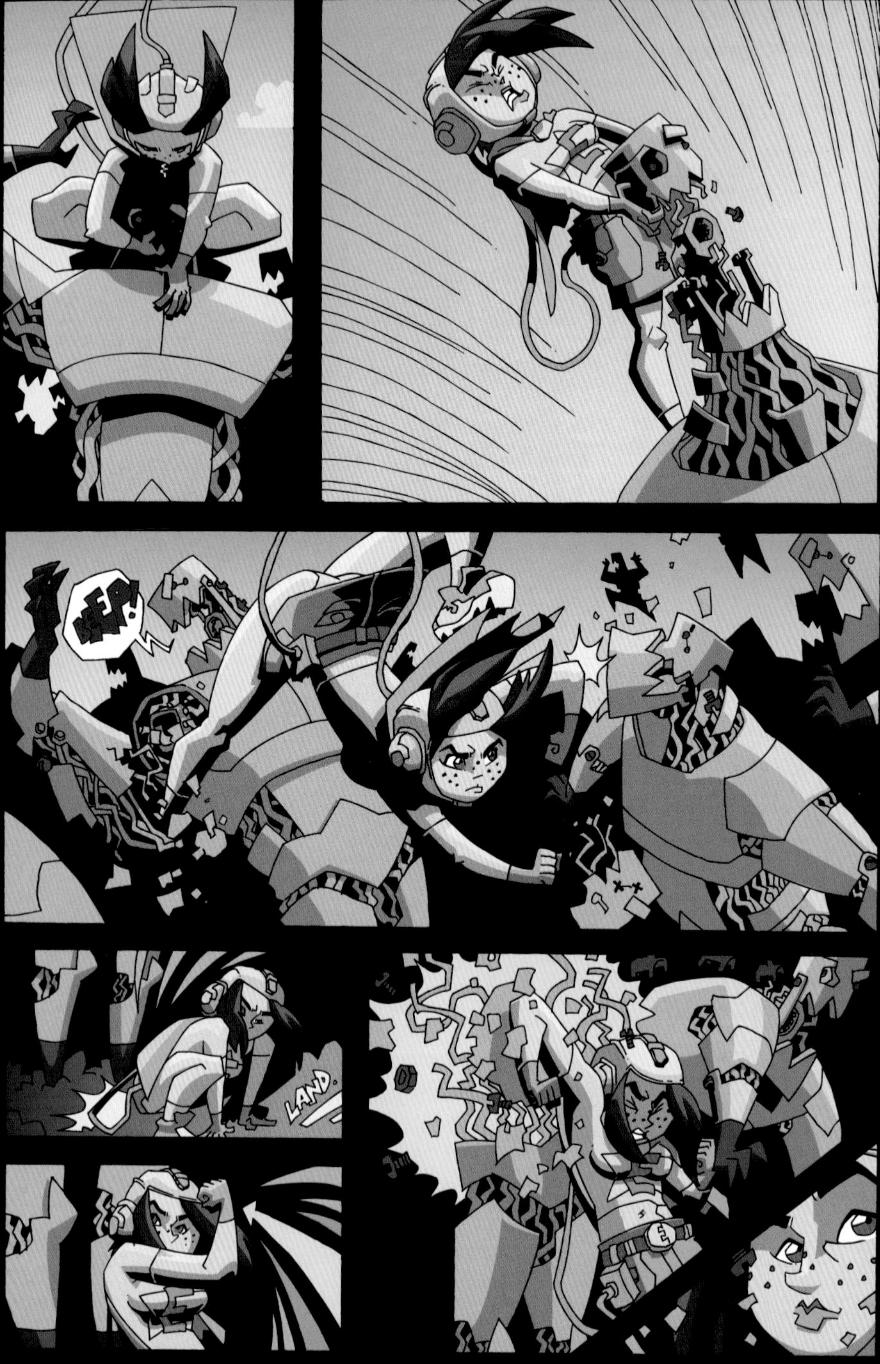
BEEP!
LAND.

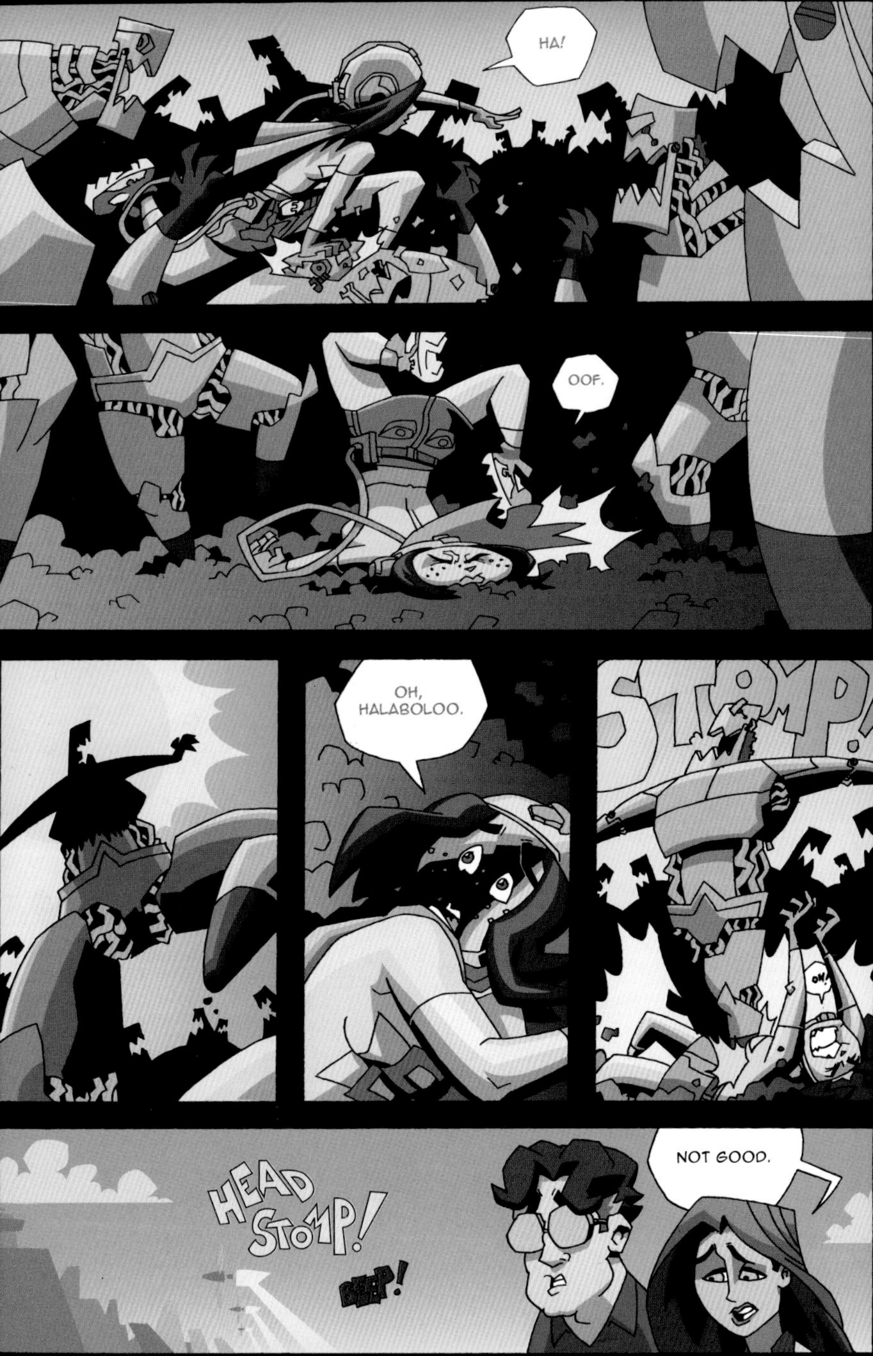
HA!
OOF.
OH, HALABOLOO.
STOMP!
OH!
HEAD STOMP!
NOT GOOD.

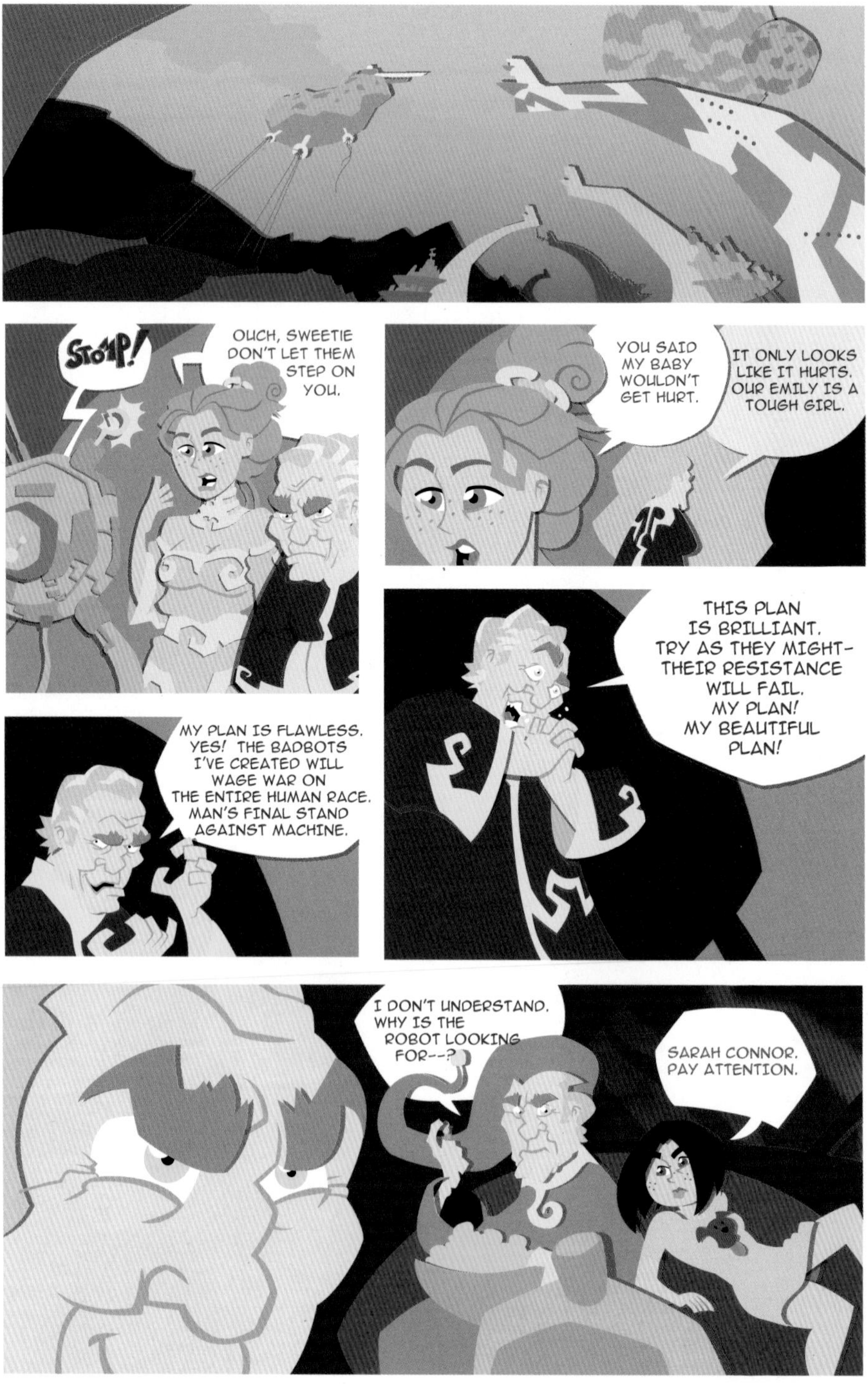
STOMP!
OUCH, SWEETIE DON'T LET THEM STEP ON YOU.
YOU SAID MY BABY WOULDN'T GET HURT.
IT ONLY LOOKS LIKE IT HURTS. OUR EMILY IS A TOUGH GIRL.
MY PLAN IS FLAWLESS. YES! THE BADBOTS I'VE CREATED WILL WAGE WAR ON THE ENTIRE HUMAN RACE. MAN'S FINAL STAND AGAINST MACHINE.
THIS PLAN IS BRILLIANT. TRY AS THEY MIGHT- THEIR RESISTANCE WILL FAIL. MY PLAN! MY BEAUTIFUL PLAN!
I DON'T UNDERSTAND. WHY IS THE ROBOT LOOKING FOR--?
SARAH CONNOR. PAY ATTENTION.

YES.

WHY AGAIN?

BECAUSE THE ROBOTS ARE WAGING WAR AGAINST THE HUMAN RACE AND THIS WOMAN WILL GIVE BIRTH TO THE LEADER OF THE FUTURE HUMAN RESISTANCE.

DUH.

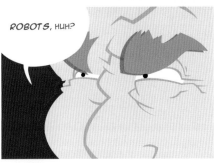

ROBOTS, HUH?

ONCE THESE ROBOTS TAKE OVER THE EARTH, SHE WILL HAVE NO CHOICE BUT TO STAY WITH US. EMILY WILL FORSAKE THOSE EARTHLINGS AND LIVE WITH HER RIGHTFUL FAMILY.

YEP, NO MORE "EVERY OTHER WEEKEND".

ARE YOU SURE SHE'S OKAY? SHE'S STILL NOT MOVING.

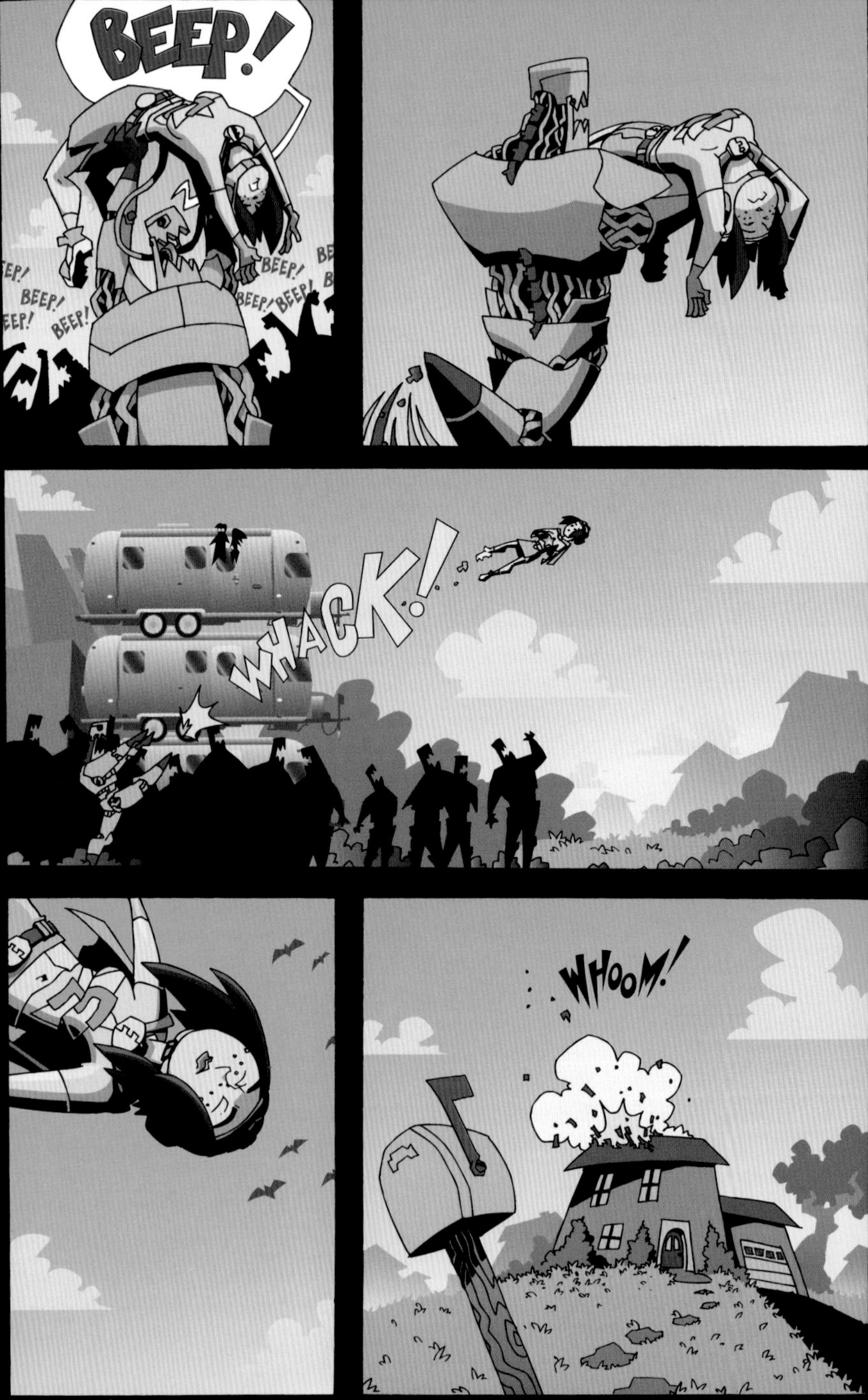
BEEP!
BEEP!
BEEP!
BEEP!
BEEP!
BEEP!
BEEP!
WHACK!
WHOOM!

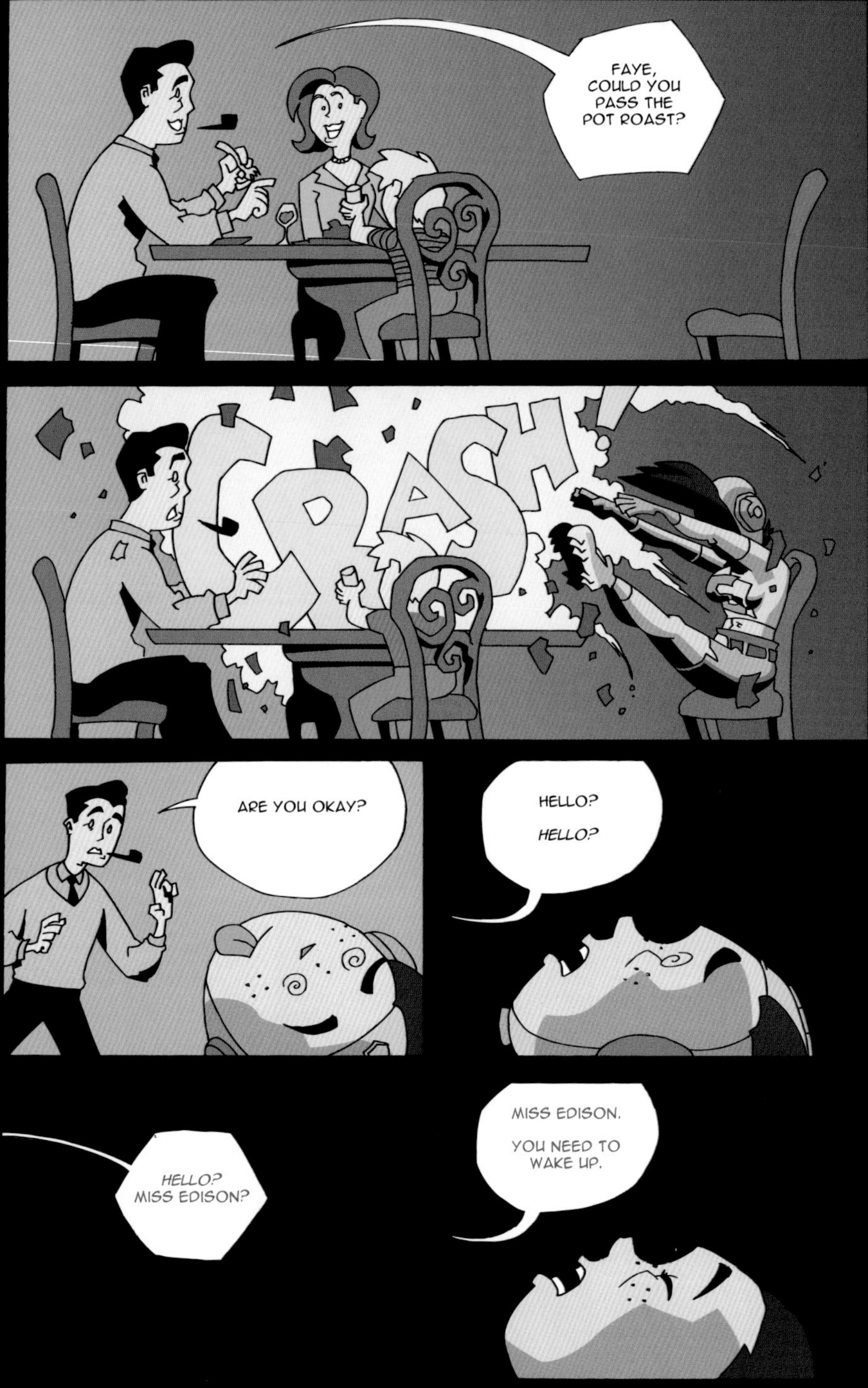
FAYE, COULD YOU PASS THE POT ROAST?
CRASH!
ARE YOU OKAY?
HELLO?
HELLO?
HELLO? MISS EDISON?
MISS EDISON.
YOU NEED TO WAKE UP.

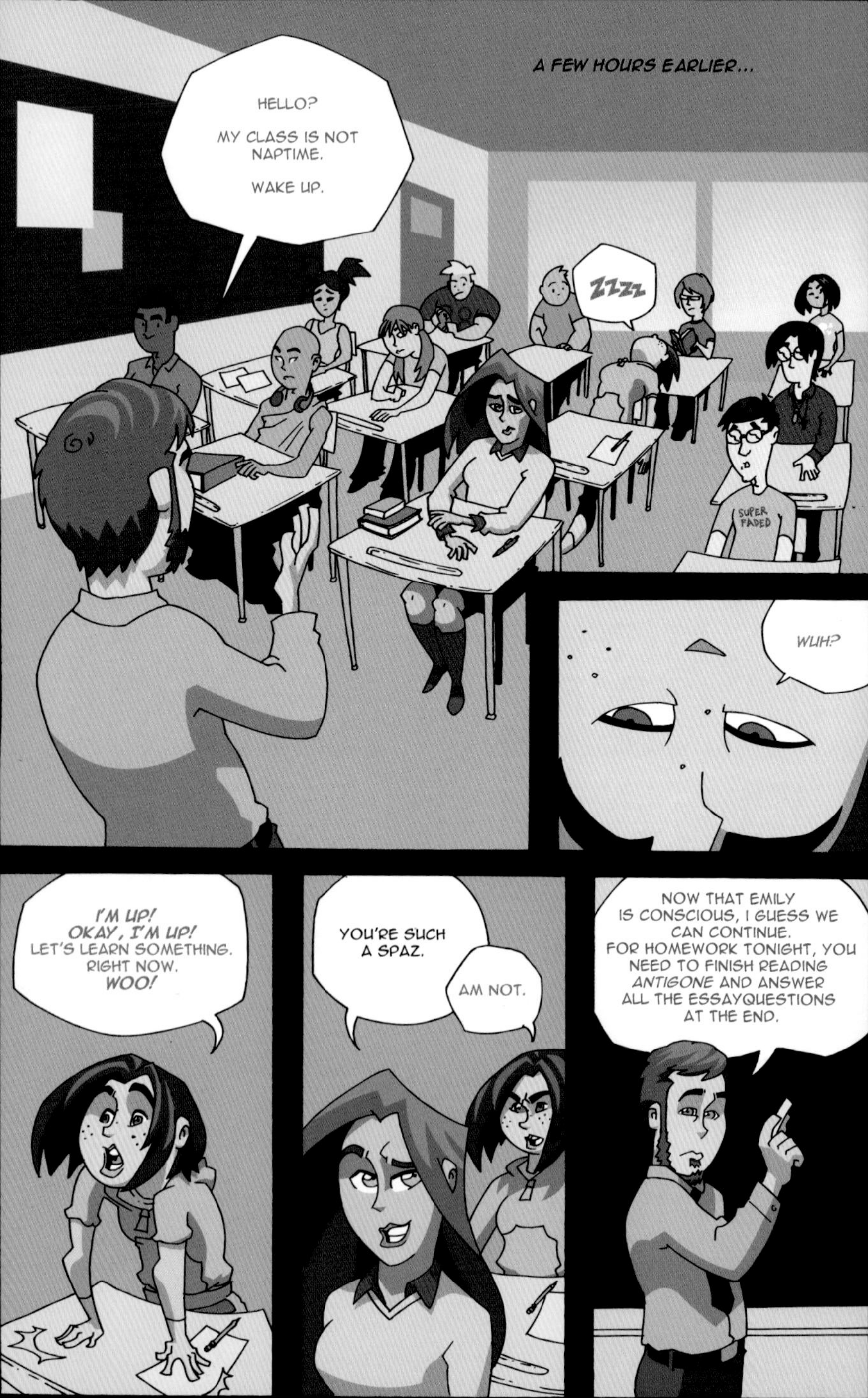
A FEW HOURS EARLIER...
HELLO? MY CLASS IS NOT NAPTIME. WAKE UP.
ZZZZ
SUPER FADED
WUH?
I'M UP! OKAY, I'M UP! LET'S LEARN SOMETHING. RIGHT NOW. WOO!
YOU'RE SUCH A SPAZ.
AM NOT.
NOW THAT EMILY IS CONSCIOUS, I GUESS WE CAN CONTINUE. FOR HOMEWORK TONIGHT, YOU NEED TO FINISH READING ANTIGONE AND ANSWER ALL THE ESSAYQUESTIONS AT THE END.

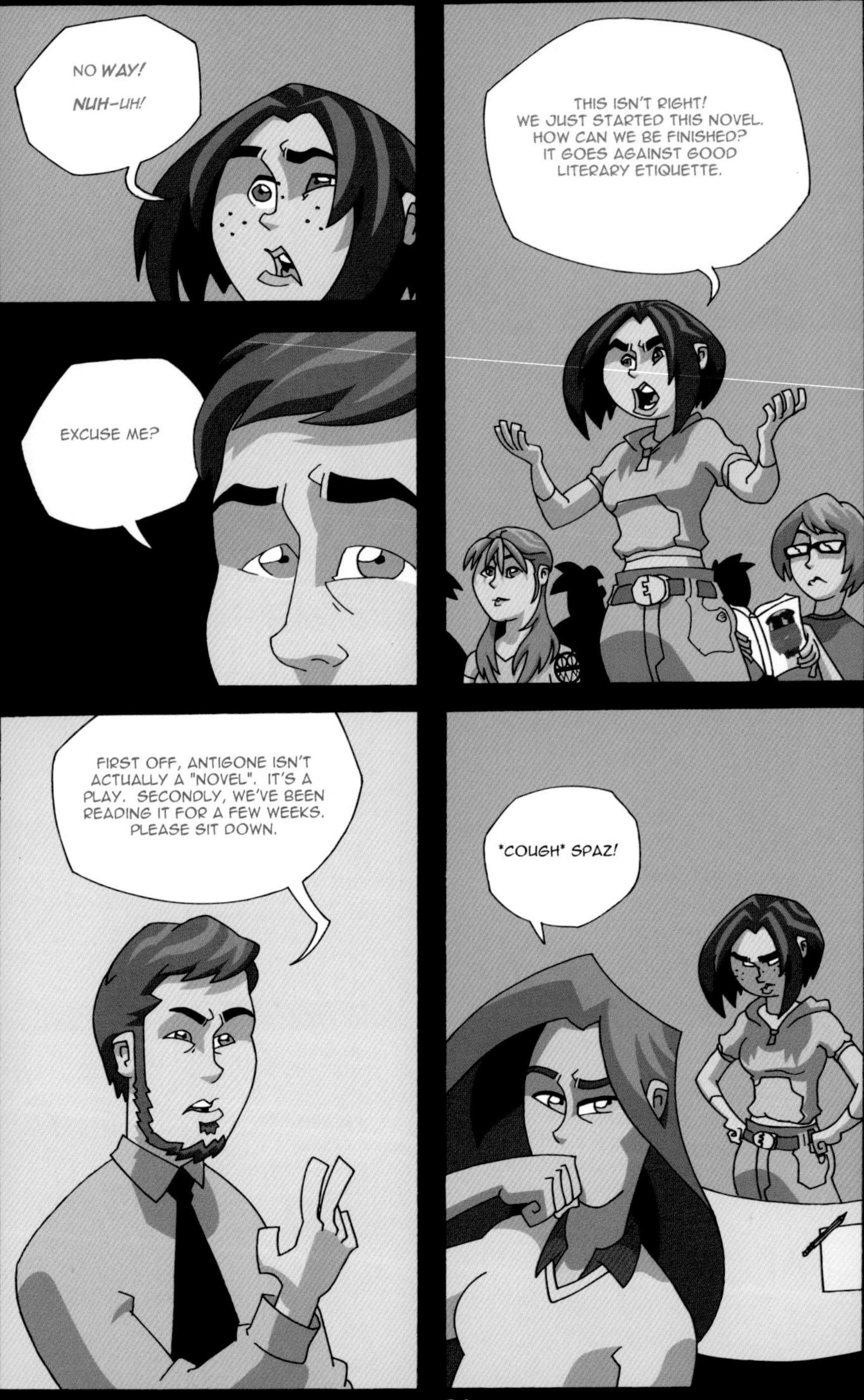
NO WAY!
NUH-UH!
THIS ISN'T RIGHT! WE JUST STARTED THIS NOVEL. HOW CAN WE BE FINISHED? IT GOES AGAINST GOOD LITERARY ETIQUETTE.
EXCUSE ME?
FIRST OFF, ANTIGONE ISN'T ACTUALLY A "NOVEL". IT'S A PLAY. SECONDLY, WE'VE BEEN READING IT FOR A FEW WEEKS. PLEASE SIT DOWN.
COUGH SPAZ!

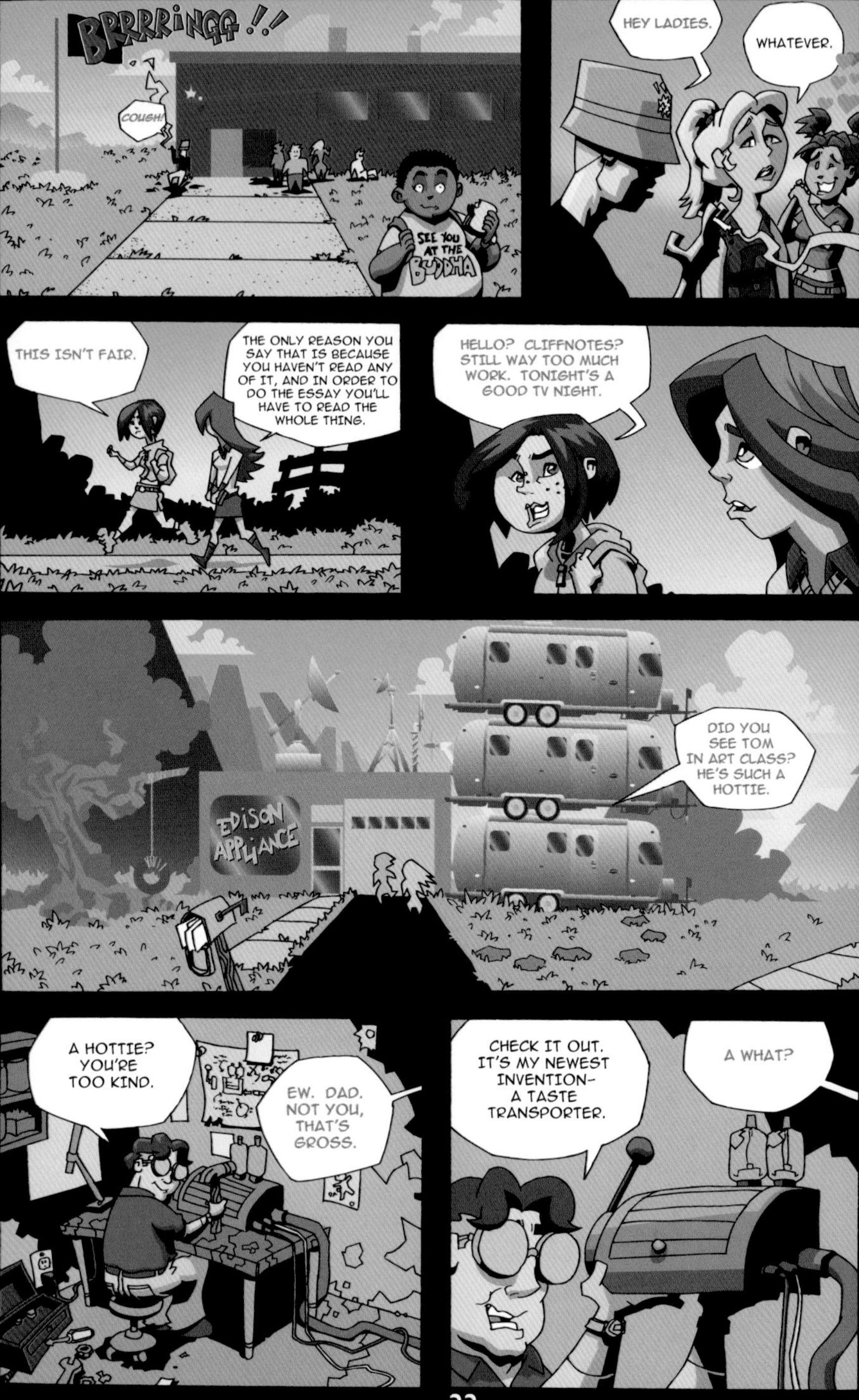
BRRRRINGG !!
COUGH!
SEE YOU AT THE BUDDHA
HEY LADIES.
WHATEVER.
THIS ISN'T FAIR.
THE ONLY REASON YOU SAY THAT IS BECAUSE YOU HAVEN'T READ ANY OF IT, AND IN ORDER TO DO THE ESSAY YOU'LL HAVE TO READ THE WHOLE THING.
HELLO? CLIFFNOTES? STILL WAY TOO MUCH WORK. TONIGHT'S A GOOD TV NIGHT.
EDISON APPLIANCE
DID YOU SEE TOM IN ART CLASS? HE'S SUCH A HOTTIE.
A HOTTIE? YOU'RE TOO KIND.
EW. DAD. NOT YOU, THAT'S GROSS.
CHECK IT OUT. IT'S MY NEWEST INVENTION- A TASTE TRANSPORTER.
A WHAT?

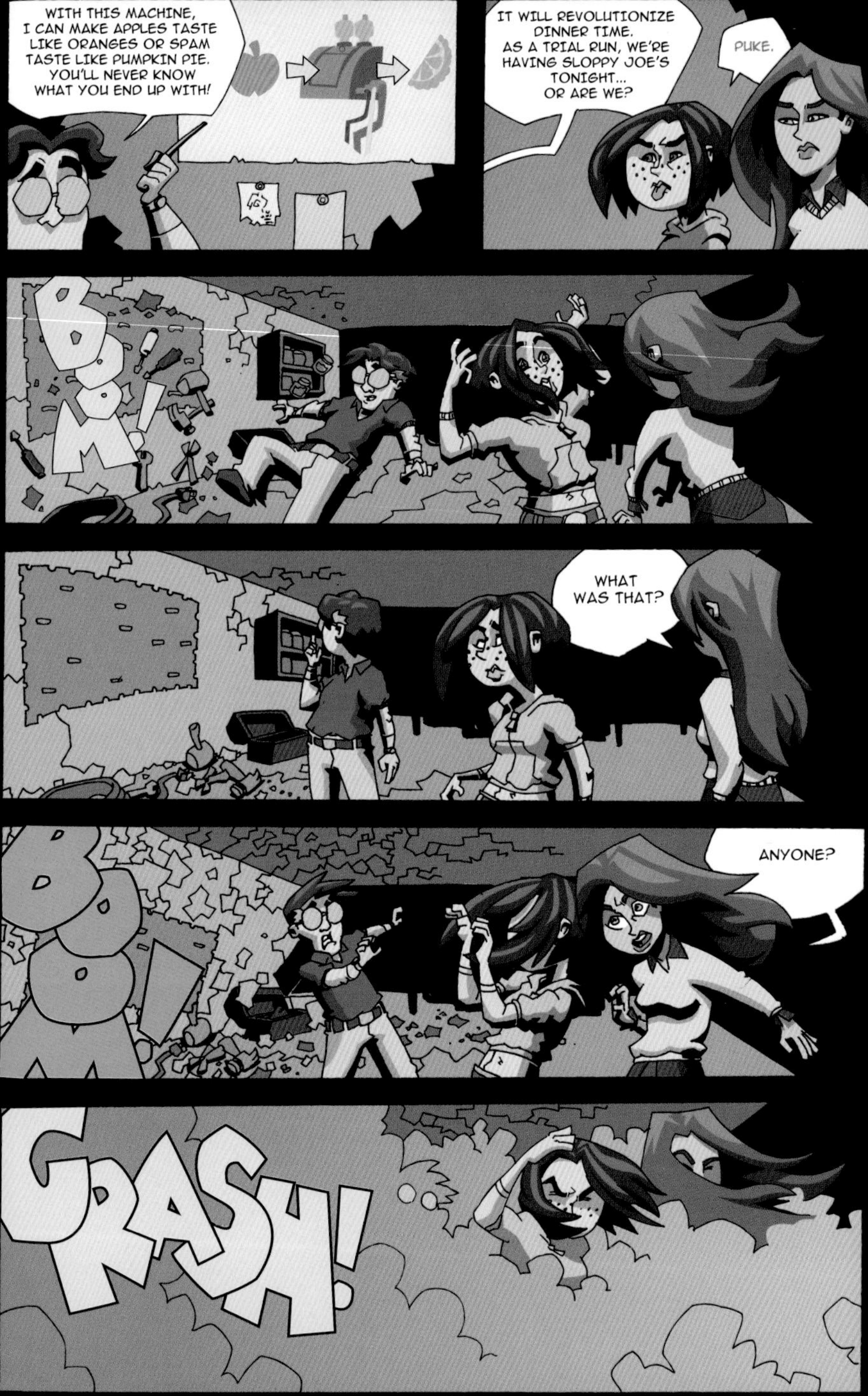
WITH THIS MACHINE, I CAN MAKE APPLES TASTE LIKE ORANGES OR SPAM TASTE LIKE PUMPKIN PIE. YOU'LL NEVER KNOW WHAT YOU END UP WITH!
IT WILL REVOLUTIONIZE DINNER TIME. AS A TRIAL RUN, WE'RE HAVING SLOPPY JOE'S TONIGHT... OR ARE WE?
PUKE.
BOOM!
WHAT WAS THAT?
BOOOM!
ANYONE?
CRASH!

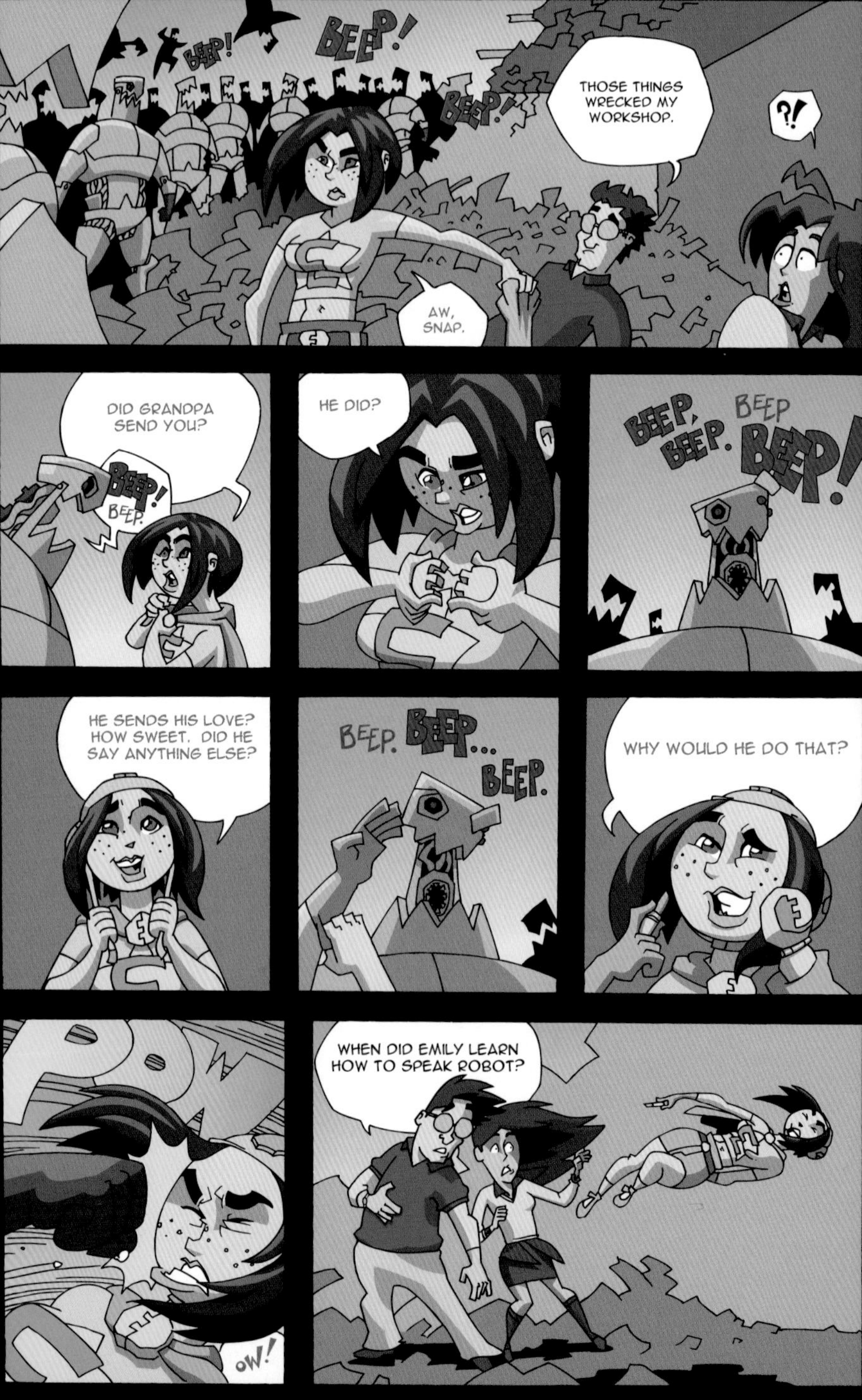
BEEP!
BEEP!
BEEP!
THOSE THINGS WRECKED MY WORKSHOP.
?!
AW, SNAP.
DID GRANDPA SEND YOU?
BEEP! BEEP.
HE DID?
BEEP, BEEP. BEEP BEEP!
HE SENDS HIS LOVE? HOW SWEET. DID HE SAY ANYTHING ELSE?
BEEP. BEEP... BEEP.
WHY WOULD HE DO THAT?
OW!
WHEN DID EMILY LEARN HOW TO SPEAK ROBOT?

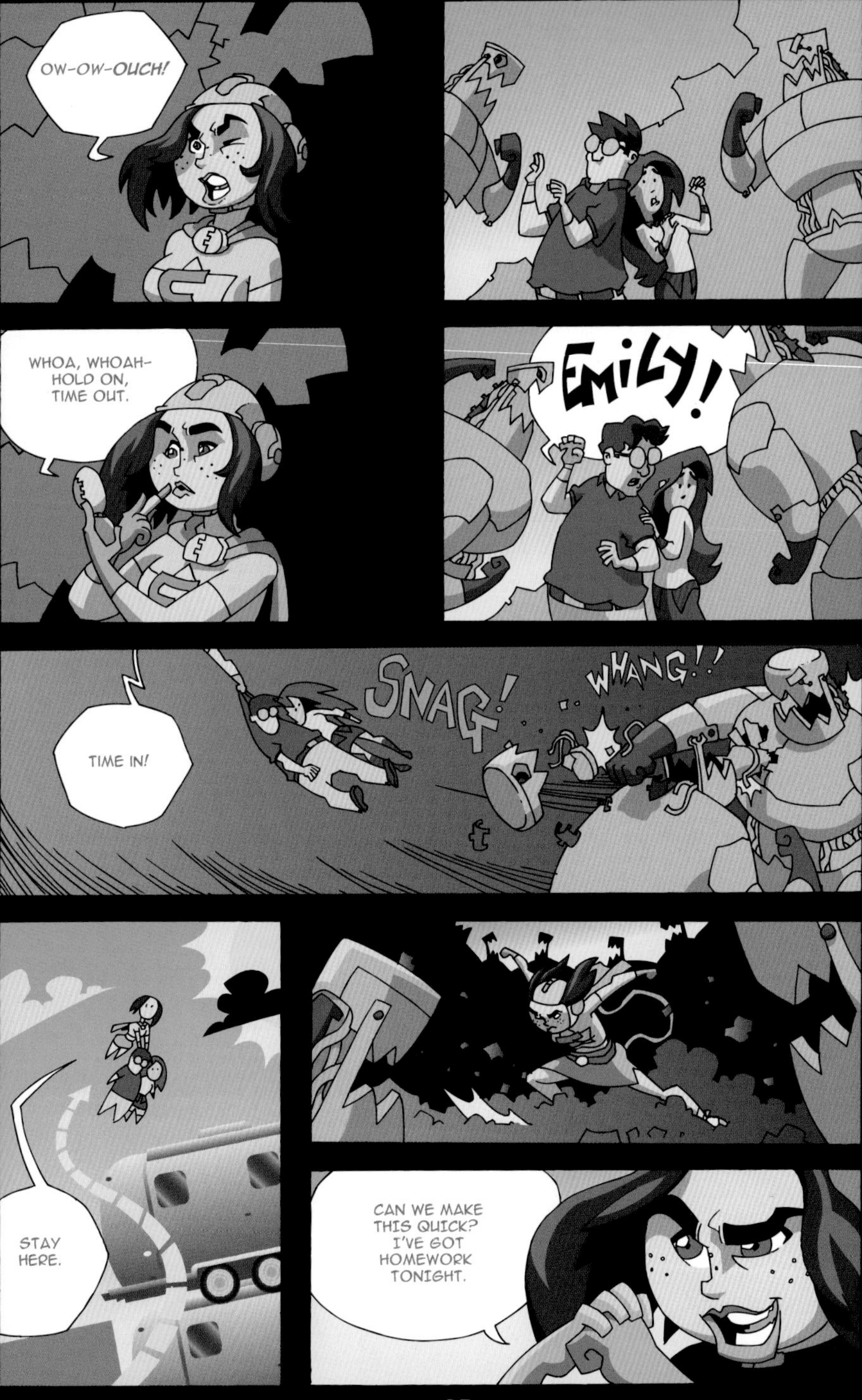

OW-OW-OUCH!
WHOA, WHOAH-
HOLD ON,
TIME OUT.
EMILY!
TIME IN!
SNAG!
WHANG!!
STAY
HERE.
CAN WE MAKE
THIS QUICK?
I'VE GOT
HOMEWORK
TONIGHT.

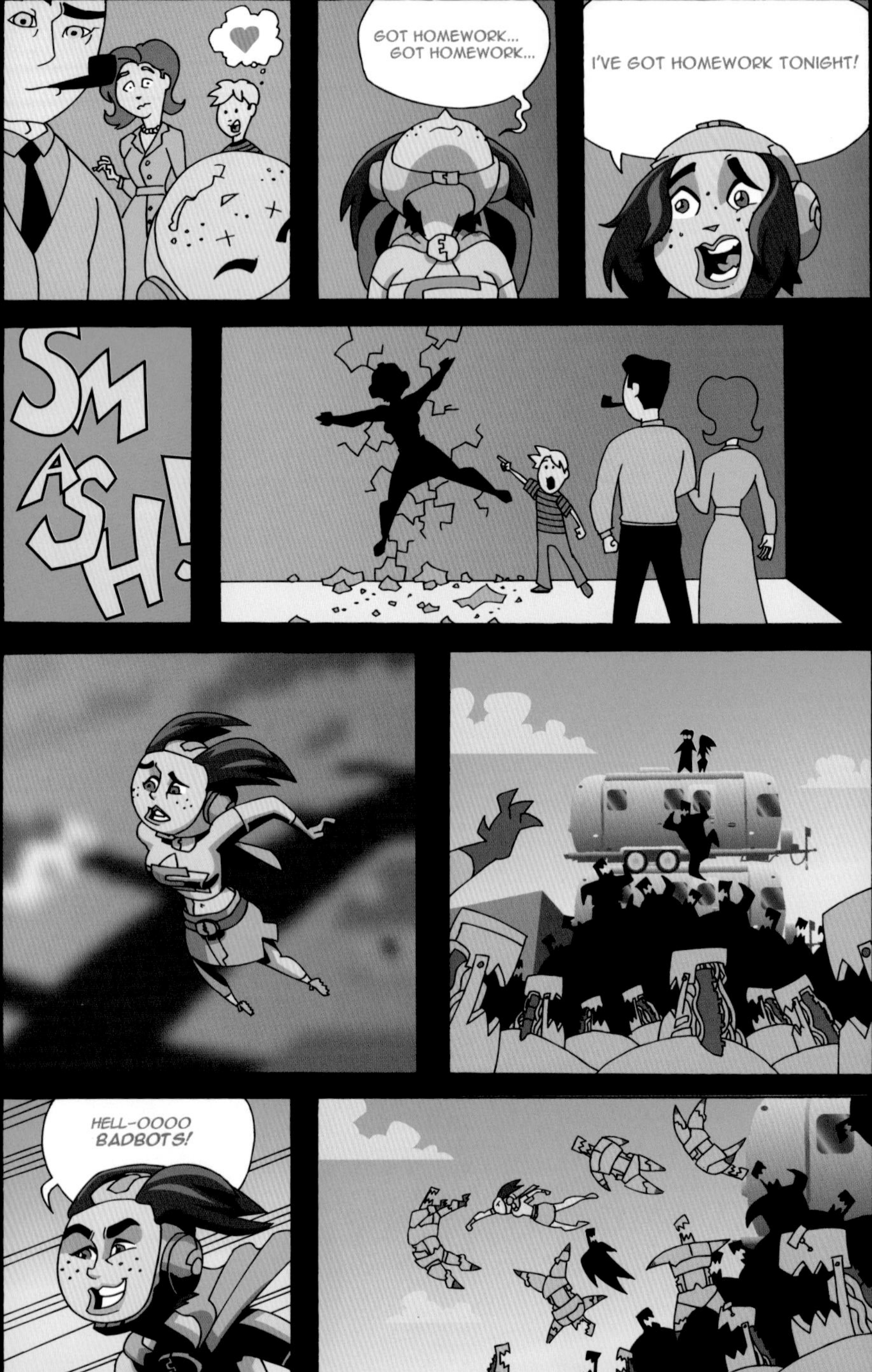
GOT HOMEWORK...
GOT HOMEWORK...
I'VE GOT HOMEWORK TONIGHT!
SMASH!
HELL-OOOO BADBOTS!

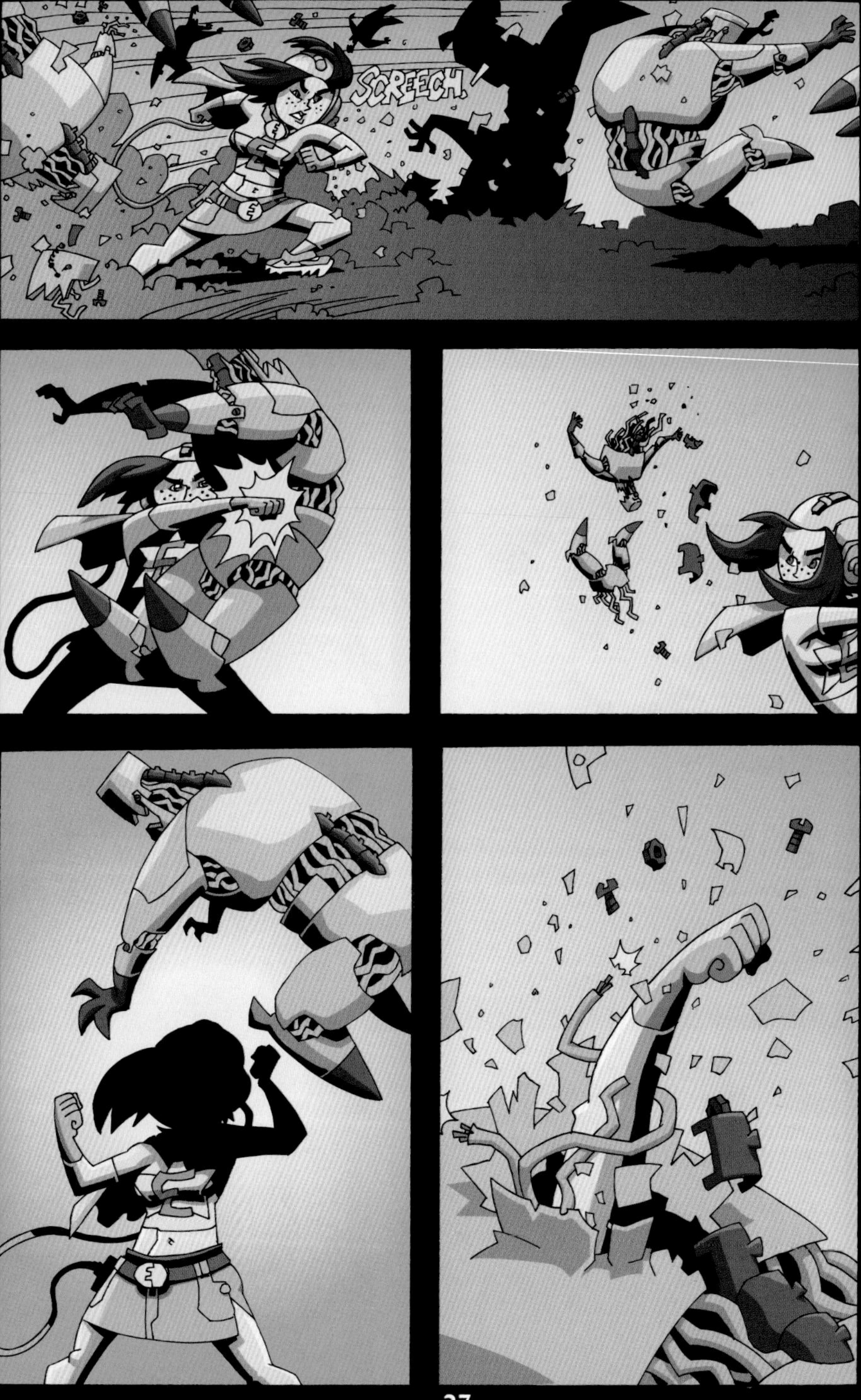
SCREECH!

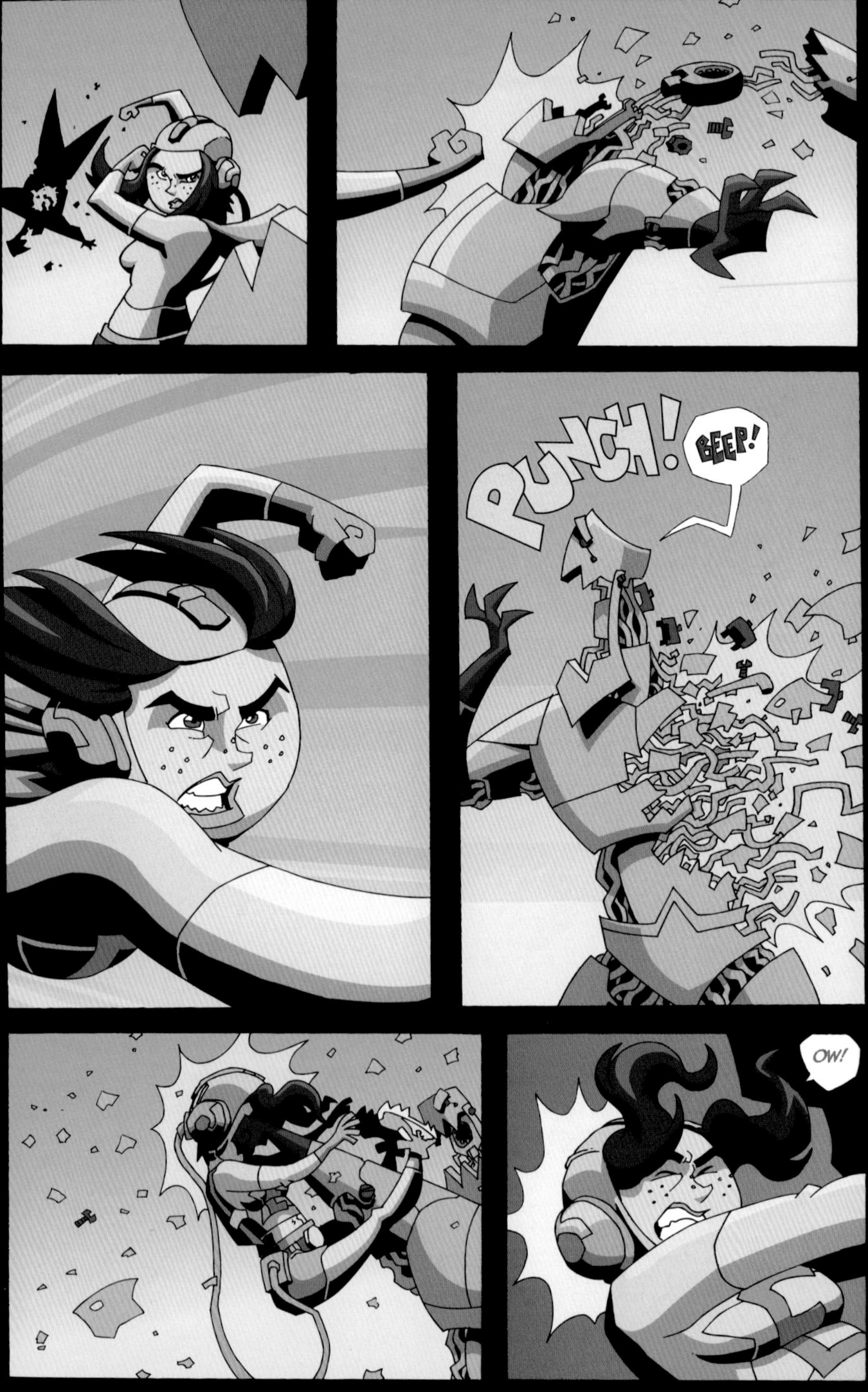
PUNCH!
BEEP!
OW!

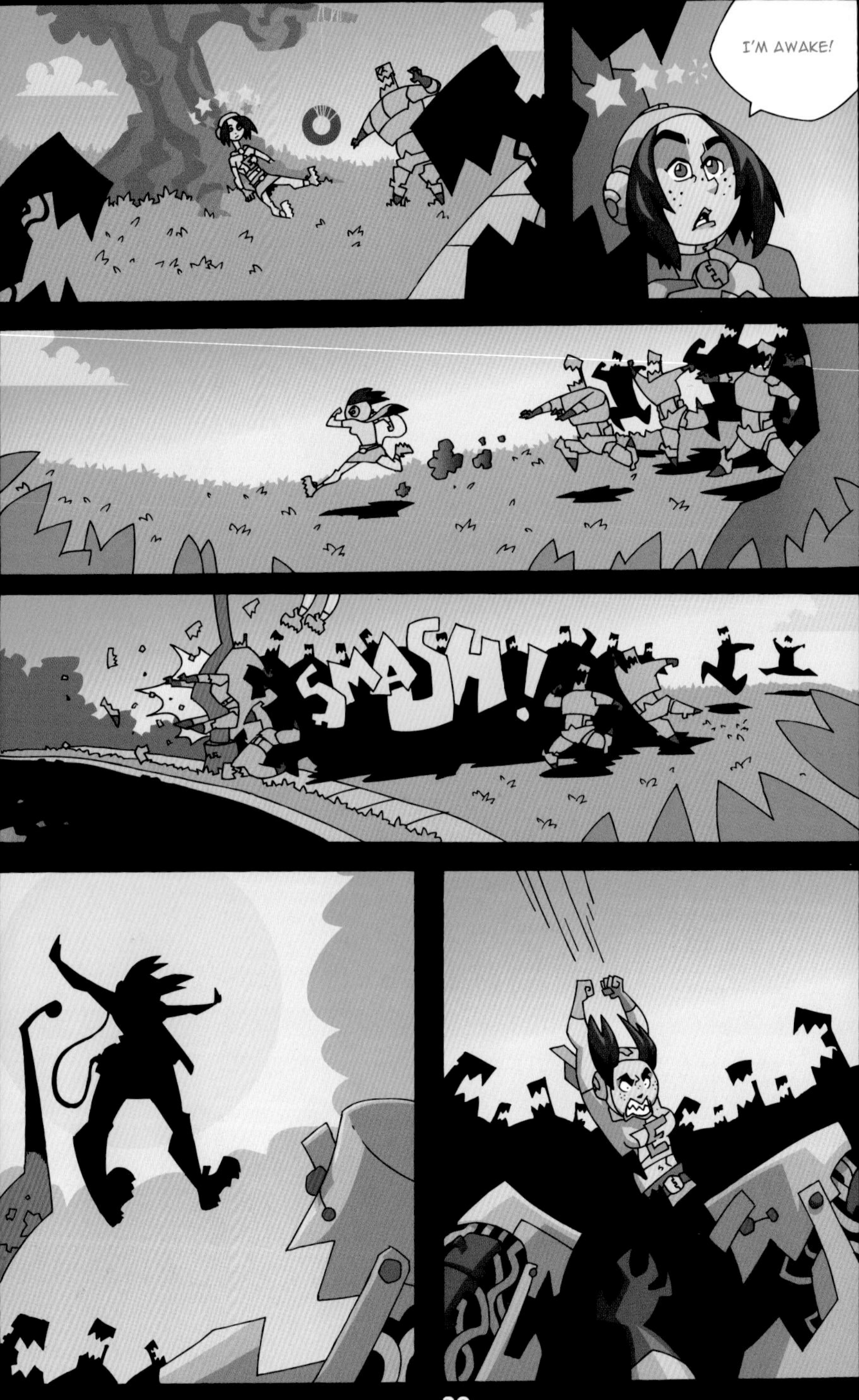
I'M AWAKE!
SMASH!

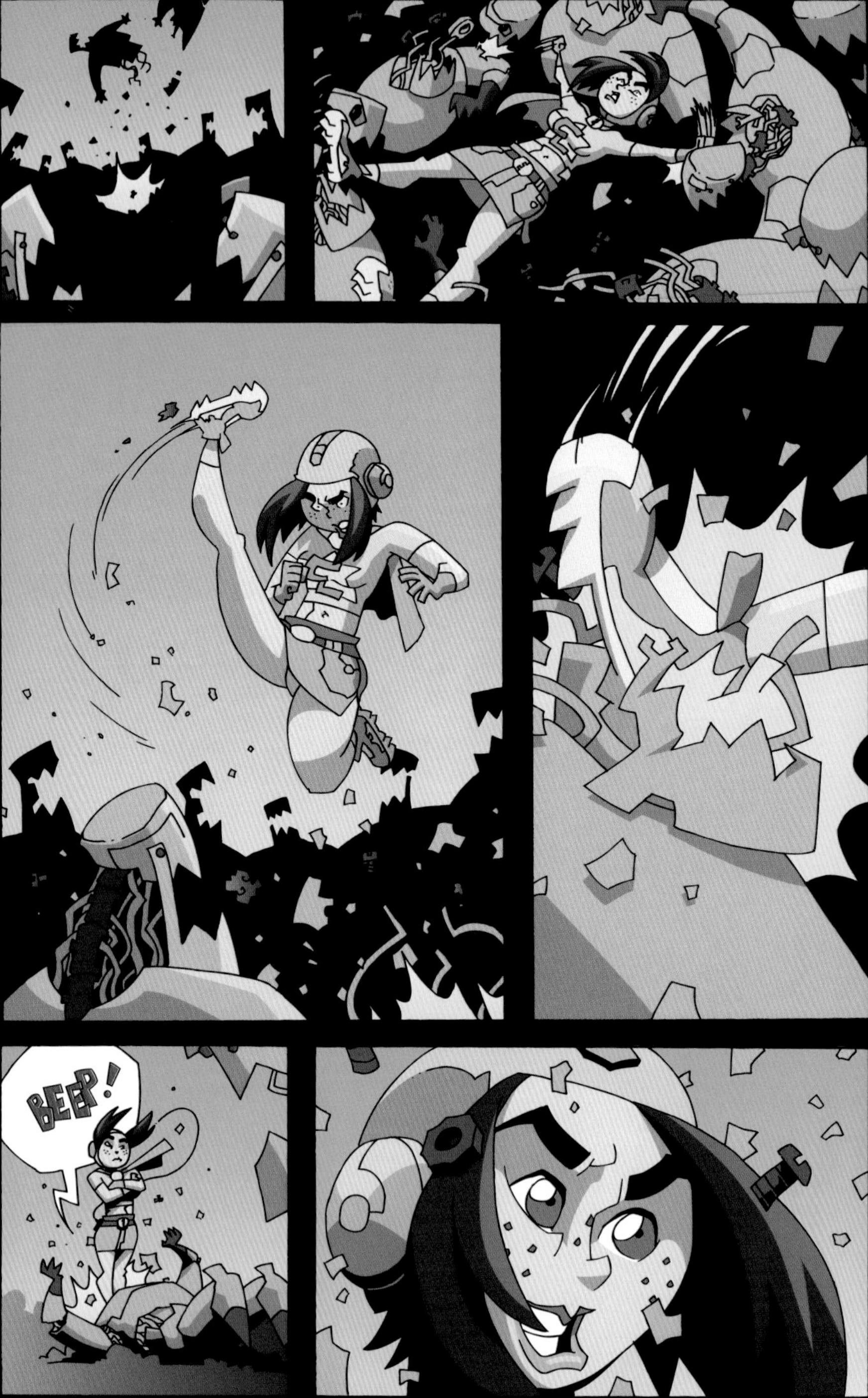
BEEP!

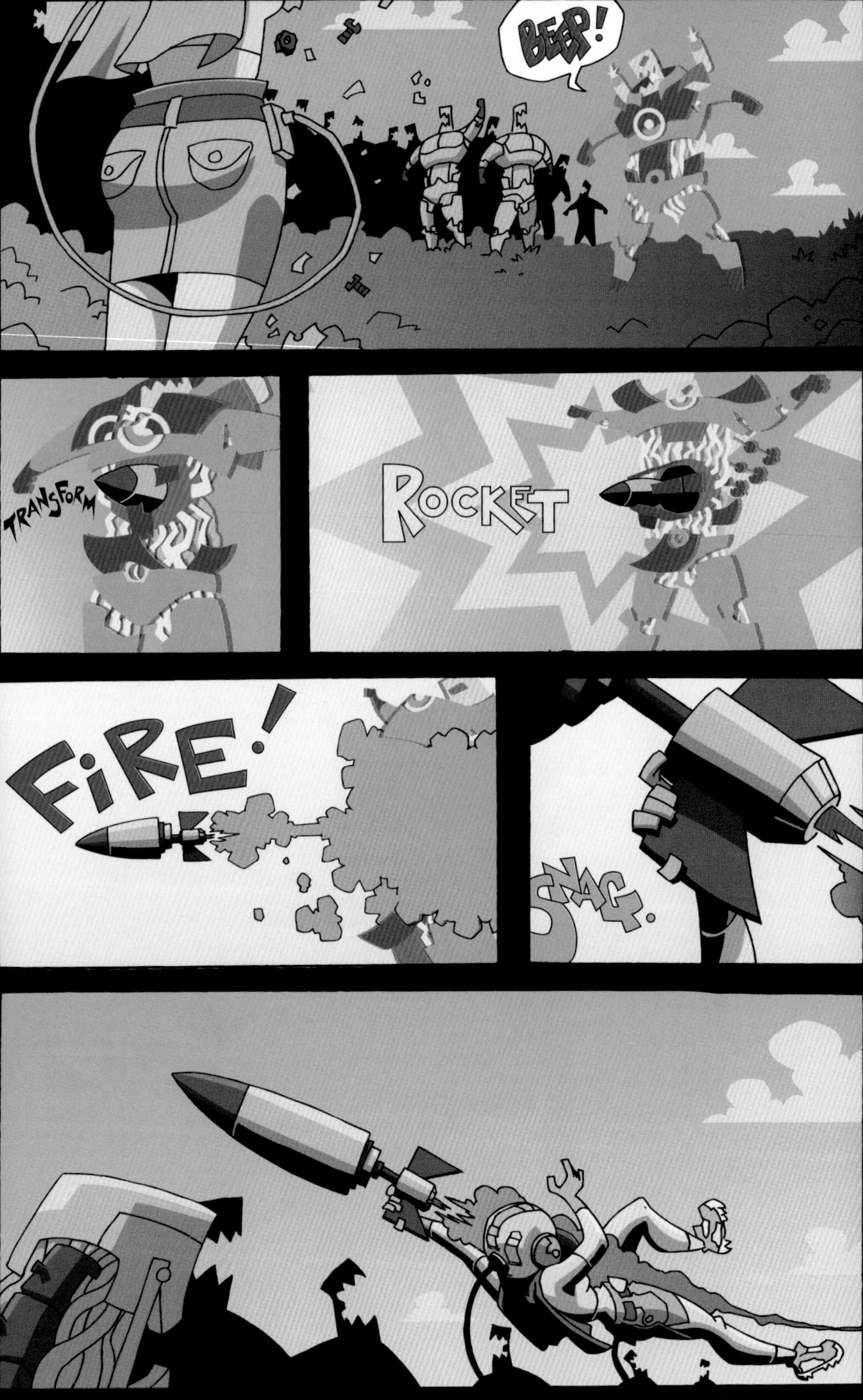
BEEP!
TRANSFORM
ROCKET
FIRE!
SNAG.

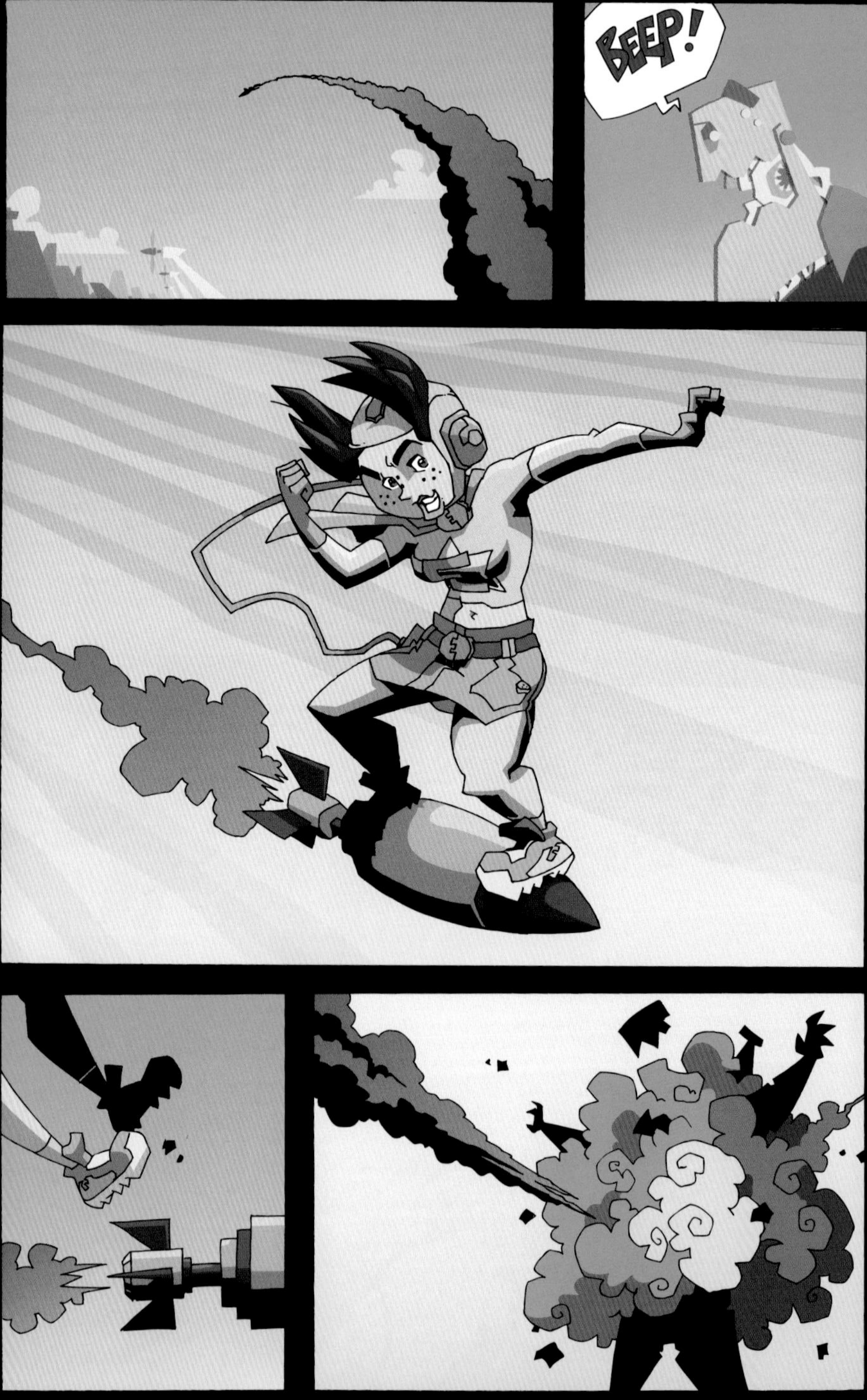
BEEP!

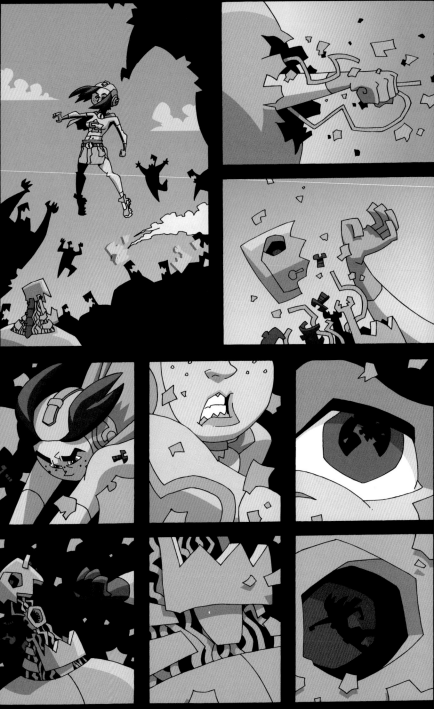

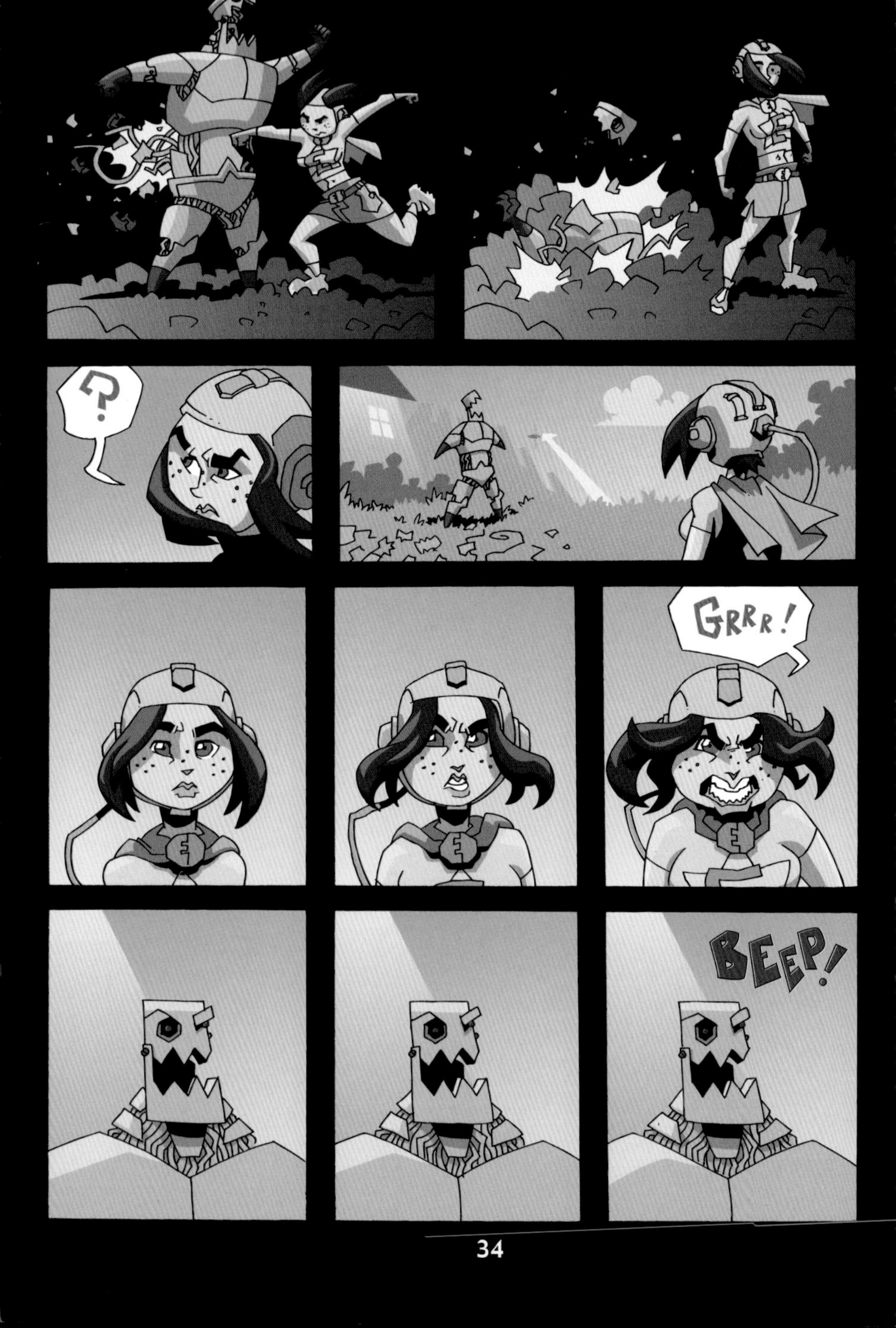
?
GRRR!
BEEP!

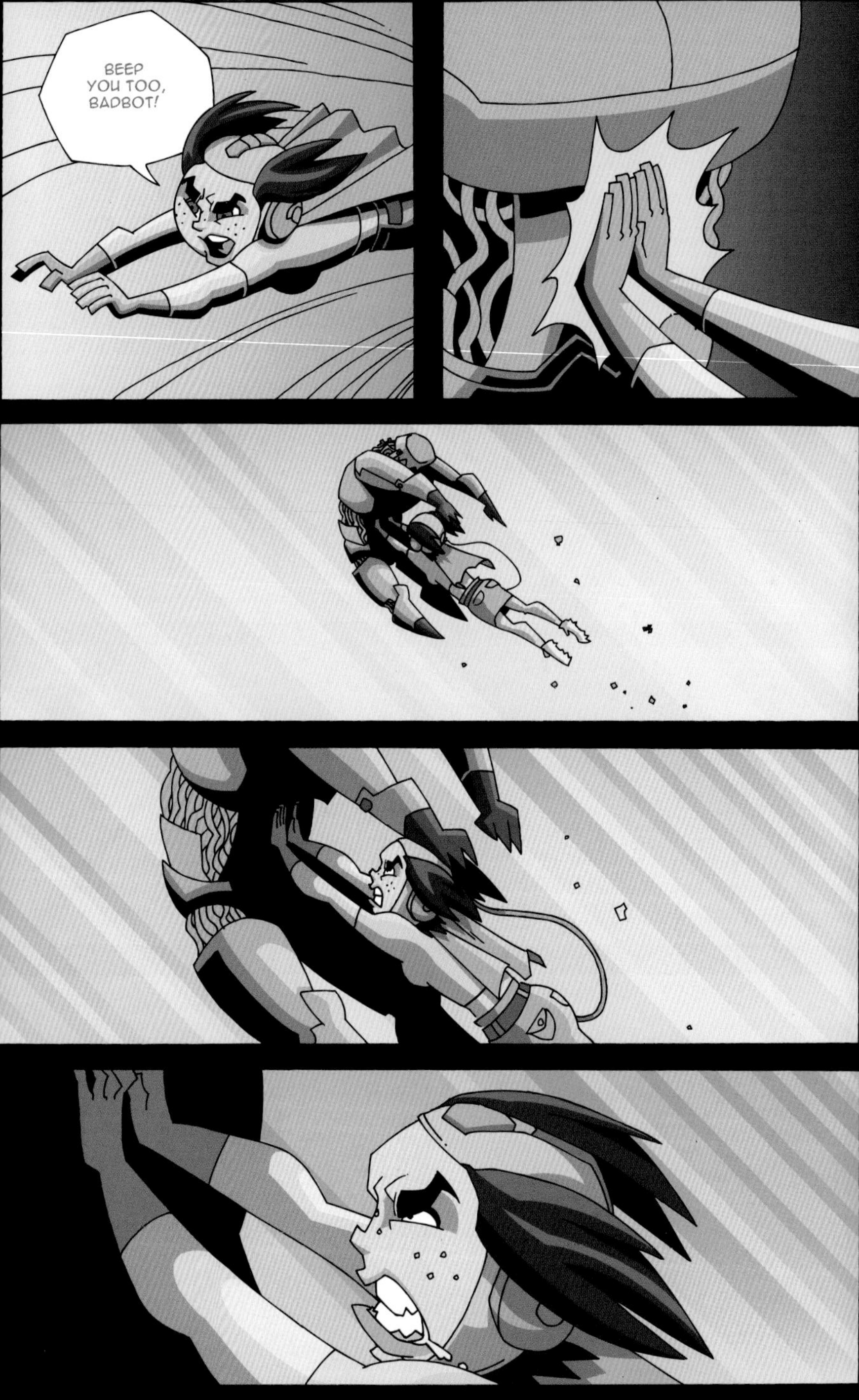
BEEP
YOU TOO,
BADBOT!

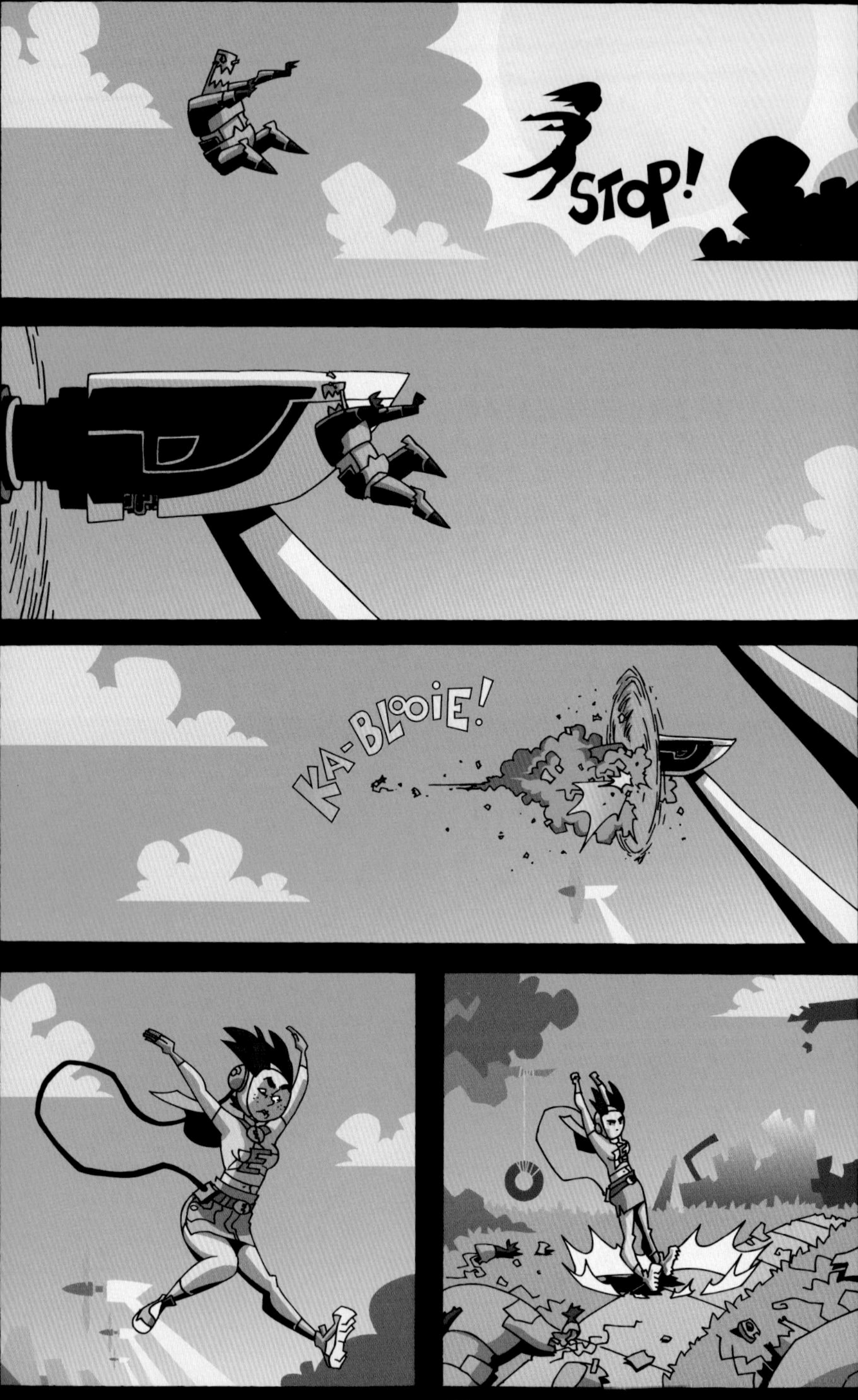
STOP!
KA-BLOOIE!

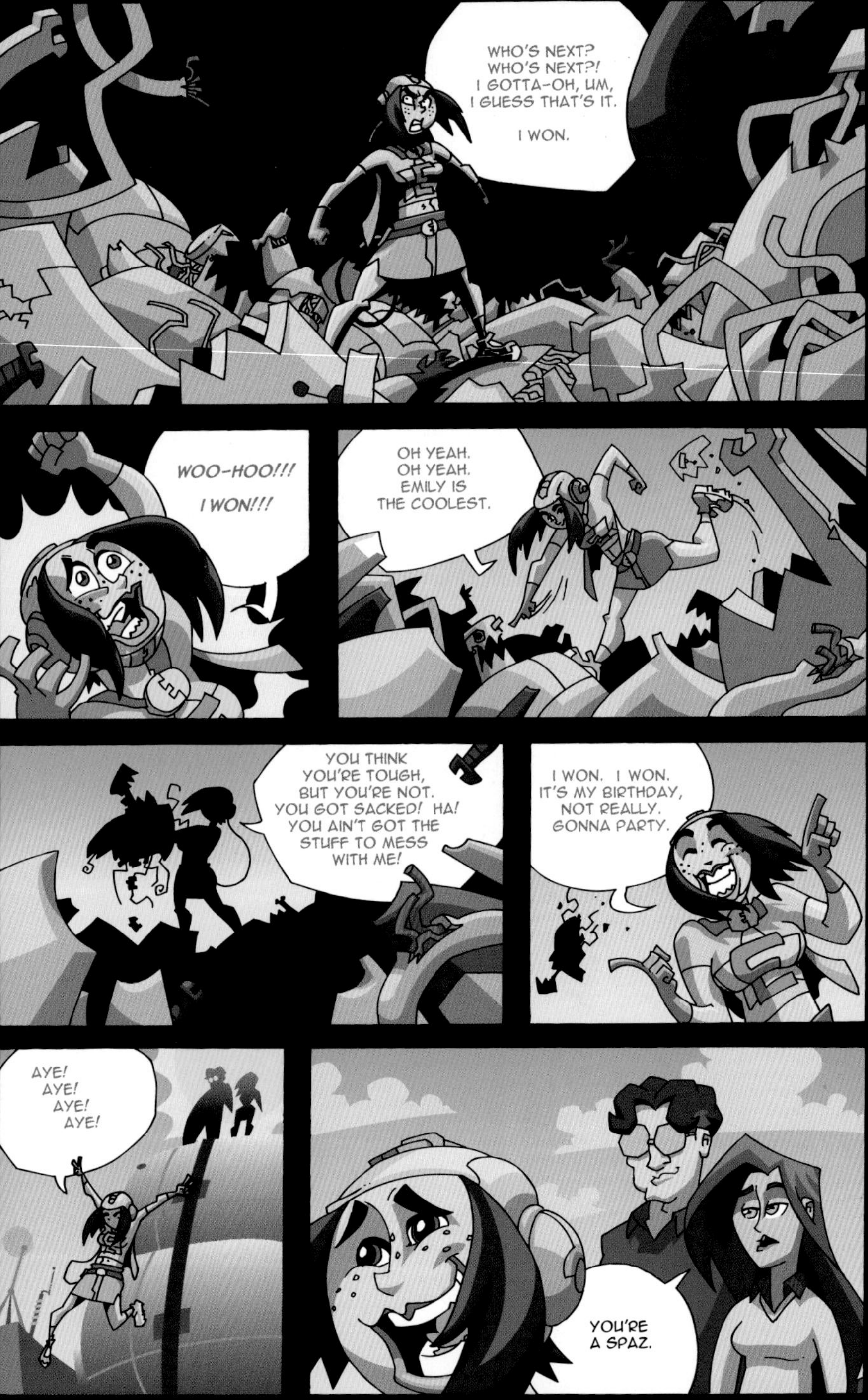
WHO'S NEXT? WHO'S NEXT?! I GOTTA-OH, UM, I GUESS THAT'S IT.
I WON.
WOO-HOO!!!
I WON!!!
OH YEAH. OH YEAH. EMILY IS THE COOLEST.
YOU THINK YOU'RE TOUGH, BUT YOU'RE NOT. YOU GOT SACKED! HA! YOU AIN'T GOT THE STUFF TO MESS WITH ME!
I WON. I WON. IT'S MY BIRTHDAY, NOT REALLY. GONNA PARTY.
AYE! AYE! AYE! AYE!
YOU'RE A SPAZ.

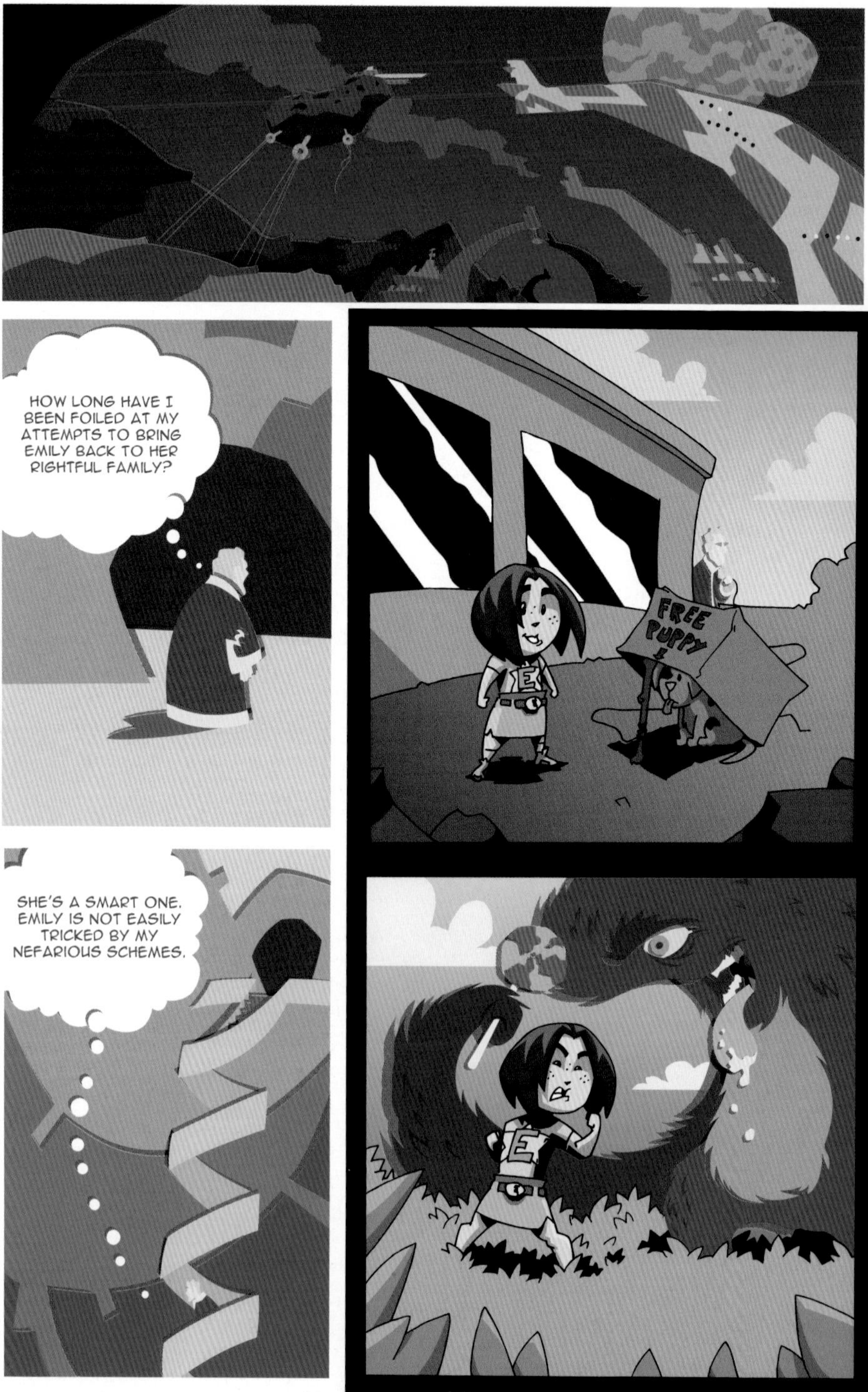
HOW LONG HAVE I BEEN FOILED AT MY ATTEMPTS TO BRING EMILY BACK TO HER RIGHTFUL FAMILY?
FREE PUPPY
SHE'S A SMART ONE. EMILY IS NOT EASILY TRICKED BY MY NEFARIOUS SCHEMES.

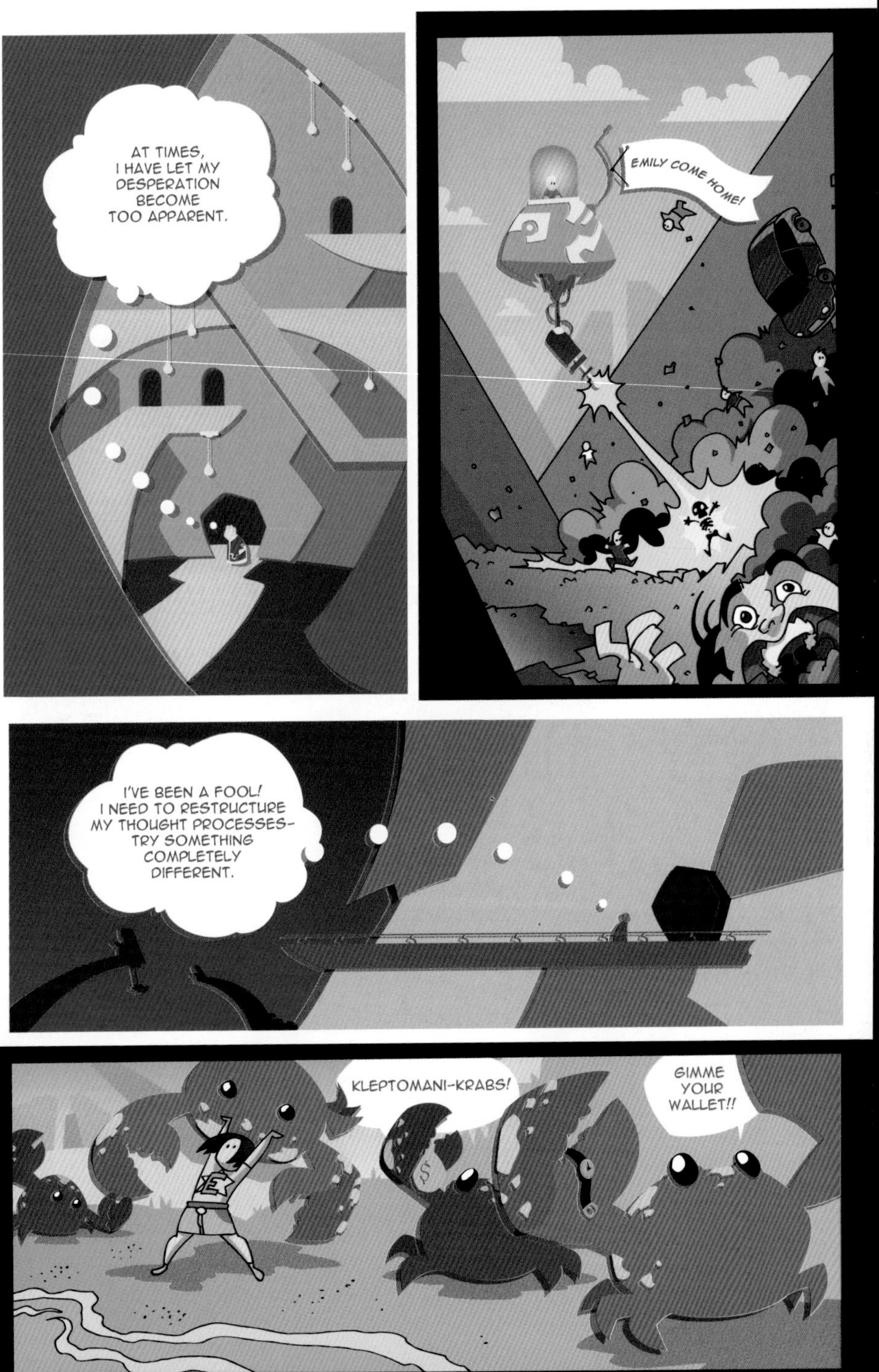
AT TIMES, I HAVE LET MY DESPERATION BECOME TOO APPARENT.
EMILY COME HOME!
I'VE BEEN A FOOL! I NEED TO RESTRUCTURE MY THOUGHT PROCESSES- TRY SOMETHING COMPLETELY DIFFERENT.
KLEPTOMANI-KRABS!
GIMME YOUR WALLET!!

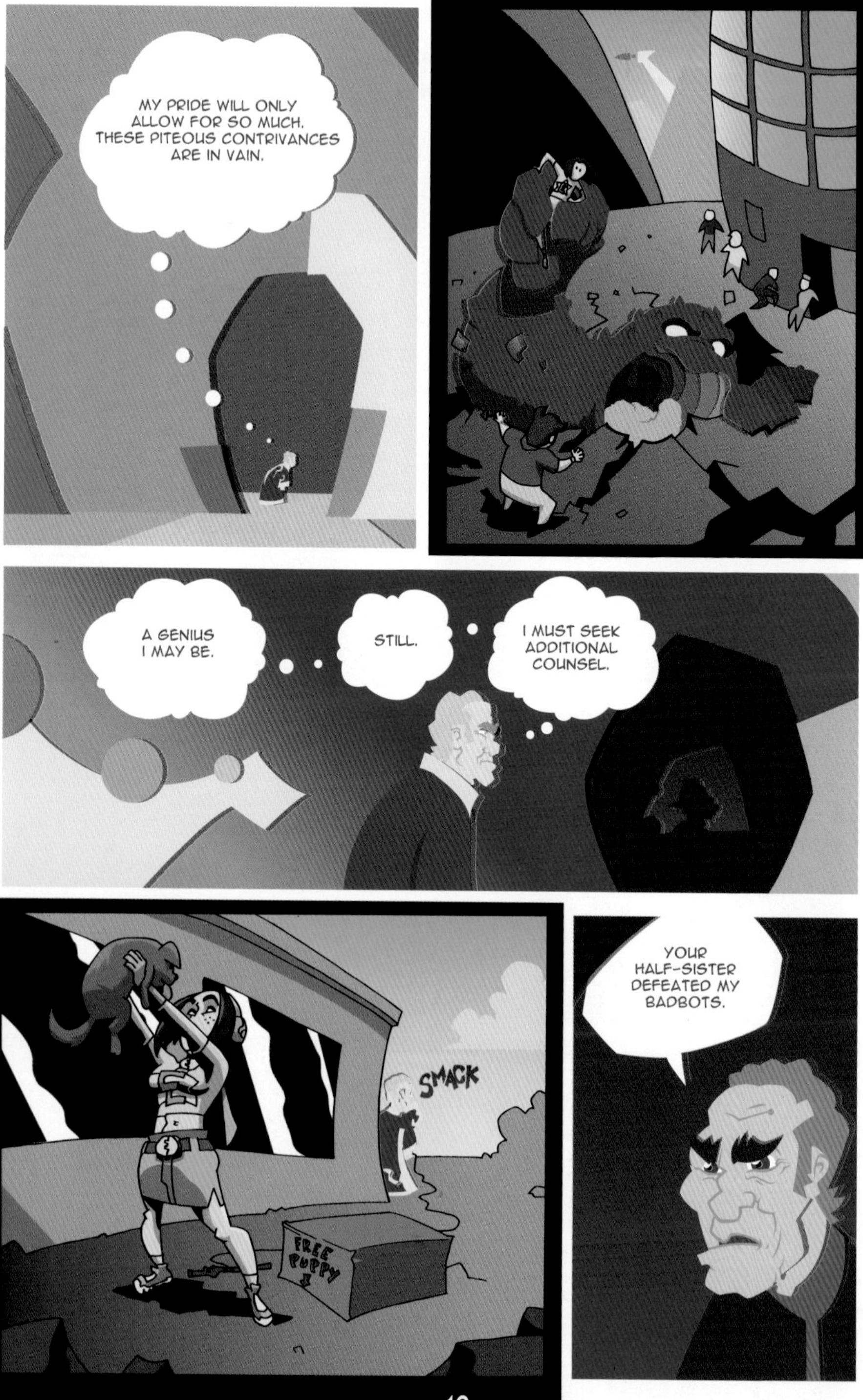
MY PRIDE WILL ONLY ALLOW FOR SO MUCH. THESE PITEOUS CONTRIVANCES ARE IN VAIN.
A GENIUS I MAY BE.
STILL.
I MUST SEEK ADDITIONAL COUNSEL.
SMACK
FREE PUPPY
YOUR HALF-SISTER DEFEATED MY BADBOTS.

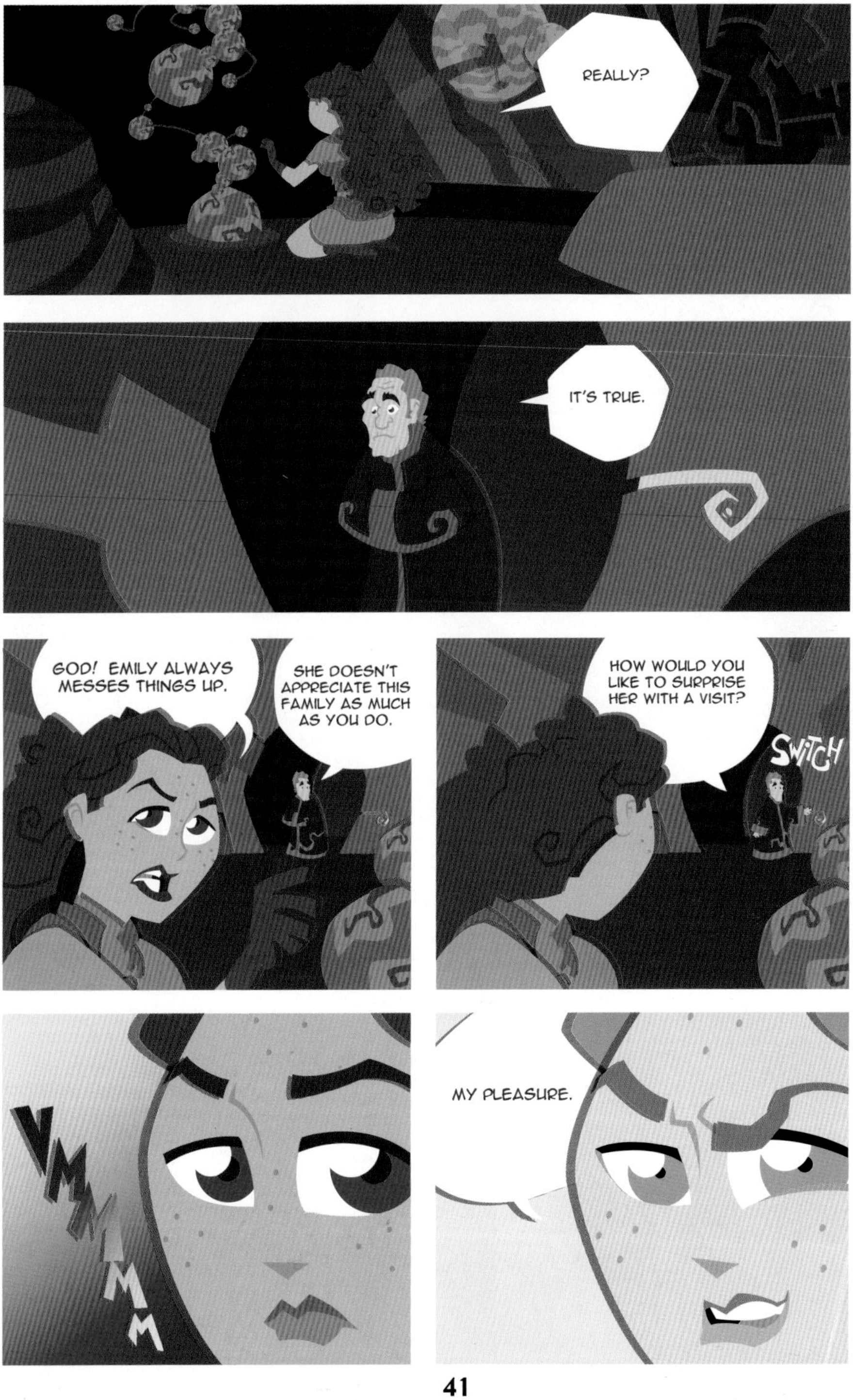
REALLY?
IT'S TRUE.
GOD! EMILY ALWAYS MESSES THINGS UP.
SHE DOESN'T APPRECIATE THIS FAMILY AS MUCH AS YOU DO.
HOW WOULD YOU LIKE TO SURPRISE HER WITH A VISIT?
SWITCH
VMMMMM
MY PLEASURE.

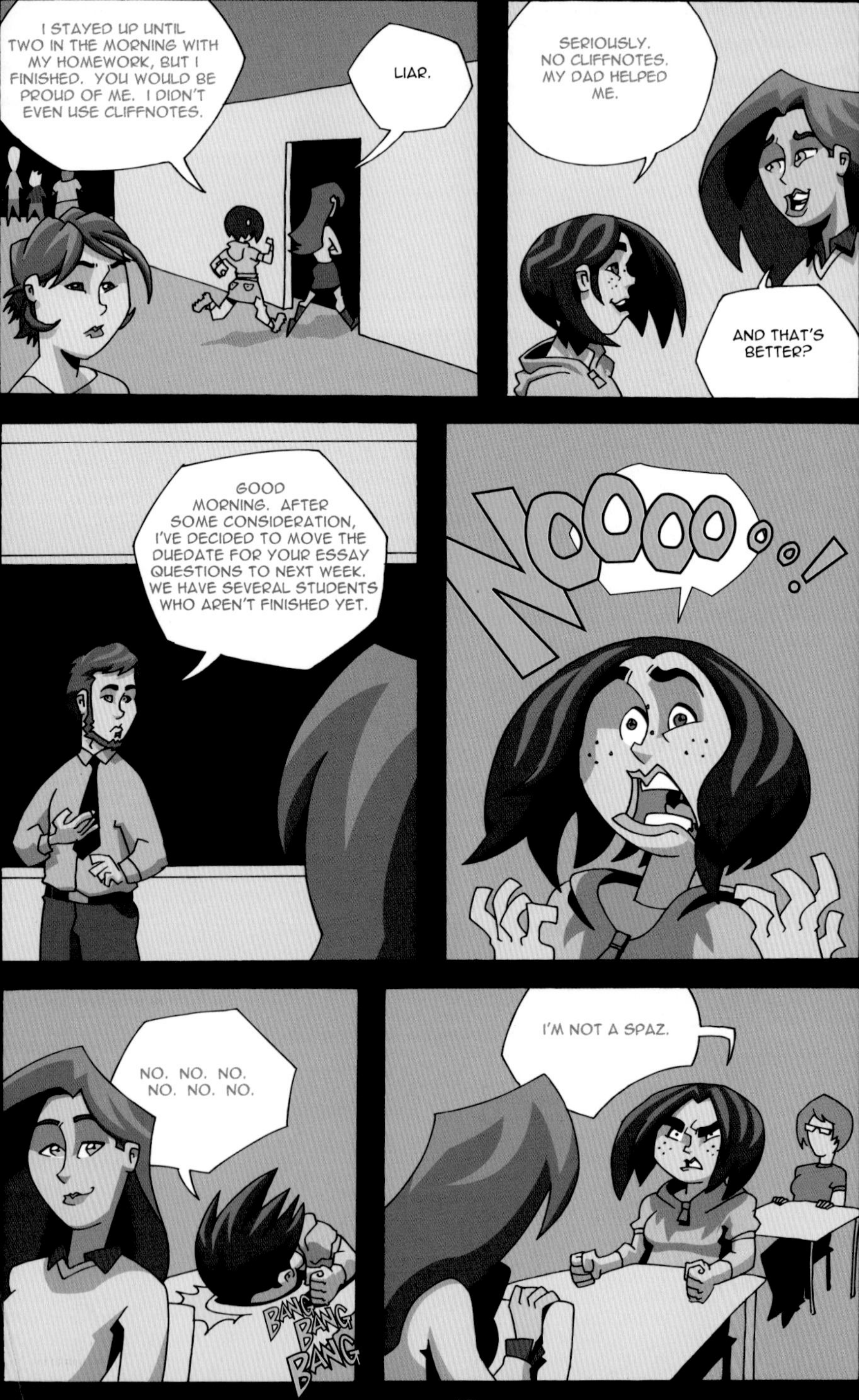
I STAYED UP UNTIL TWO IN THE MORNING WITH MY HOMEWORK, BUT I FINISHED. YOU WOULD BE PROUD OF ME. I DIDN'T EVEN USE CLIFFNOTES.
LIAR.
SERIOUSLY. NO CLIFFNOTES. MY DAD HELPED ME.
AND THAT'S BETTER?
GOOD MORNING. AFTER SOME CONSIDERATION, I'VE DECIDED TO MOVE THE DUEDATE FOR YOUR ESSAY QUESTIONS TO NEXT WEEK. WE HAVE SEVERAL STUDENTS WHO AREN'T FINISHED YET.
NOOOOOoo!
NO. NO. NO. NO. NO. NO.
BANG BANG BANG
I'M NOT A SPAZ.

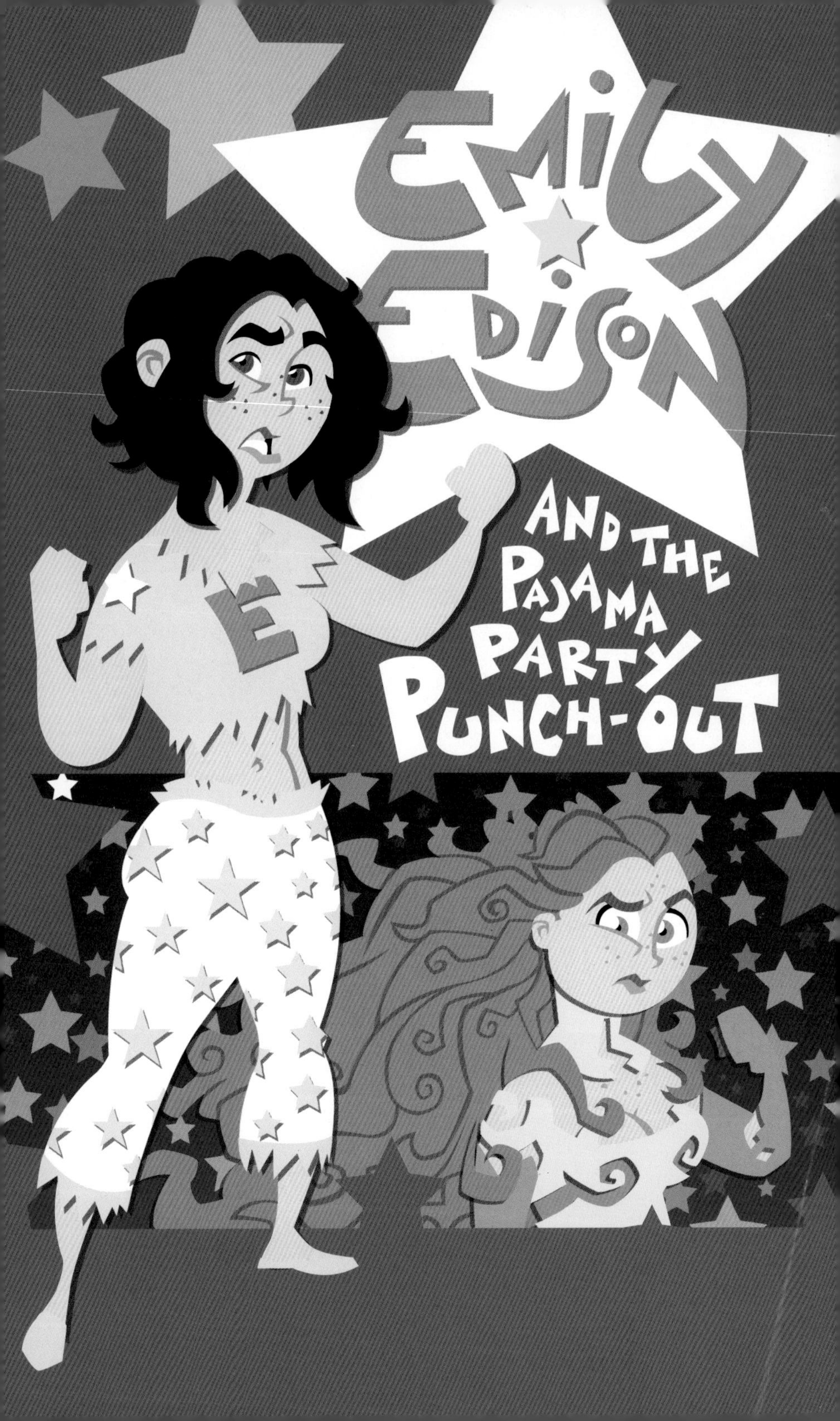

Emily Edison
And the Pajama Party Punch-Out

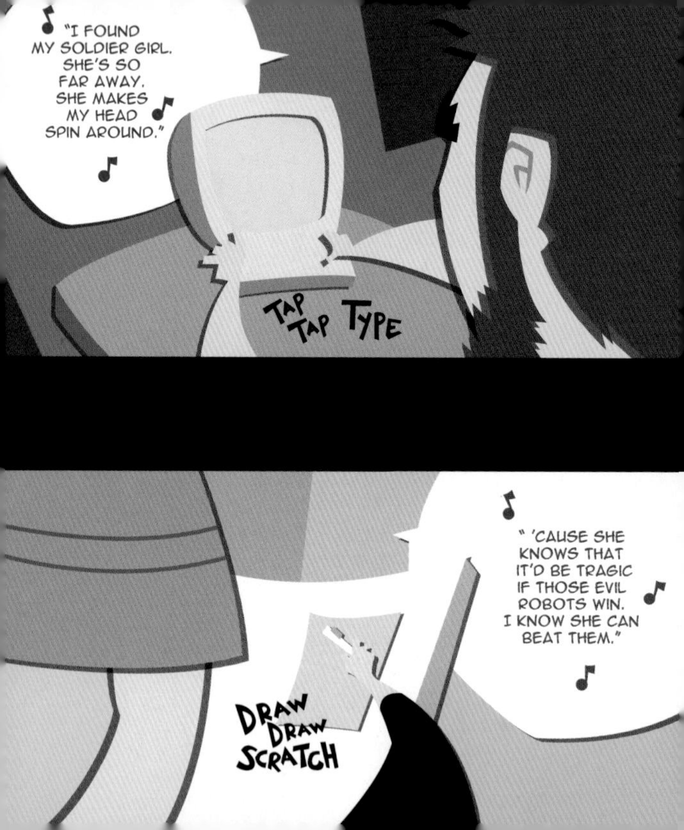
"I FOUND MY SOLDIER GIRL. SHE'S SO FAR AWAY. SHE MAKES MY HEAD SPIN AROUND."
TAP TAP TYPE
" 'CAUSE SHE KNOWS THAT IT'D BE TRAGIC IF THOSE EVIL ROBOTS WIN. I KNOW SHE CAN BEAT THEM."
DRAW DRAW SCRATCH

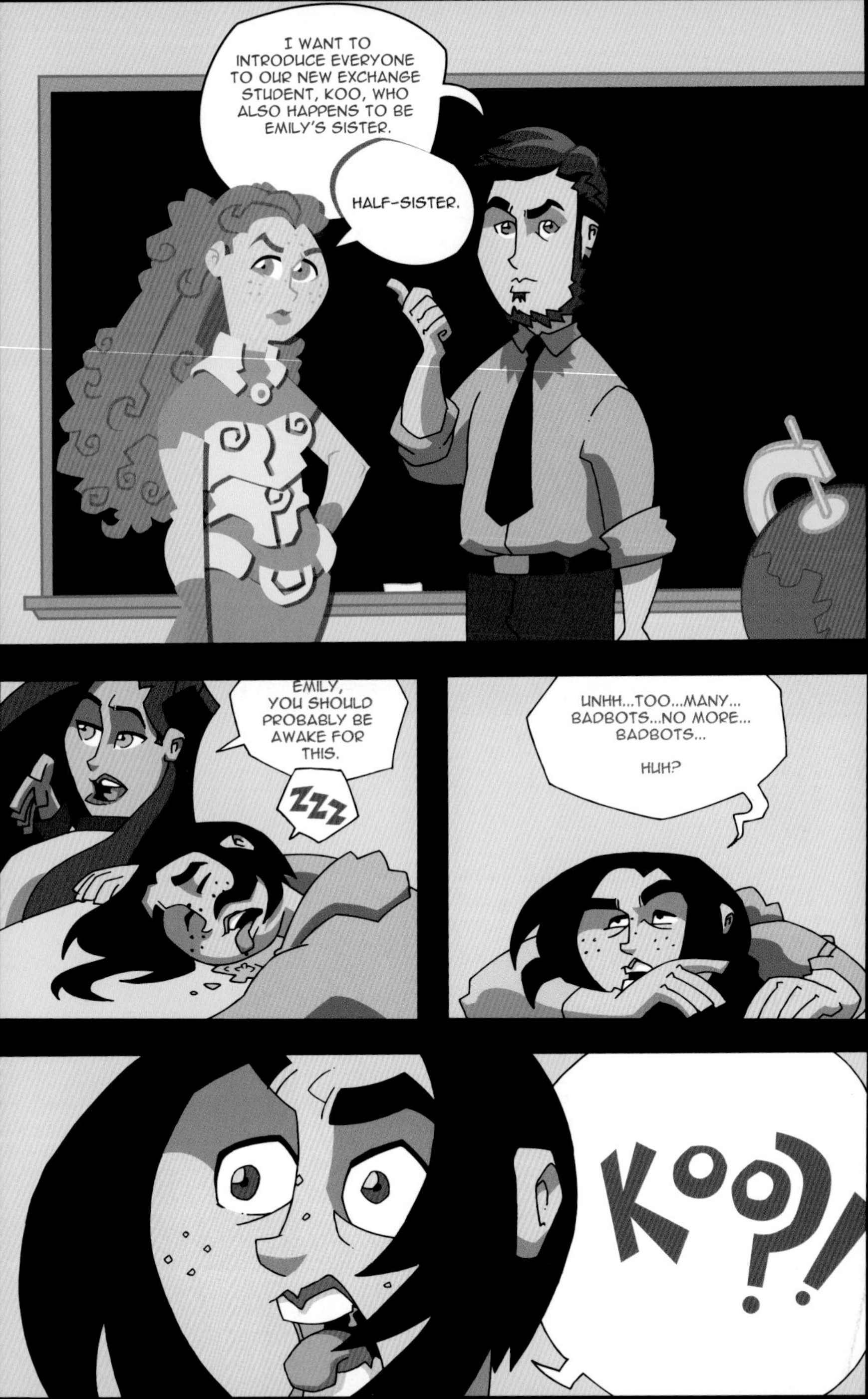
I WANT TO INTRODUCE EVERYONE TO OUR NEW EXCHANGE STUDENT, KOO, WHO ALSO HAPPENS TO BE EMILY'S SISTER.
HALF-SISTER.
EMILY, YOU SHOULD PROBABLY BE AWAKE FOR THIS.
ZZZ
UNHH...TOO...MANY... BADBOTS...NO MORE... BADBOTS...
HUH?
KOO?!

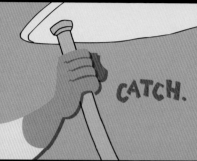

MOLLY, EVERYONE, GET OUT OF HERE, NOW!

CATCH.

I'LL PRETEND I DIDN'T JUST SEE YOU THROW A DESK ACROSS THE ROOM.

I SHOULD HAVE TOLD YOU IN ADVANCE. EMILY IS ASHAMED TO ASSOCIATE WITH OUR SIDE OF THE FAMILY.

SET.

I APOLOGIZE FOR EMILY'S ACTIONS.

SIT.

UM...OKAY THEN, LET'S GET STARTED.

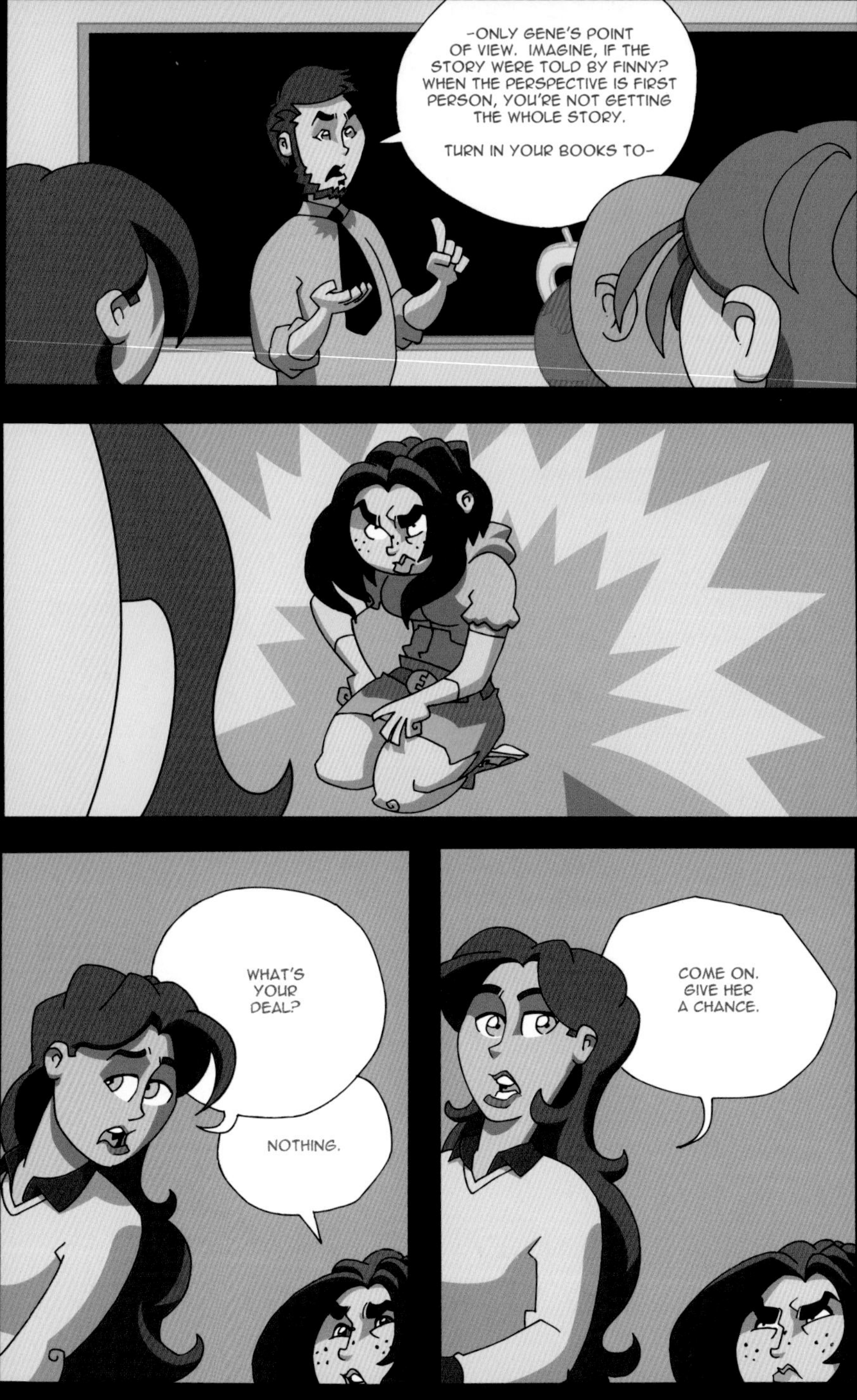
-ONLY GENE'S POINT OF VIEW. IMAGINE, IF THE STORY WERE TOLD BY FINNY? WHEN THE PERSPECTIVE IS FIRST PERSON, YOU'RE NOT GETTING THE WHOLE STORY.
TURN IN YOUR BOOKS TO-
WHAT'S YOUR DEAL?
NOTHING.
COME ON. GIVE HER A CHANCE.

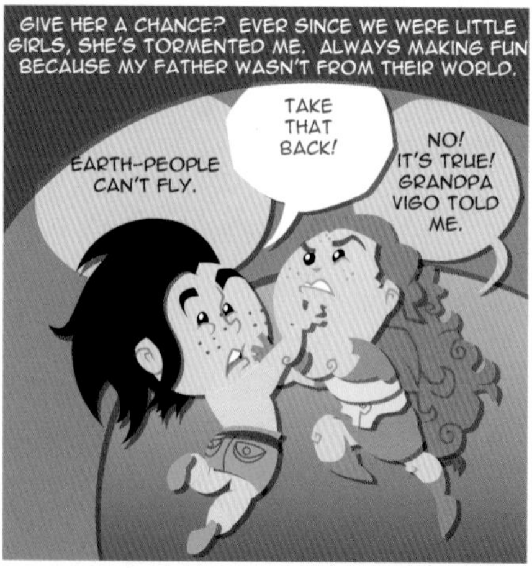
GIVE HER A CHANCE? EVER SINCE WE WERE LITTLE GIRLS, SHE'S TORMENTED ME. ALWAYS MAKING FUN BECAUSE MY FATHER WASN'T FROM THEIR WORLD.
EARTH-PEOPLE CAN'T FLY.
TAKE THAT BACK!
NO! IT'S TRUE! GRANDPA VIGO TOLD ME.

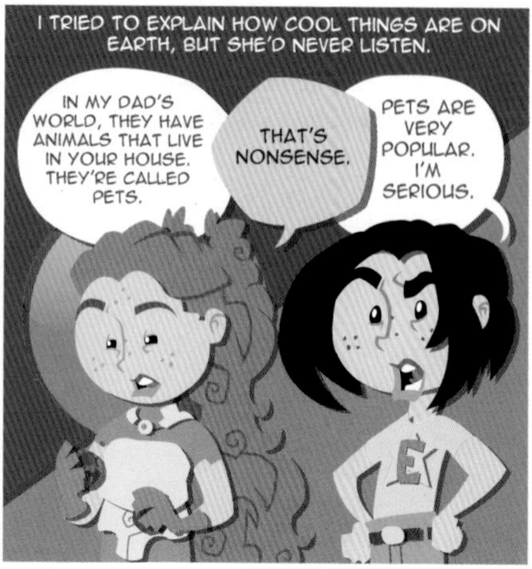
I TRIED TO EXPLAIN HOW COOL THINGS ARE ON EARTH, BUT SHE'D NEVER LISTEN.
IN MY DAD'S WORLD, THEY HAVE ANIMALS THAT LIVE IN YOUR HOUSE. THEY'RE CALLED PETS.
THAT'S NONSENSE.
PETS ARE VERY POPULAR. I'M SERIOUS.

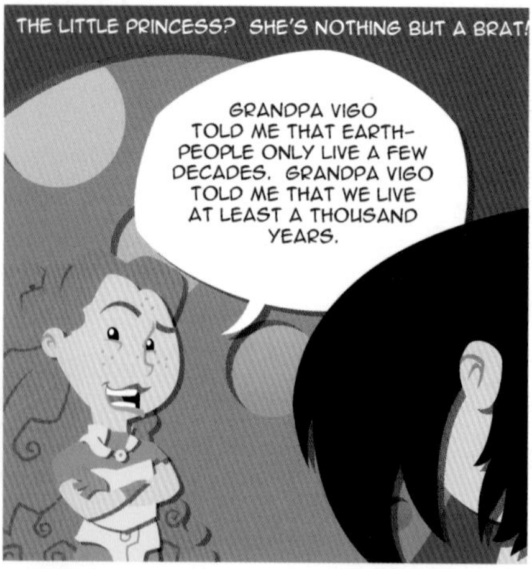
THE LITTLE PRINCESS? SHE'S NOTHING BUT A BRAT!
GRANDPA VIGO TOLD ME THAT EARTH-PEOPLE ONLY LIVE A FEW DECADES. GRANDPA VIGO TOLD ME THAT WE LIVE AT LEAST A THOUSAND YEARS.

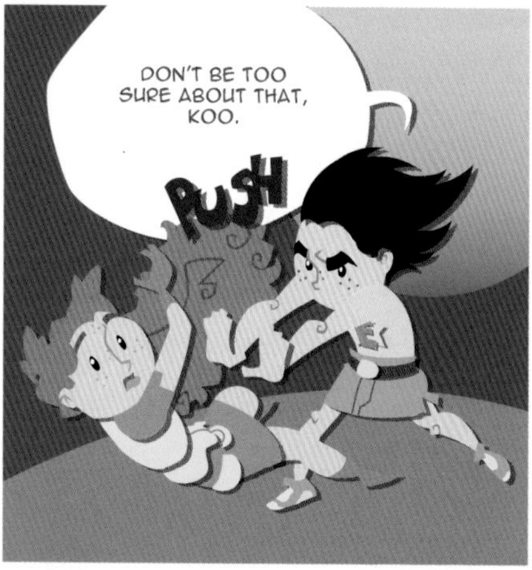
DON'T BE TOO SURE ABOUT THAT, KOO.
PUSH

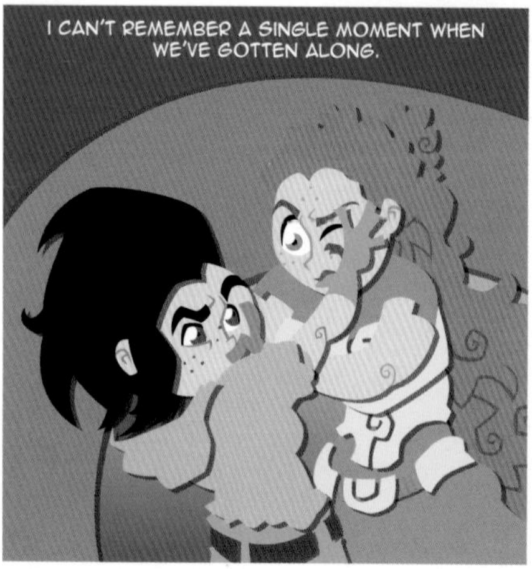
I CAN'T REMEMBER A SINGLE MOMENT WHEN WE'VE GOTTEN ALONG.

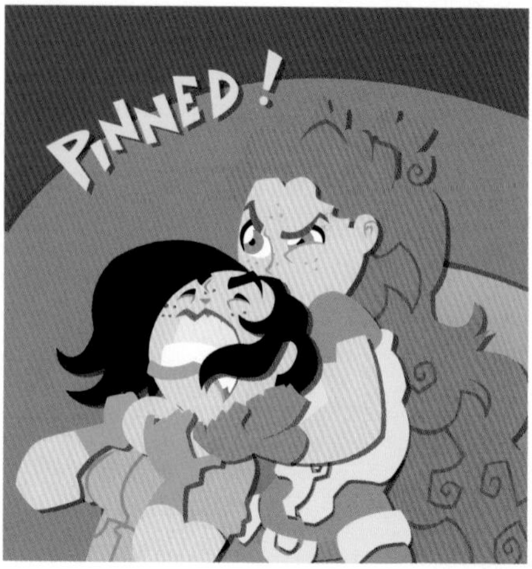
PINNED!

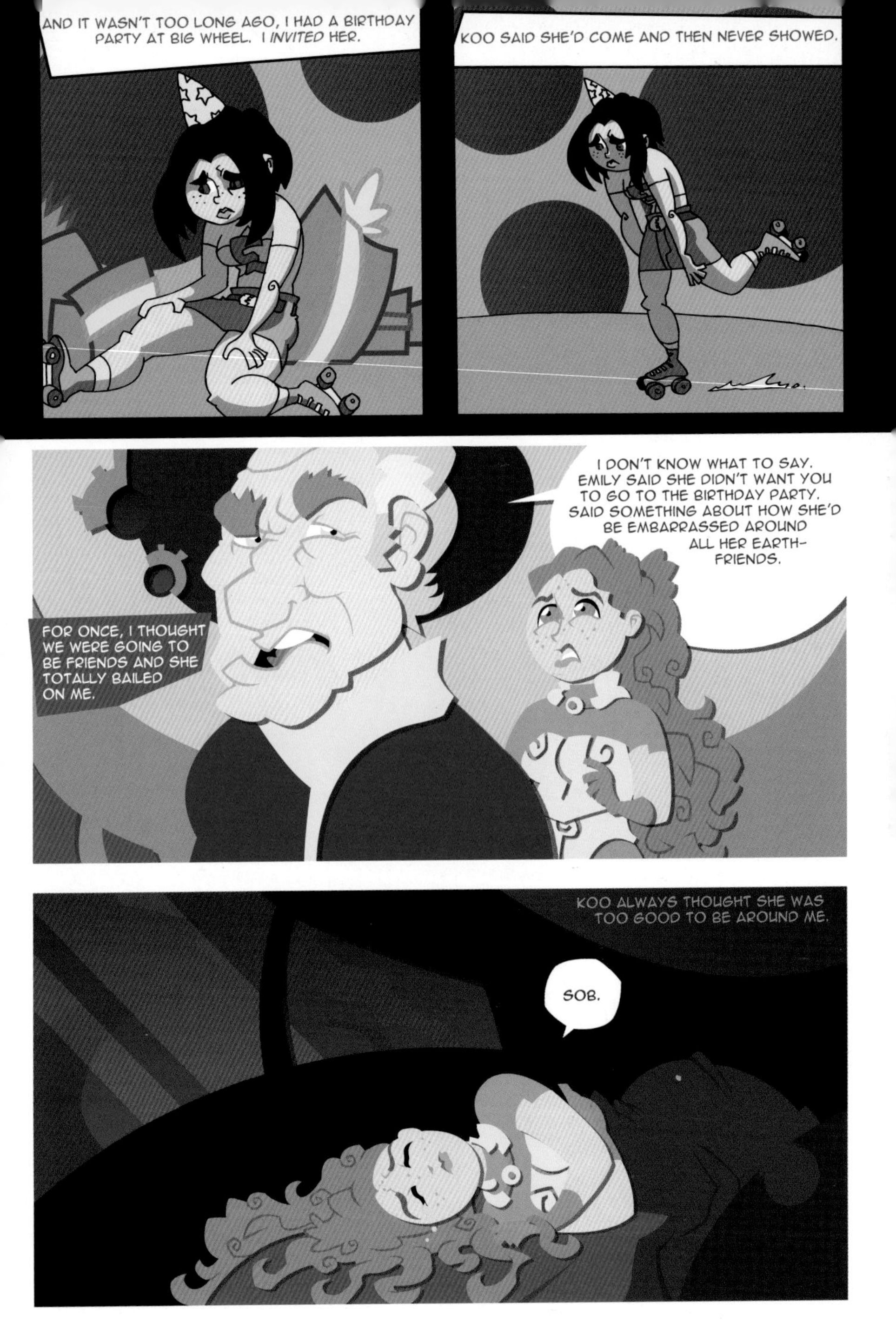
AND IT WASN'T TOO LONG AGO, I HAD A BIRTHDAY PARTY AT BIG WHEEL. I *INVITED* HER.
KOO SAID SHE'D COME AND THEN NEVER SHOWED.
FOR ONCE, I THOUGHT WE WERE GOING TO BE FRIENDS AND SHE TOTALLY BAILED ON ME.
I DON'T KNOW WHAT TO SAY. EMILY SAID SHE DIDN'T WANT YOU TO GO TO THE BIRTHDAY PARTY. SAID SOMETHING ABOUT HOW SHE'D BE EMBARRASSED AROUND ALL HER EARTH-FRIENDS.
KOO ALWAYS THOUGHT SHE WAS TOO GOOD TO BE AROUND ME.
SOB.

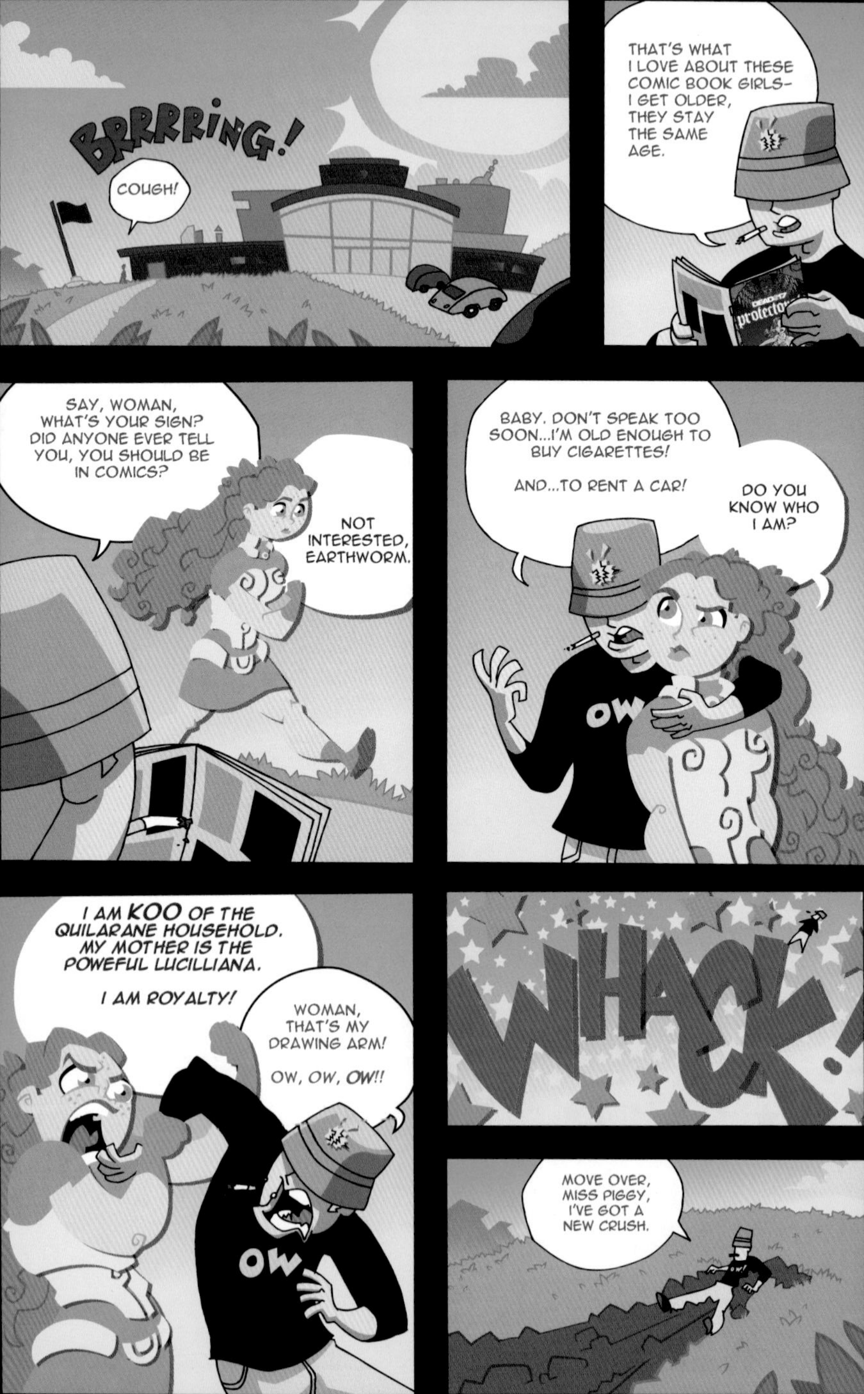
BRRRRING!
COUGH!
THAT'S WHAT I LOVE ABOUT THESE COMIC BOOK GIRLS- I GET OLDER, THEY STAY THE SAME AGE.
SAY, WOMAN, WHAT'S YOUR SIGN? DID ANYONE EVER TELL YOU, YOU SHOULD BE IN COMICS?
NOT INTERESTED, EARTHWORM.
BABY. DON'T SPEAK TOO SOON...I'M OLD ENOUGH TO BUY CIGARETTES!
AND...TO RENT A CAR!
DO YOU KNOW WHO I AM?
OW
I AM KOO OF THE QUILARANE HOUSEHOLD. MY MOTHER IS THE POWEFUL LUCILLIANA.
I AM ROYALTY!
WOMAN, THAT'S MY DRAWING ARM!
OW, OW, OW!!
OW
WHACK!
MOVE OVER, MISS PIGGY, I'VE GOT A NEW CRUSH.

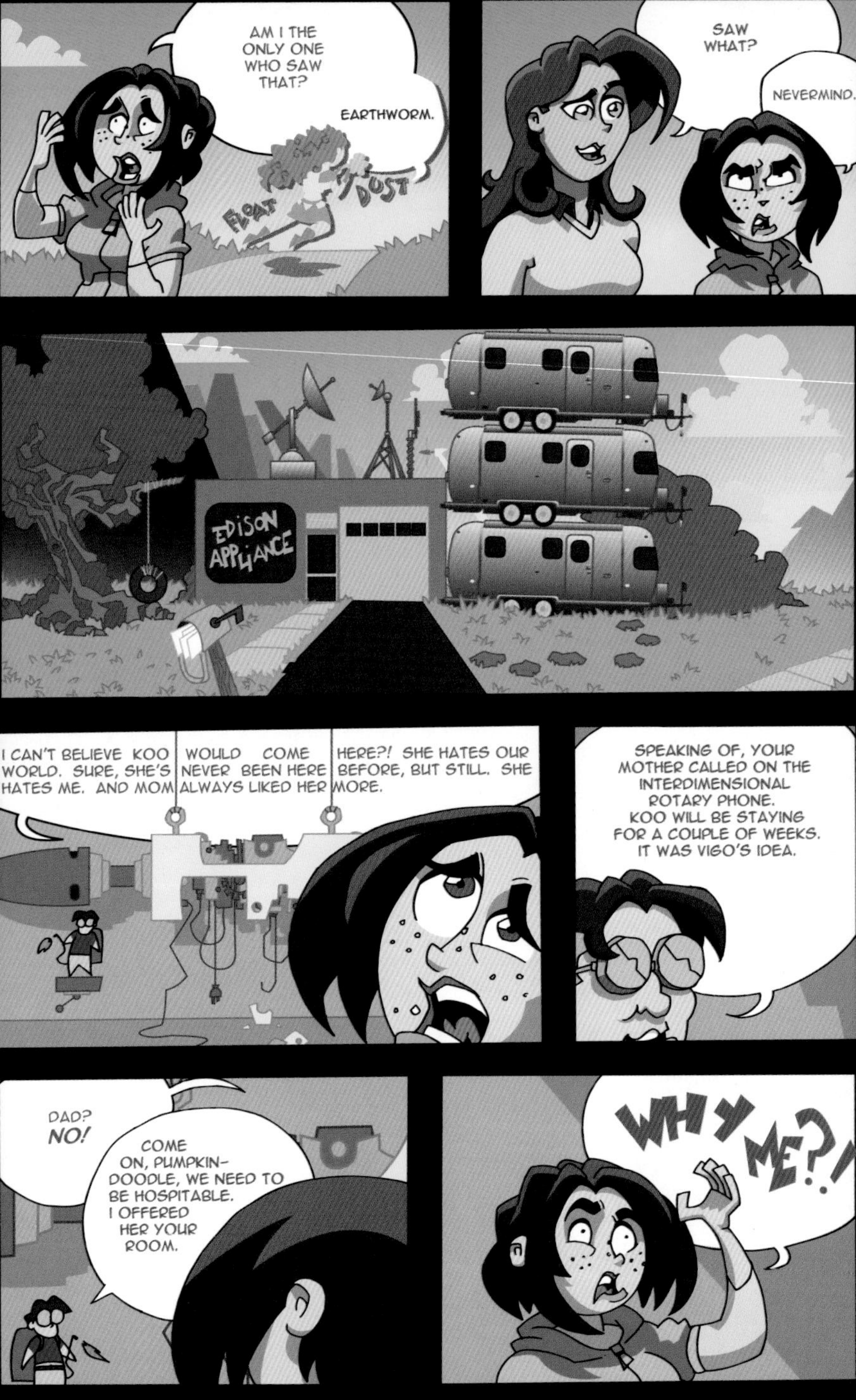
AM I THE ONLY ONE WHO SAW THAT?
EARTHWORM.
FLOAT
DUST
SAW WHAT?
NEVERMIND.
EDISON APPLIANCE
I CAN'T BELIEVE KOO WOULD COME HERE?! SHE HATES OUR WORLD. SURE, SHE'S NEVER BEEN HERE BEFORE, BUT STILL. SHE HATES ME. AND MOM ALWAYS LIKED HER MORE.
SPEAKING OF, YOUR MOTHER CALLED ON THE INTERDIMENSIONAL ROTARY PHONE. KOO WILL BE STAYING FOR A COUPLE OF WEEKS. IT WAS VIGO'S IDEA.
DAD? NO!
COME ON, PUMPKIN-DOODLE, WE NEED TO BE HOSPITABLE. I OFFERED HER YOUR ROOM.
WHY ME?!

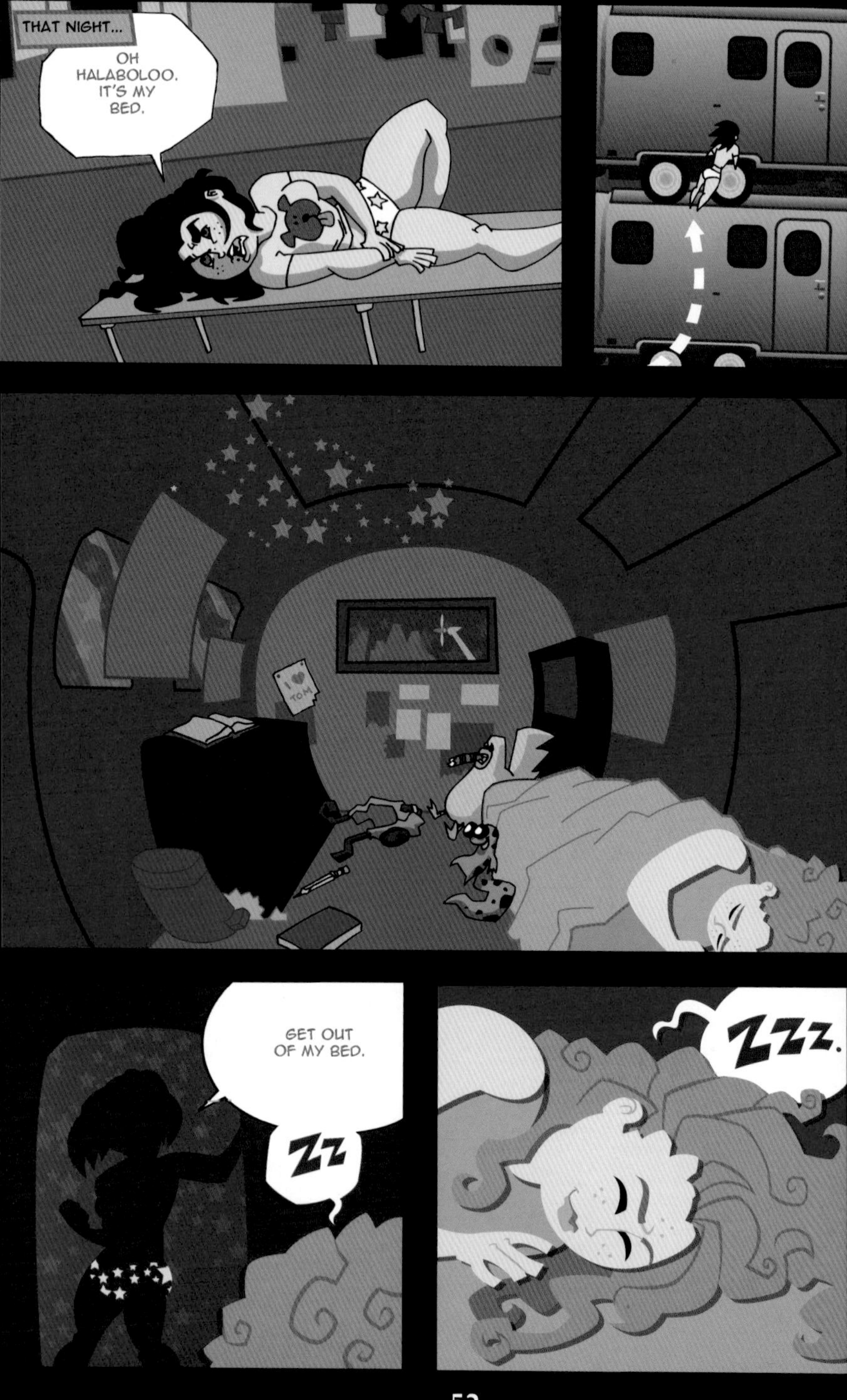
THAT NIGHT...
OH HALABOLOO. IT'S MY BED.
I ♥ TOM
GET OUT OF MY BED.
ZZ
ZZZ.

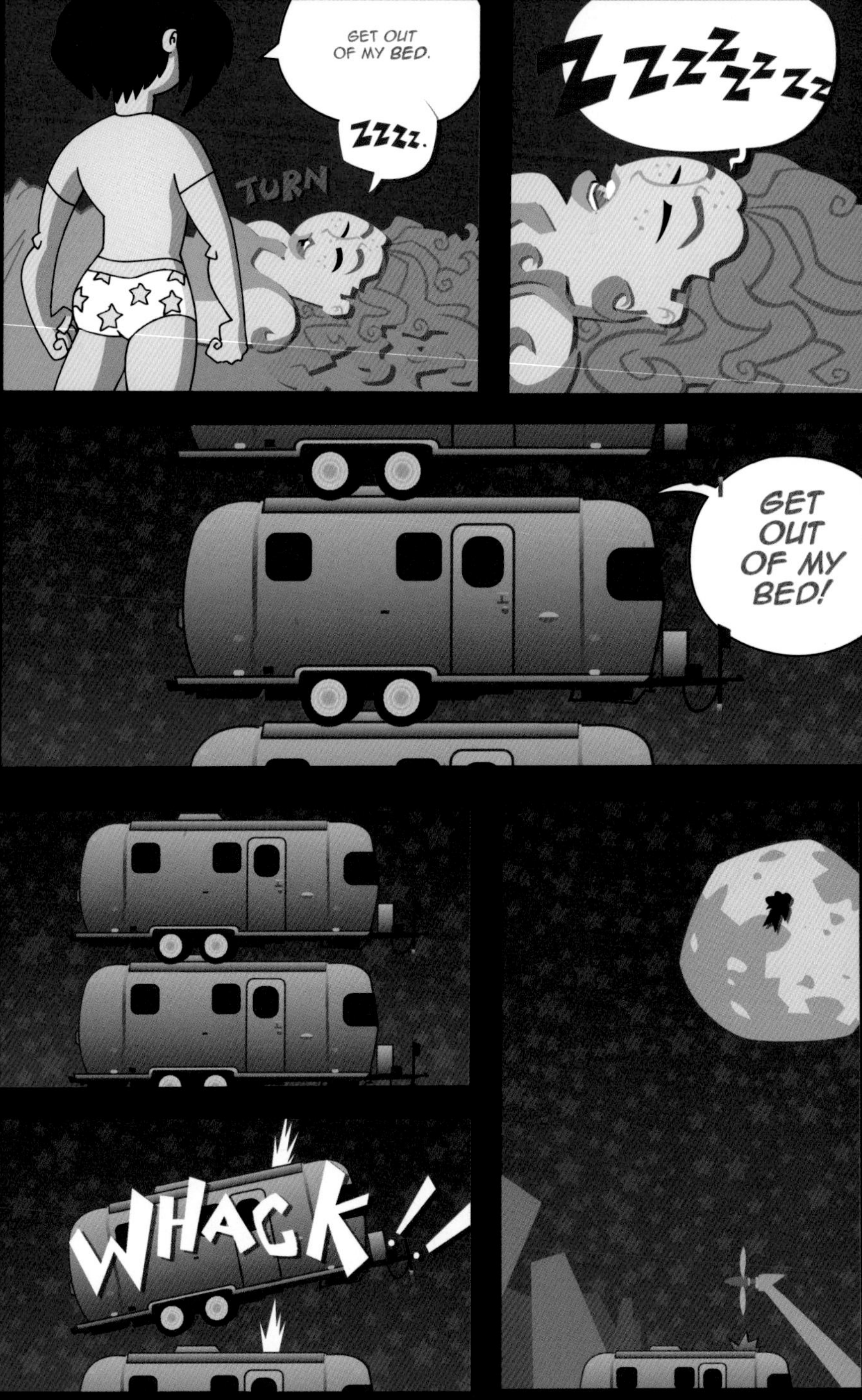
GET OUT OF MY BED.
ZZZZ.
TURN
ZZZZZZZZZ
GET OUT OF MY BED!
WHACK!!

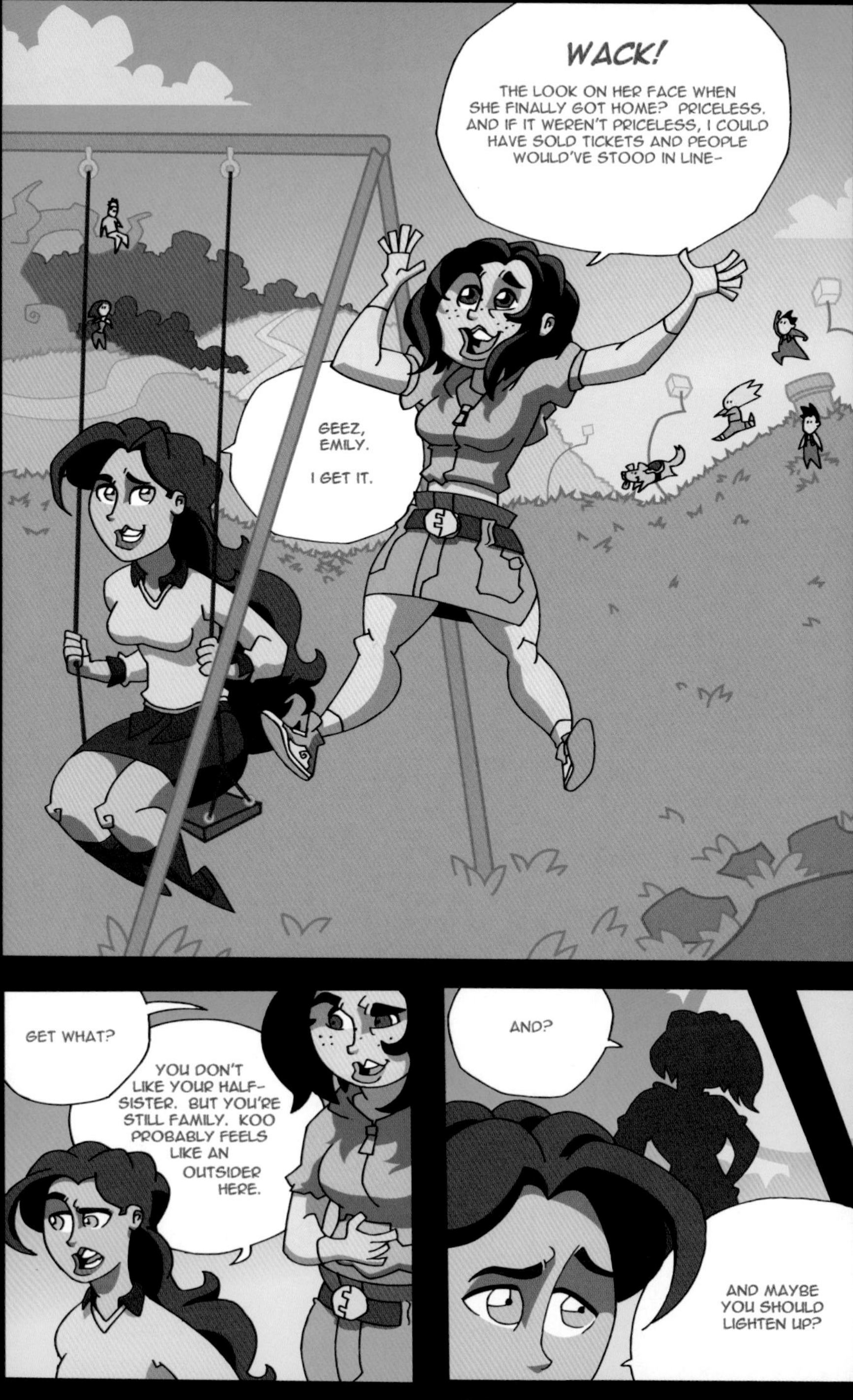
WACK!
THE LOOK ON HER FACE WHEN SHE FINALLY GOT HOME? PRICELESS. AND IF IT WEREN'T PRICELESS, I COULD HAVE SOLD TICKETS AND PEOPLE WOULD'VE STOOD IN LINE-
GEEZ, EMILY. I GET IT.
GET WHAT?
YOU DON'T LIKE YOUR HALF-SISTER. BUT YOU'RE STILL FAMILY. KOO PROBABLY FEELS LIKE AN OUTSIDER HERE.
AND?
AND MAYBE YOU SHOULD LIGHTEN UP?

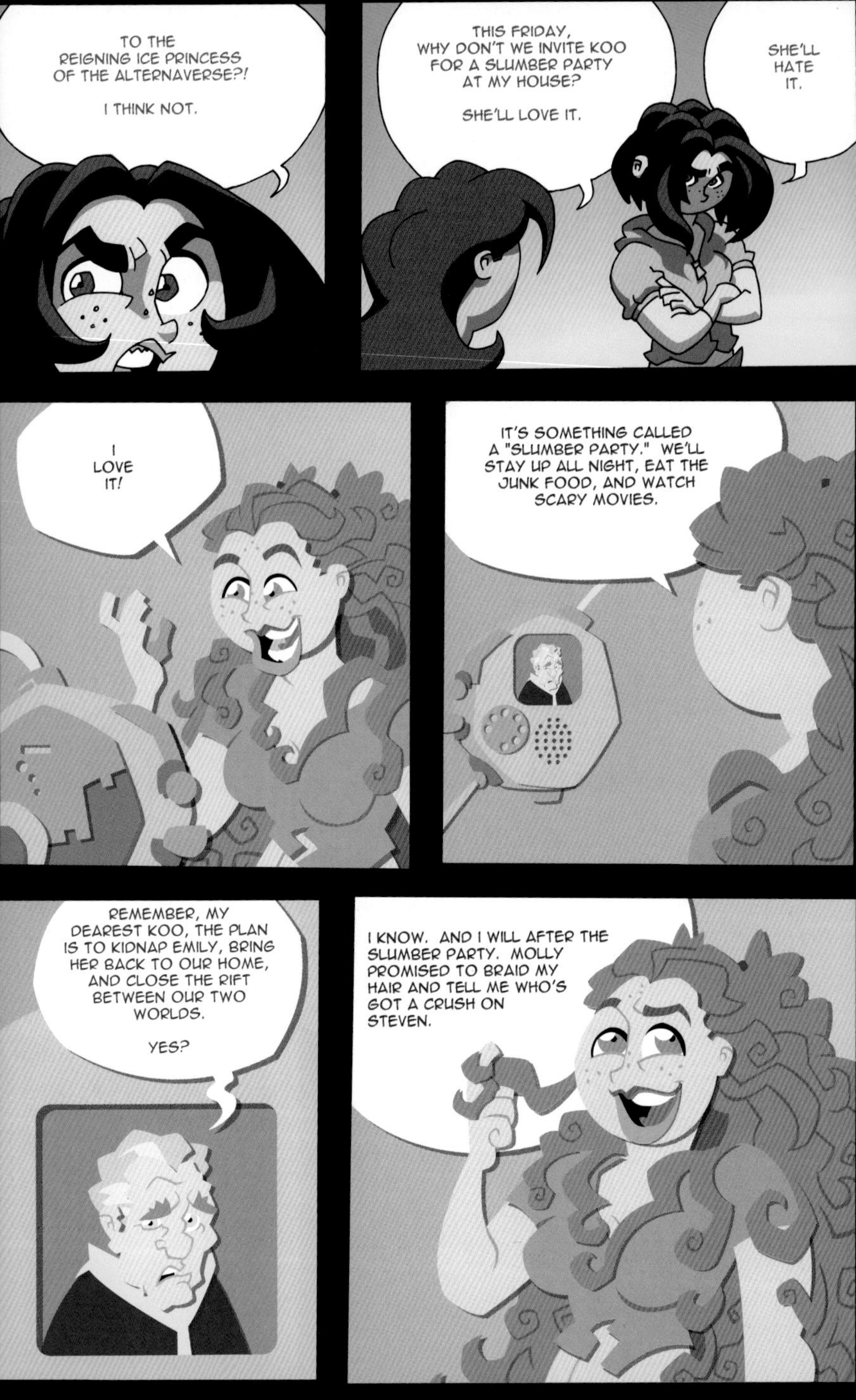
TO THE REIGNING ICE PRINCESS OF THE ALTERNAVERSE?! I THINK NOT.
THIS FRIDAY, WHY DON'T WE INVITE KOO FOR A SLUMBER PARTY AT MY HOUSE? SHE'LL LOVE IT.
SHE'LL HATE IT.
I LOVE IT!
IT'S SOMETHING CALLED A "SLUMBER PARTY." WE'LL STAY UP ALL NIGHT, EAT THE JUNK FOOD, AND WATCH SCARY MOVIES.
REMEMBER, MY DEAREST KOO, THE PLAN IS TO KIDNAP EMILY, BRING HER BACK TO OUR HOME, AND CLOSE THE RIFT BETWEEN OUR TWO WORLDS. YES?
I KNOW. AND I WILL AFTER THE SLUMBER PARTY. MOLLY PROMISED TO BRAID MY HAIR AND TELL ME WHO'S GOT A CRUSH ON STEVEN.

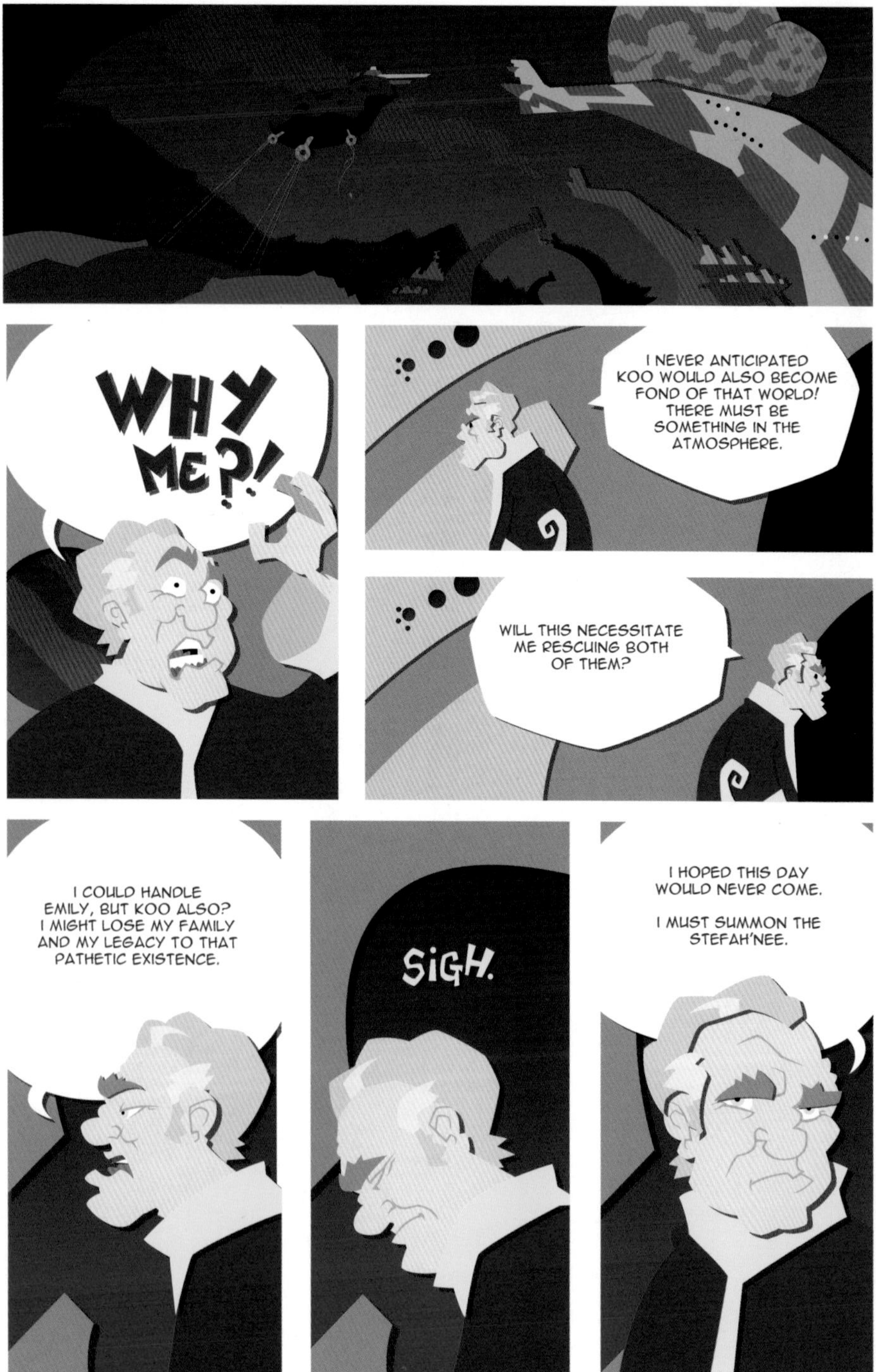
WHY ME?!
I NEVER ANTICIPATED KOO WOULD ALSO BECOME FOND OF THAT WORLD! THERE MUST BE SOMETHING IN THE ATMOSPHERE.
WILL THIS NECESSITATE ME RESCUING BOTH OF THEM?
I COULD HANDLE EMILY, BUT KOO ALSO? I MIGHT LOSE MY FAMILY AND MY LEGACY TO THAT PATHETIC EXISTENCE.
SIGH.
I HOPED THIS DAY WOULD NEVER COME.
I MUST SUMMON THE STEFAH'NEE.

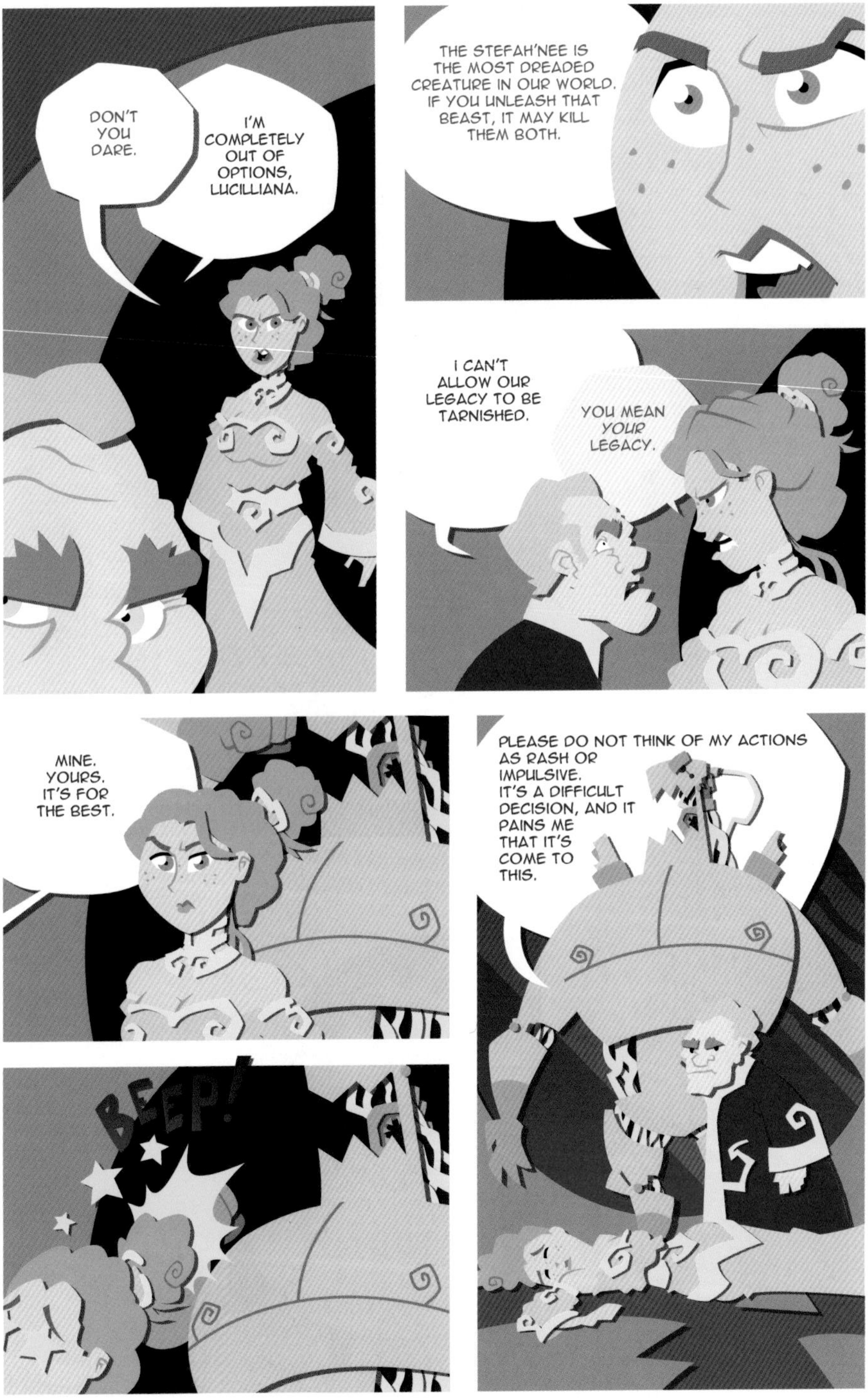
DON'T YOU DARE.
I'M COMPLETELY OUT OF OPTIONS, LUCILLIANA.
THE STEFAH'NEE IS THE MOST DREADED CREATURE IN OUR WORLD. IF YOU UNLEASH THAT BEAST, IT MAY KILL THEM BOTH.
I CAN'T ALLOW OUR LEGACY TO BE TARNISHED.
YOU MEAN *YOUR* LEGACY.
MINE. YOURS. IT'S FOR THE BEST.
PLEASE DO NOT THINK OF MY ACTIONS AS RASH OR IMPULSIVE. IT'S A DIFFICULT DECISION, AND IT PAINS ME THAT IT'S COME TO THIS.
BEEP!

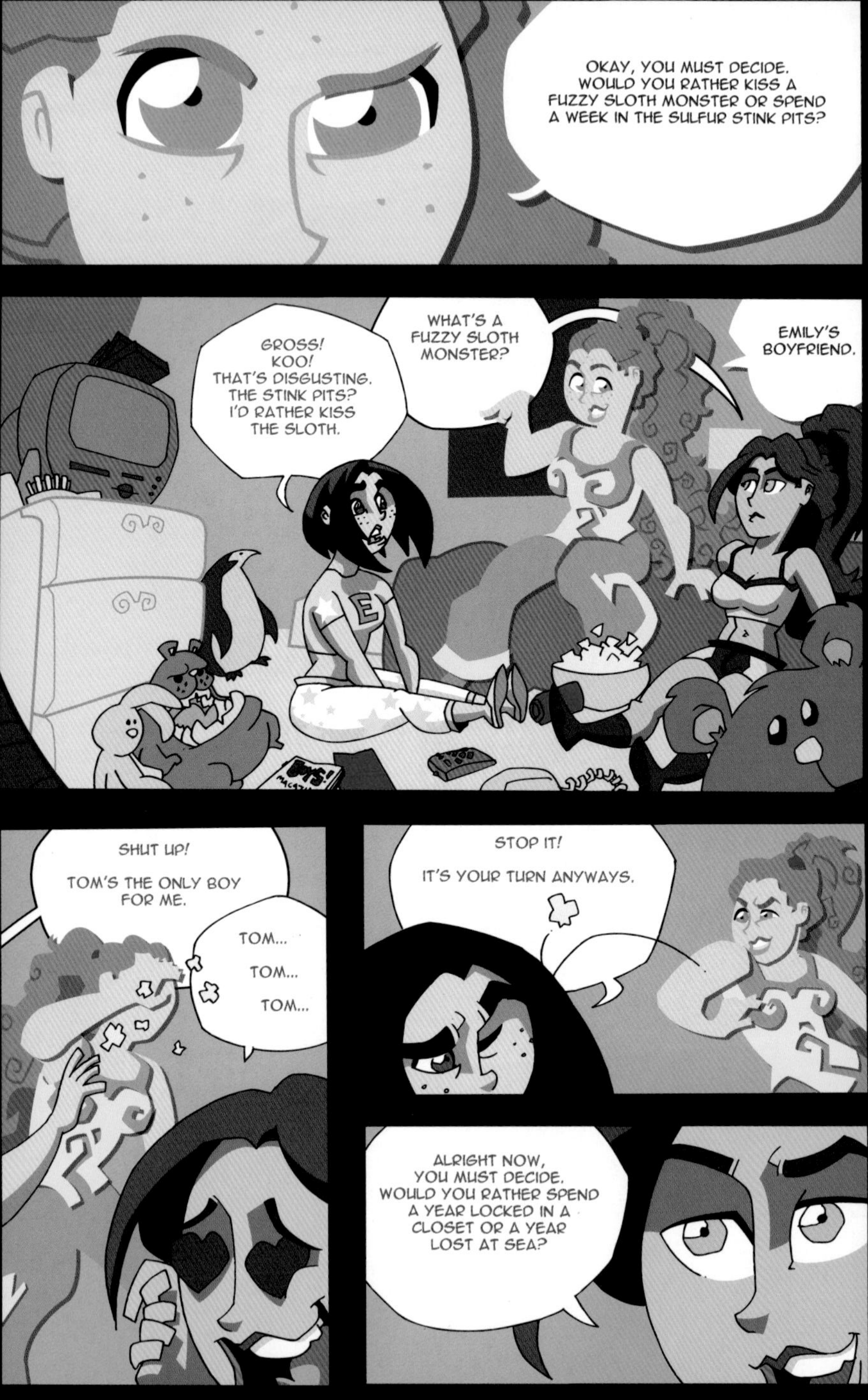
OKAY, YOU MUST DECIDE. WOULD YOU RATHER KISS A FUZZY SLOTH MONSTER OR SPEND A WEEK IN THE SULFUR STINK PITS?
GROSS! KOO! THAT'S DISGUSTING. THE STINK PITS? I'D RATHER KISS THE SLOTH.
WHAT'S A FUZZY SLOTH MONSTER?
EMILY'S BOYFRIEND.
SHUT UP!
TOM'S THE ONLY BOY FOR ME.
TOM... TOM... TOM...
STOP IT!
IT'S YOUR TURN ANYWAYS.
ALRIGHT NOW, YOU MUST DECIDE. WOULD YOU RATHER SPEND A YEAR LOCKED IN A CLOSET OR A YEAR LOST AT SEA?

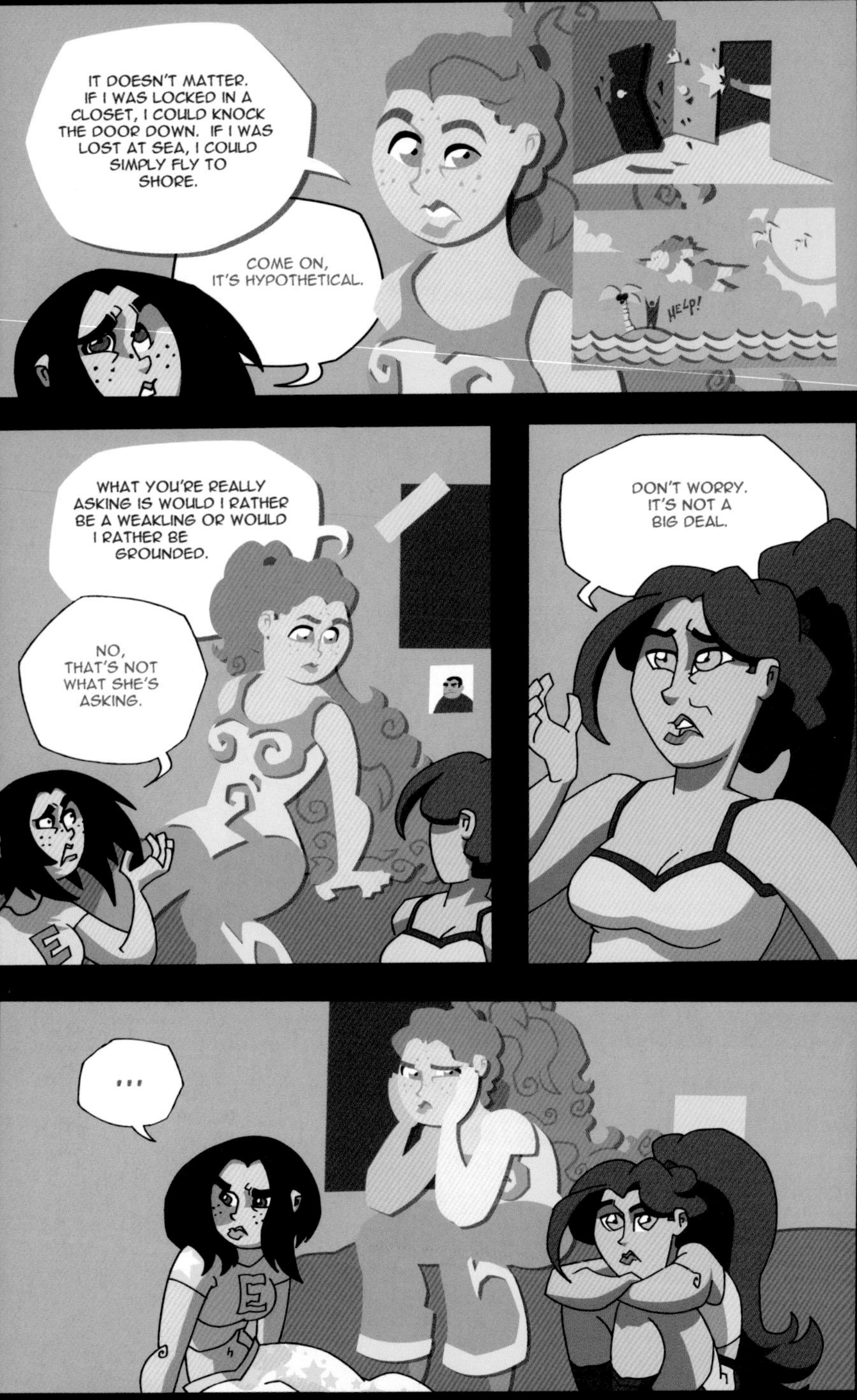
IT DOESN'T MATTER. IF I WAS LOCKED IN A CLOSET, I COULD KNOCK THE DOOR DOWN. IF I WAS LOST AT SEA, I COULD SIMPLY FLY TO SHORE.
COME ON, IT'S HYPOTHETICAL.
HELP!
WHAT YOU'RE REALLY ASKING IS WOULD I RATHER BE A WEAKLING OR WOULD I RATHER BE GROUNDED.
NO, THAT'S NOT WHAT SHE'S ASKING.
DON'T WORRY. IT'S NOT A BIG DEAL.
...

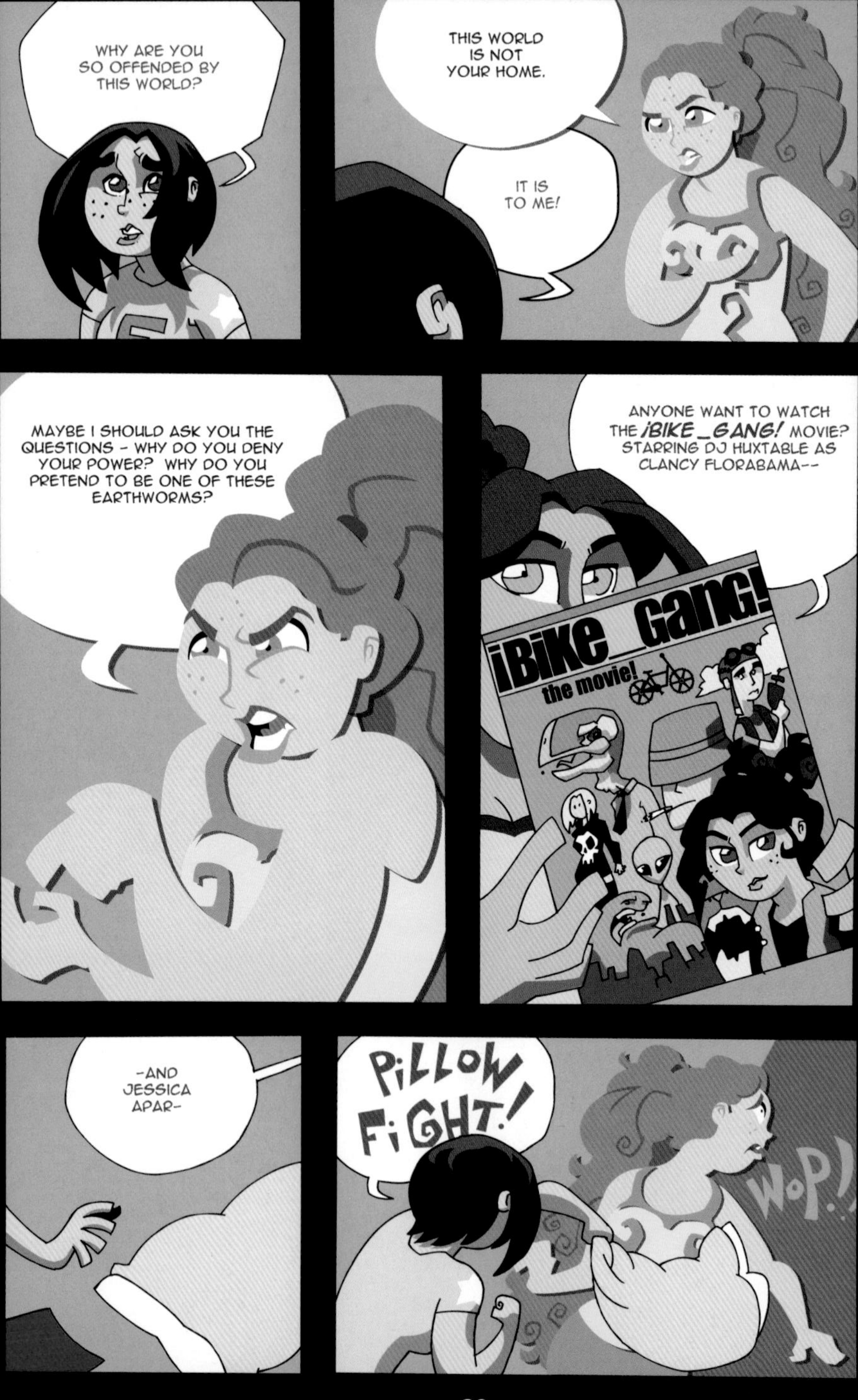
WHY ARE YOU SO OFFENDED BY THIS WORLD?
THIS WORLD IS NOT YOUR HOME.
IT IS TO ME!
MAYBE I SHOULD ASK YOU THE QUESTIONS - WHY DO YOU DENY YOUR POWER? WHY DO YOU PRETEND TO BE ONE OF THESE EARTHWORMS?
ANYONE WANT TO WATCH THE ¡BIKE_GANG! MOVIE? STARRING DJ HUXTABLE AS CLANCY FLORABAMA--
¡Bike_Gang!
the movie!
-AND JESSICA APAR-
PILLOW FIGHT!
WOP!

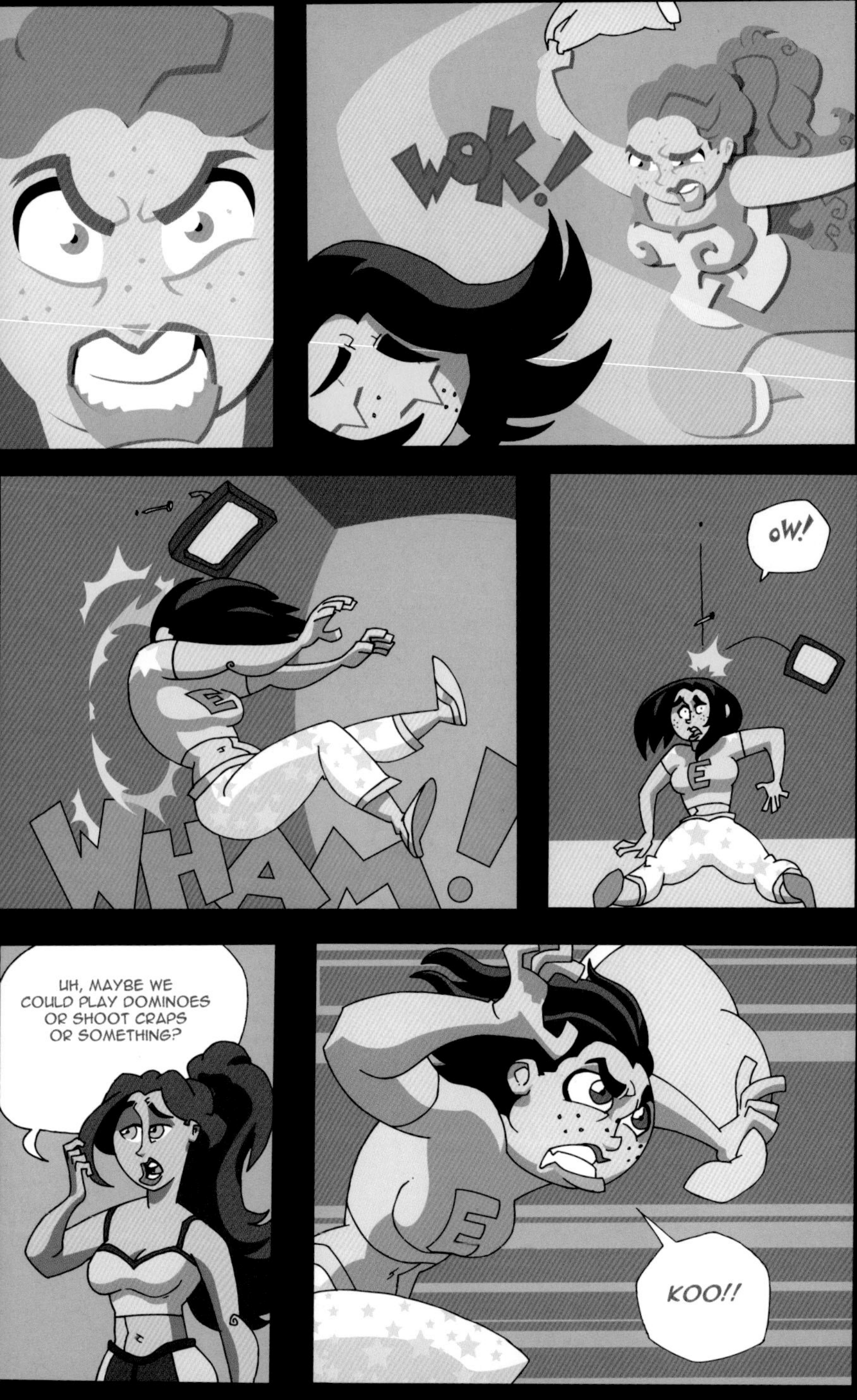
WOK!
WHAM!
OW!
UH, MAYBE WE COULD PLAY DOMINOES OR SHOOT CRAPS OR SOMETHING?
KOO!!

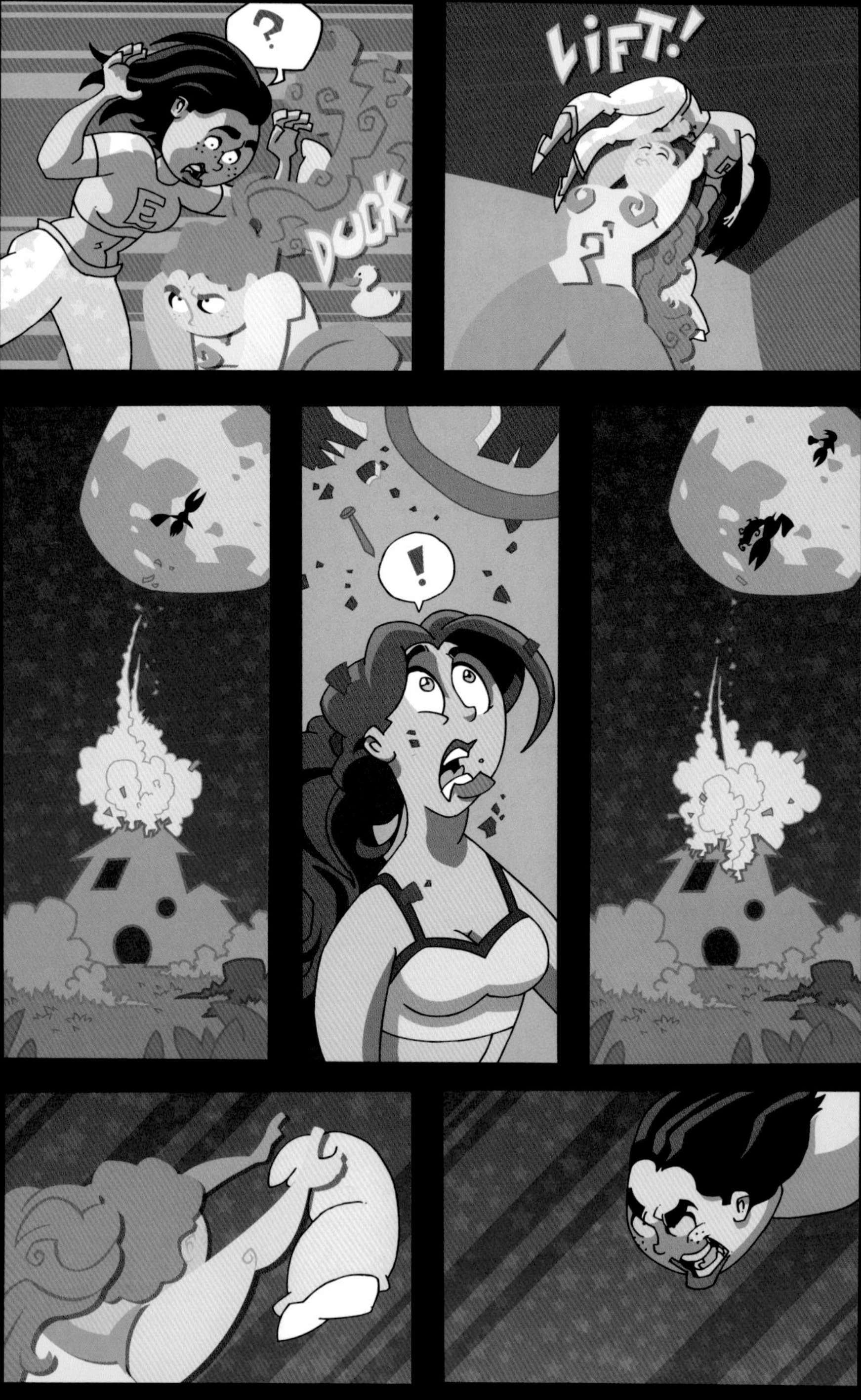
?
DUCK
LIFT!
!

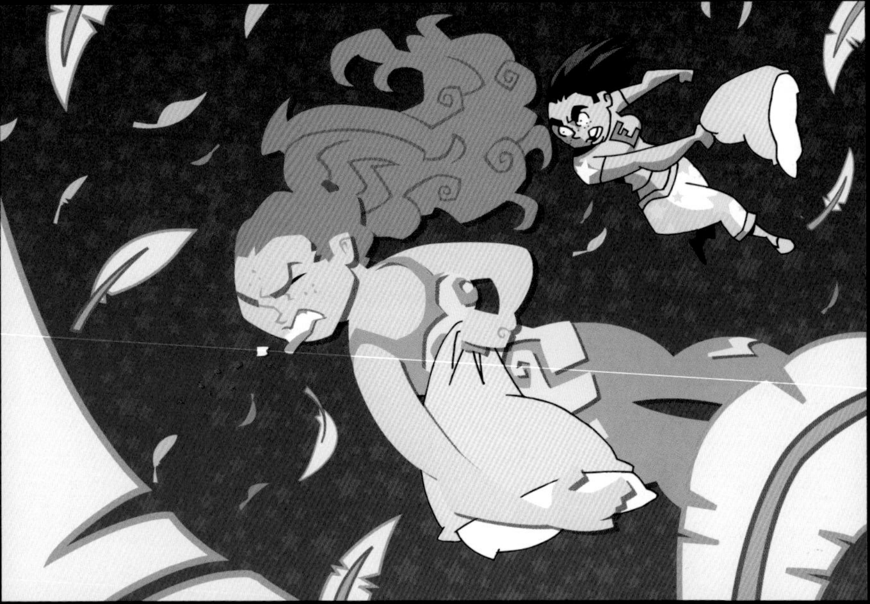

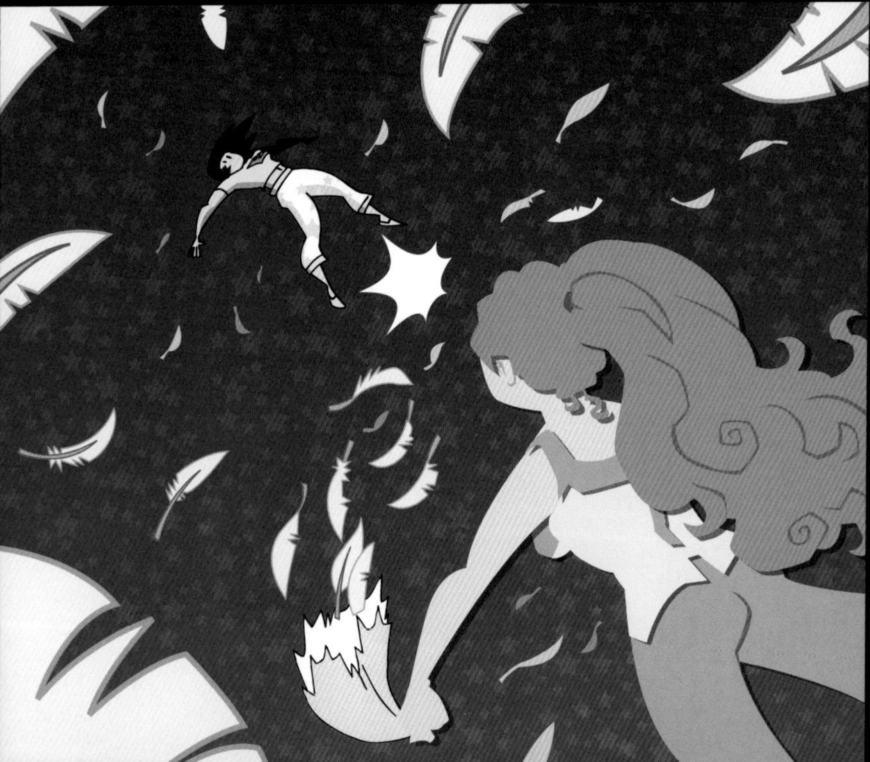

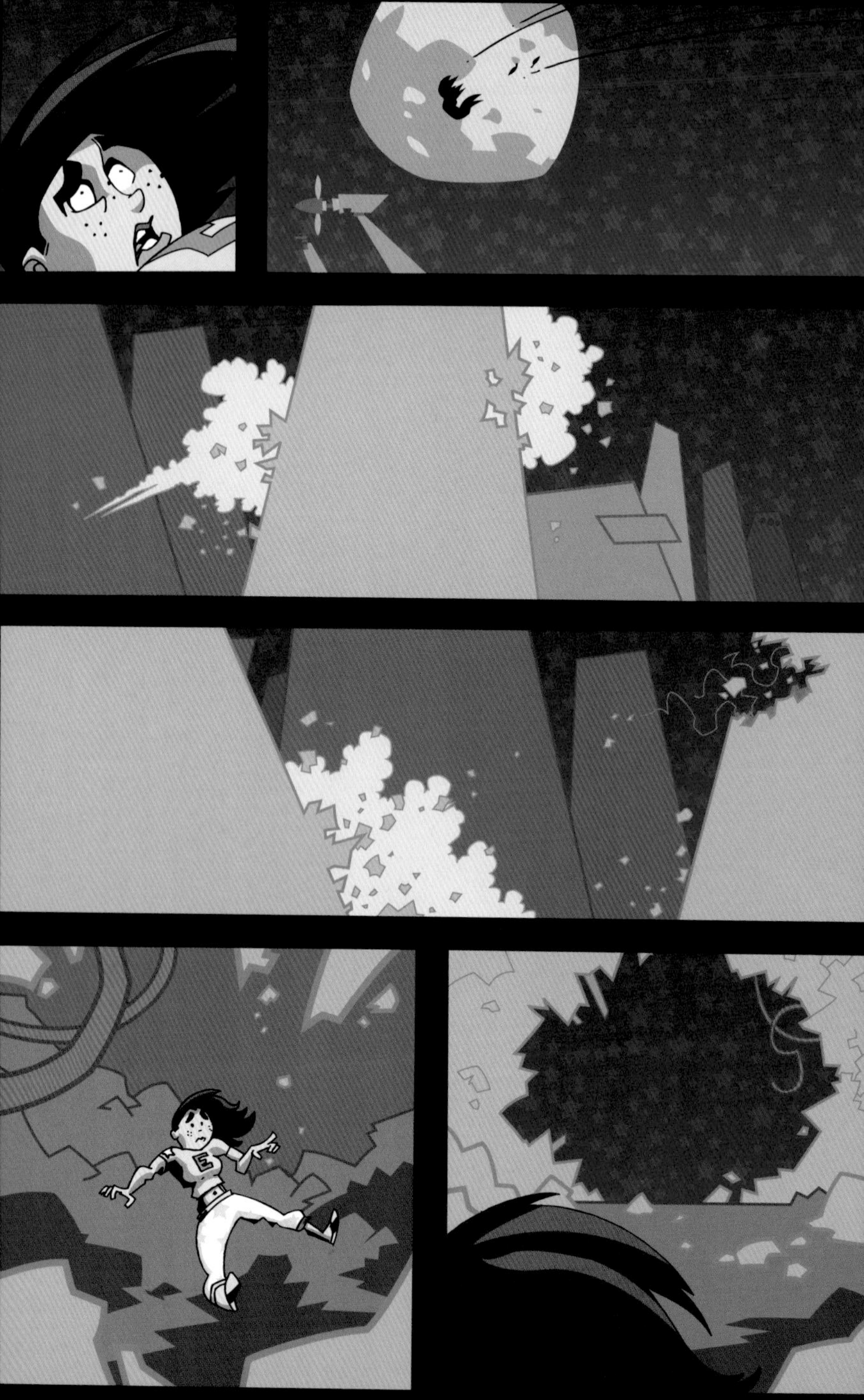

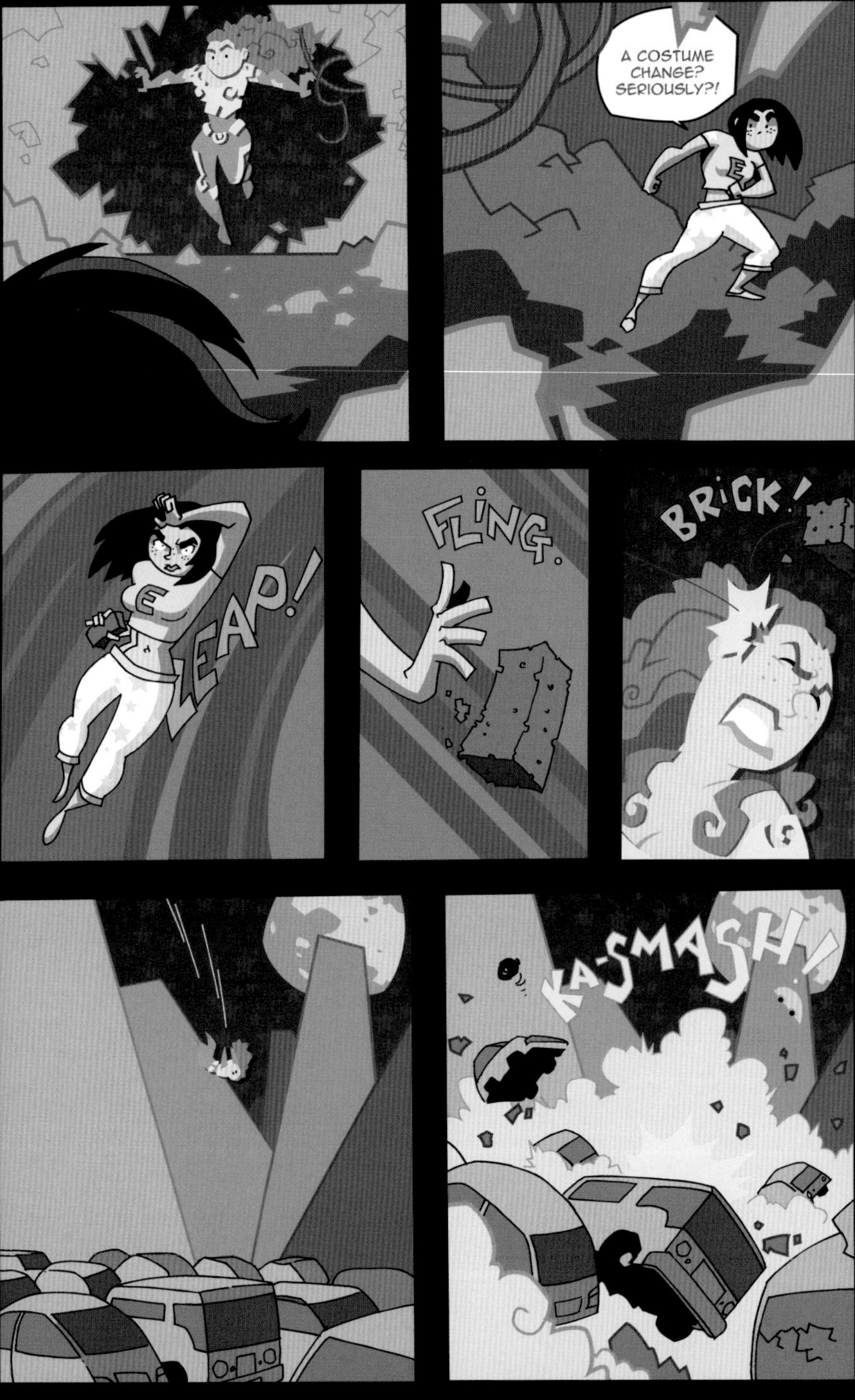
A COSTUME CHANGE? SERIOUSLY?!
LEAP!
FLING.
BRICK!
KA-SMASH!

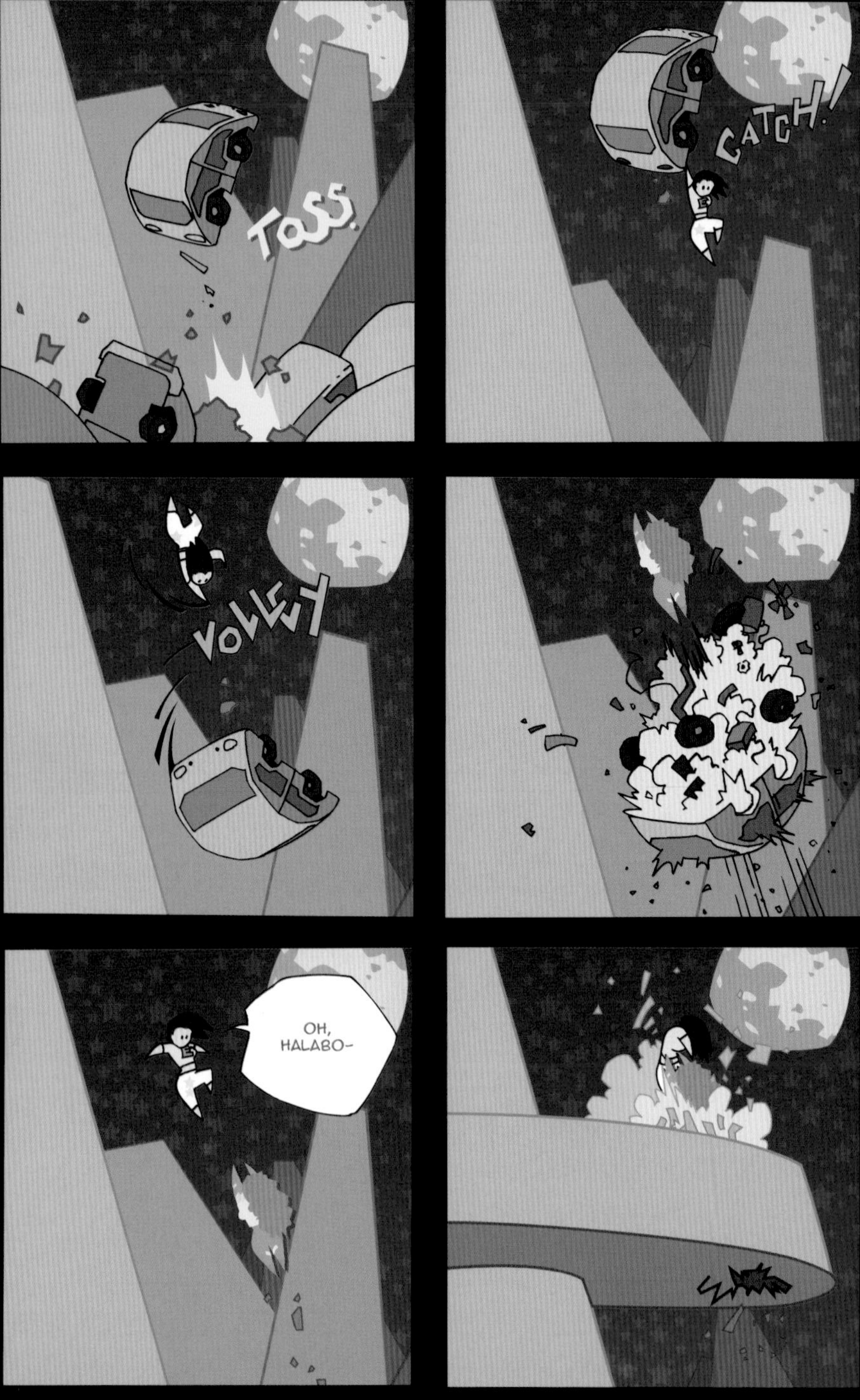
TOSS
CATCH!
VOLLEY
OH, HALABO-

THROW
SNAG.
SWIVEL
KICK!
OW!
UNGH...
THAT DIDN'T HURT.
SLAP.

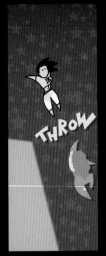

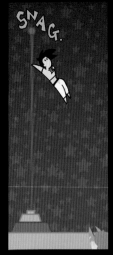

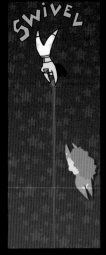

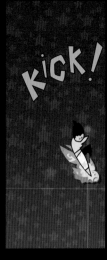

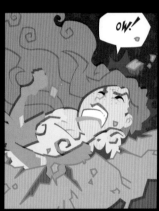

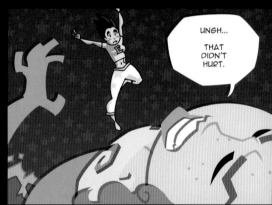

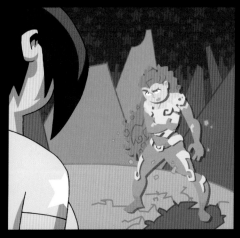

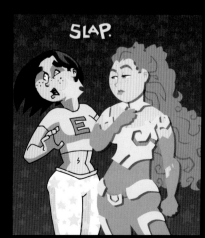

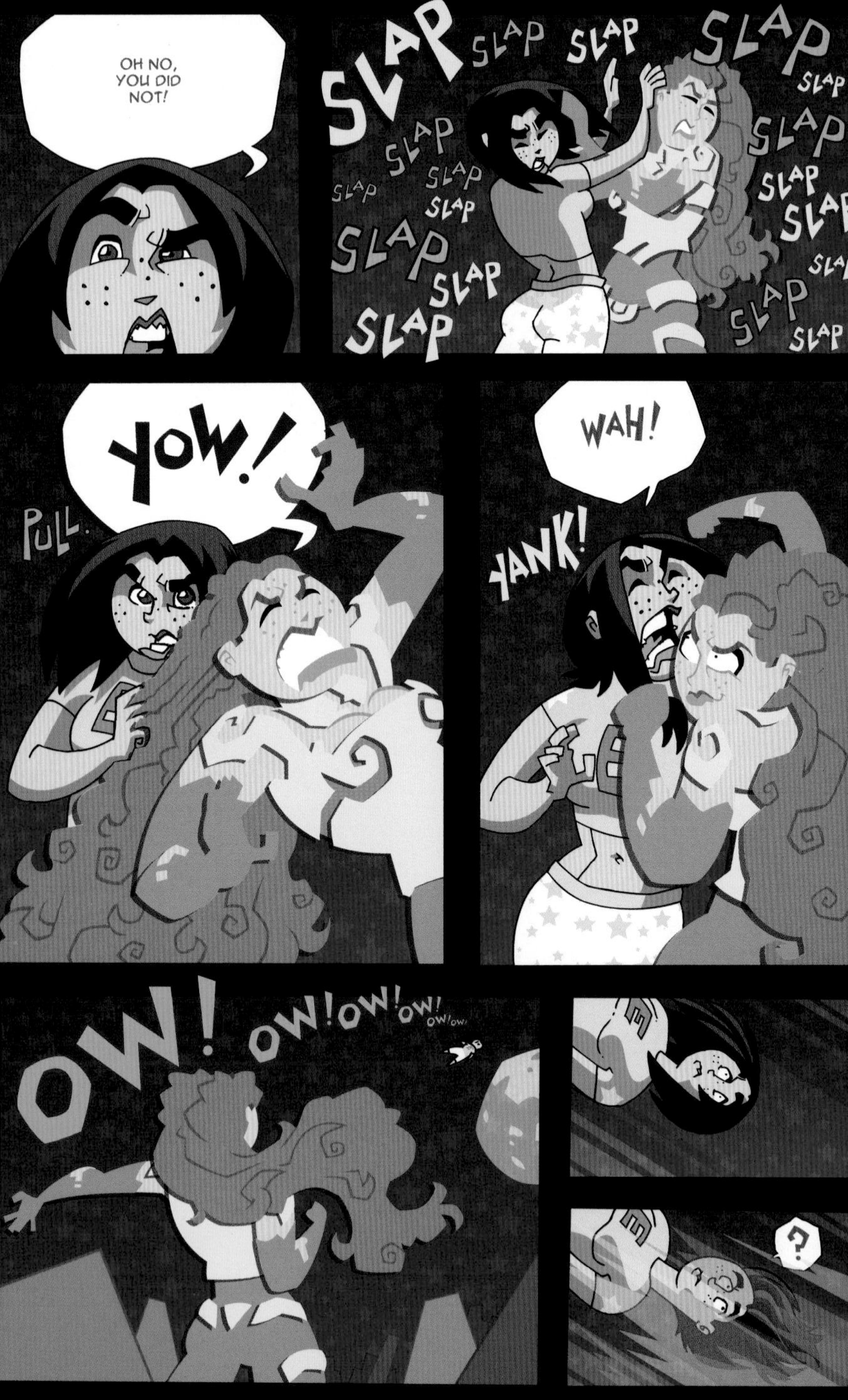
OH NO, YOU DID NOT!
SLAP SLAP SLAP SLAP SLAP SLAP SLAP SLAP SLAP SLAP SLAP SLAP SLAP SLAP SLAP SLAP SLAP SLAP
YOW!!
PULL.
WAH!
YANK!
OW! OW! OW! OW! OW! OW!
?

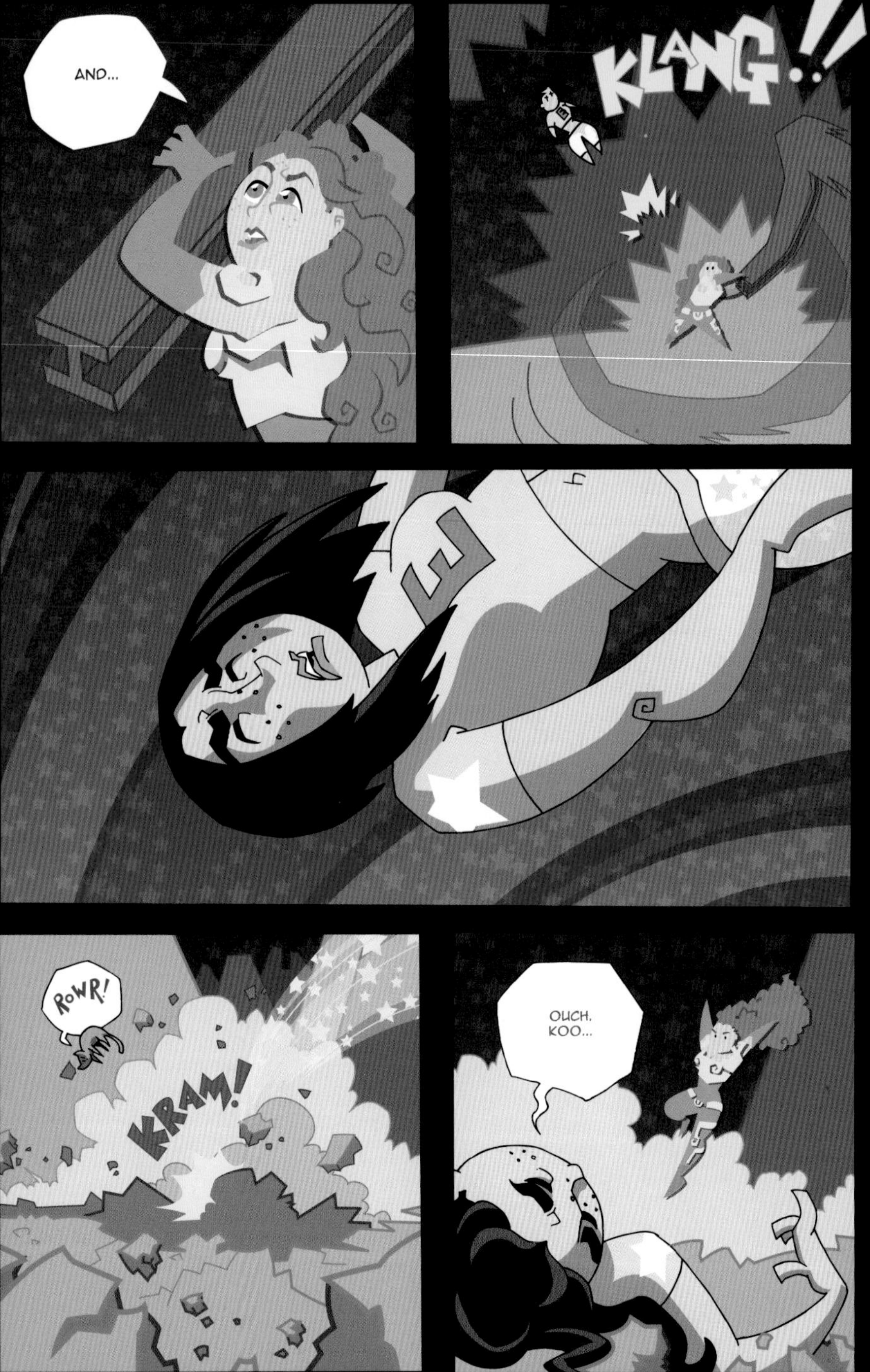
AND...
KLANG!!
ROWR!
KRAM!
OUCH, KOO...

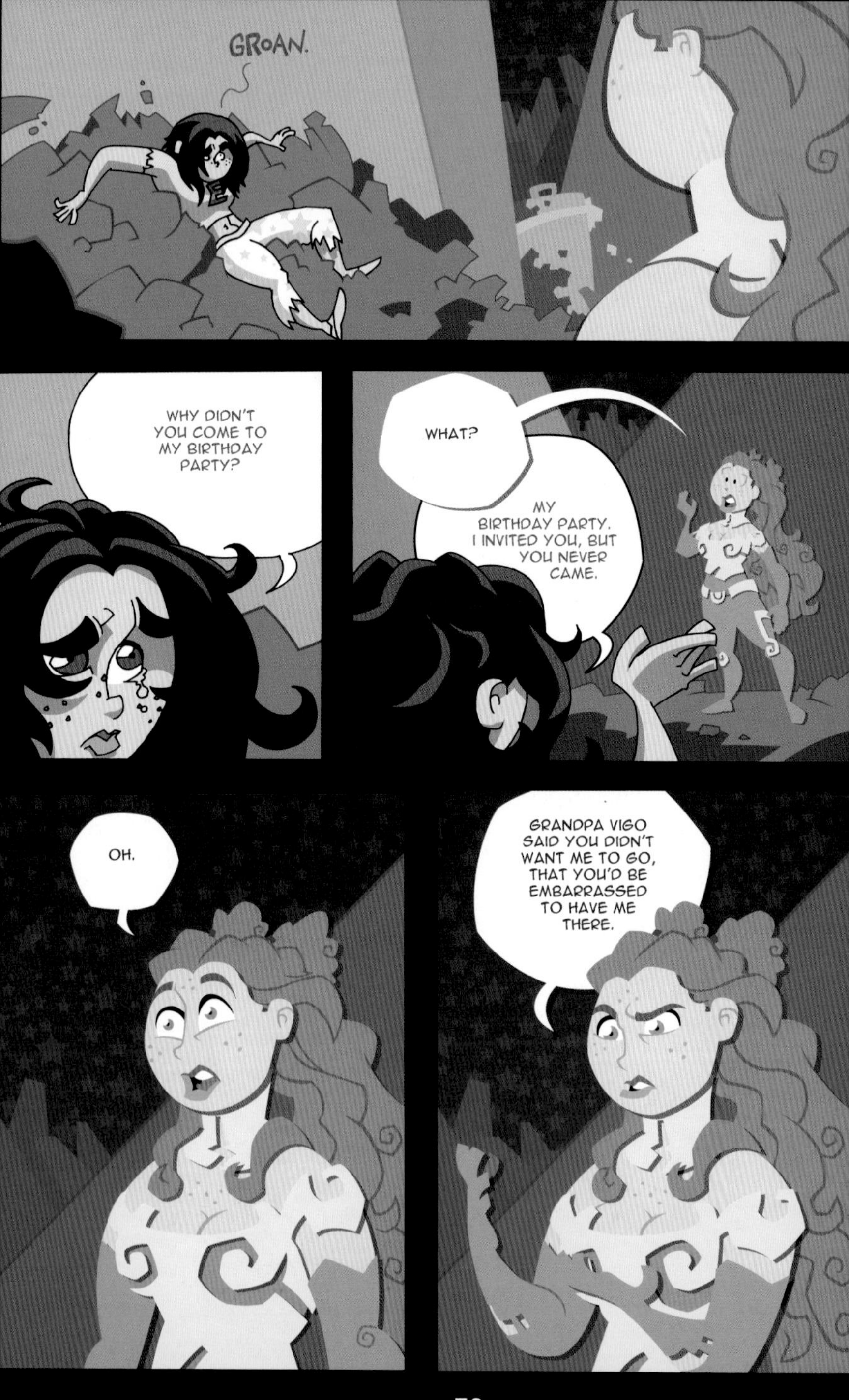
GROAN.
WHY DIDN'T YOU COME TO MY BIRTHDAY PARTY?
WHAT?
MY BIRTHDAY PARTY. I INVITED YOU, BUT YOU NEVER CAME.
OH.
GRANDPA VIGO SAID YOU DIDN'T WANT ME TO GO, THAT YOU'D BE EMBARRASSED TO HAVE ME THERE.

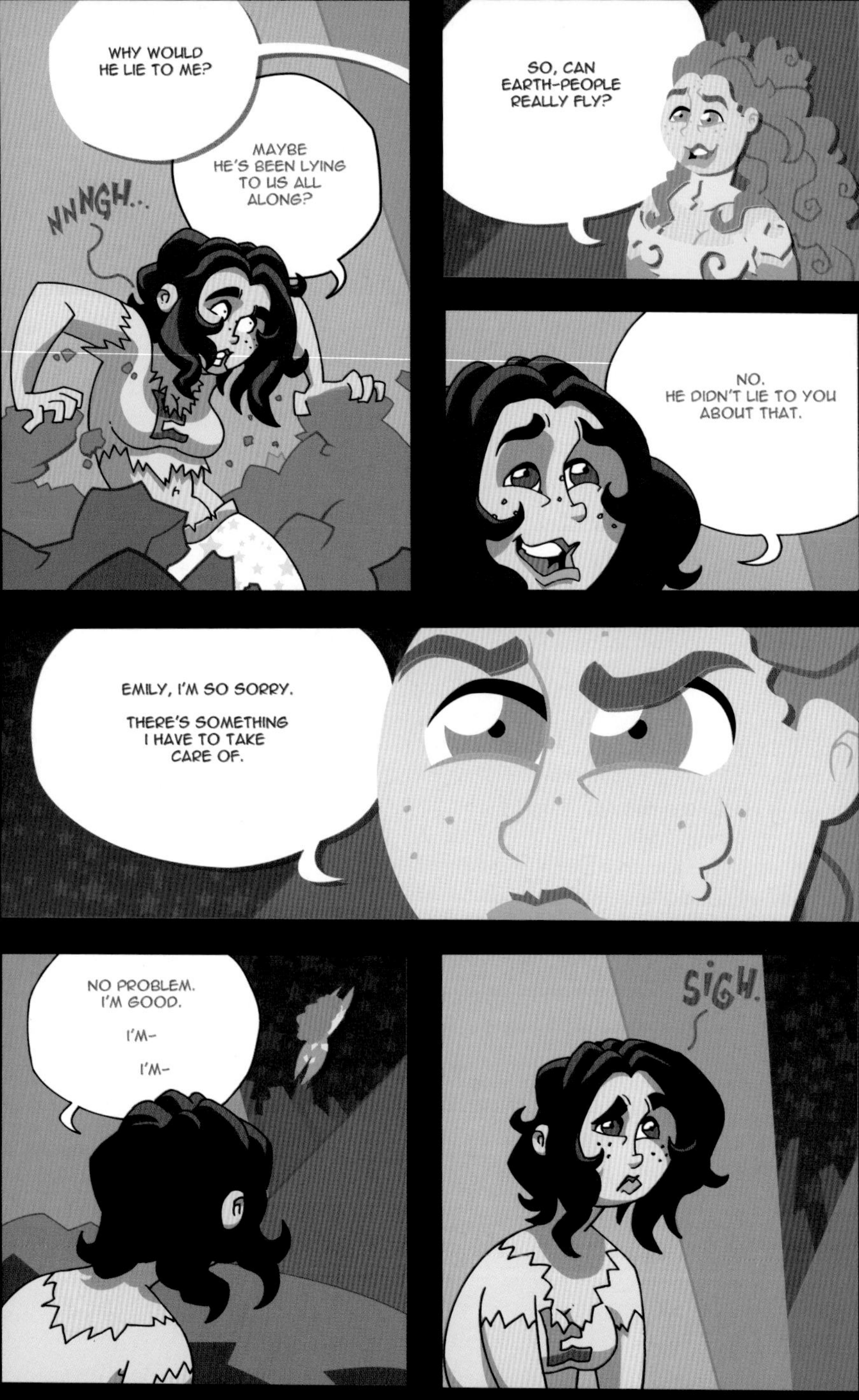

WHY WOULD HE LIE TO ME?
MAYBE HE'S BEEN LYING TO US ALL ALONG?
NNNGH...
SO, CAN EARTH-PEOPLE REALLY FLY?
NO. HE DIDN'T LIE TO YOU ABOUT THAT.
EMILY, I'M SO SORRY.
THERE'S SOMETHING I HAVE TO TAKE CARE OF.
NO PROBLEM. I'M GOOD.
I'M-
I'M-
SIGH.

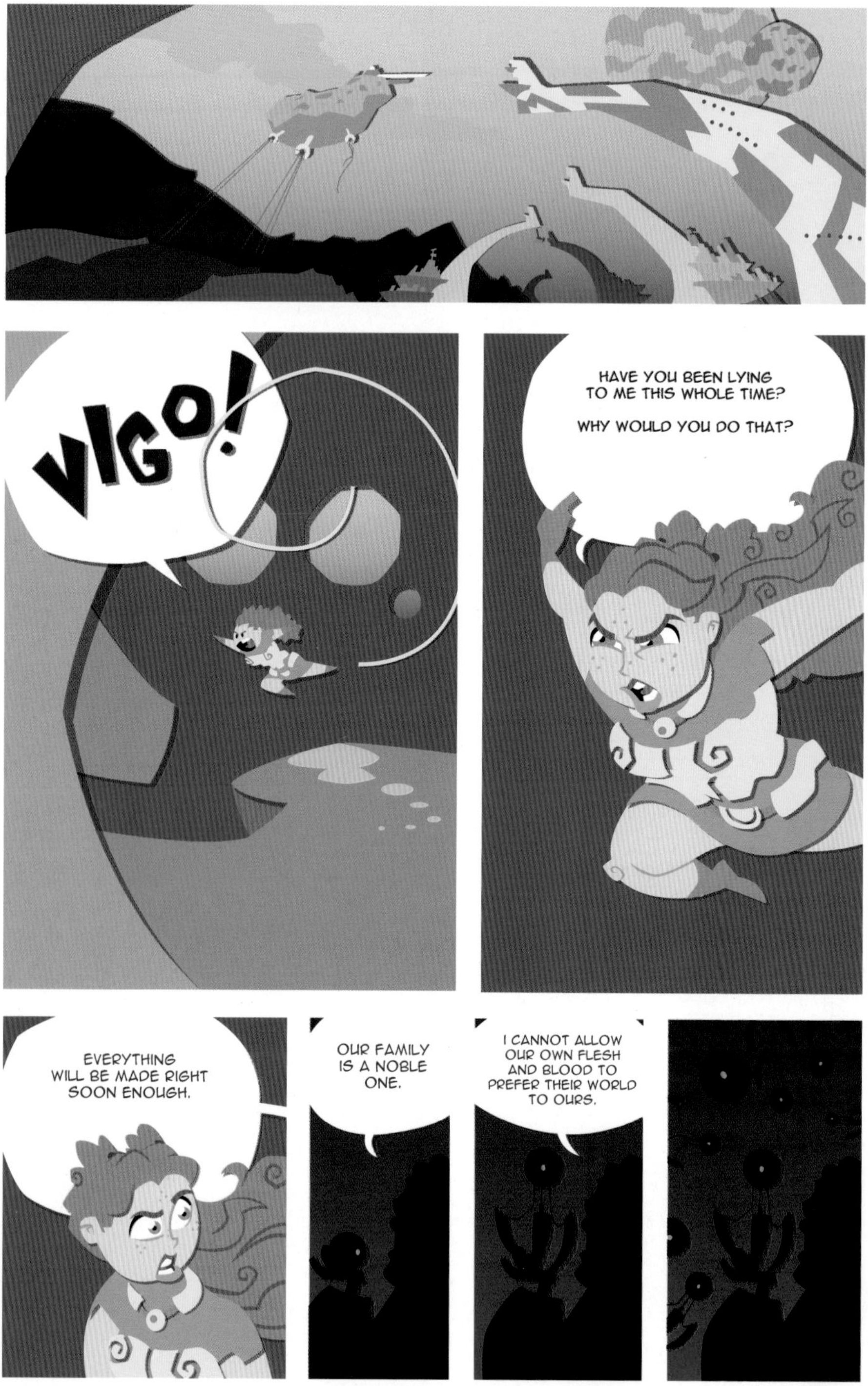
VIGO!
HAVE YOU BEEN LYING TO ME THIS WHOLE TIME?
WHY WOULD YOU DO THAT?
EVERYTHING WILL BE MADE RIGHT SOON ENOUGH.
OUR FAMILY IS A NOBLE ONE.
I CANNOT ALLOW OUR OWN FLESH AND BLOOD TO PREFER THEIR WORLD TO OURS.

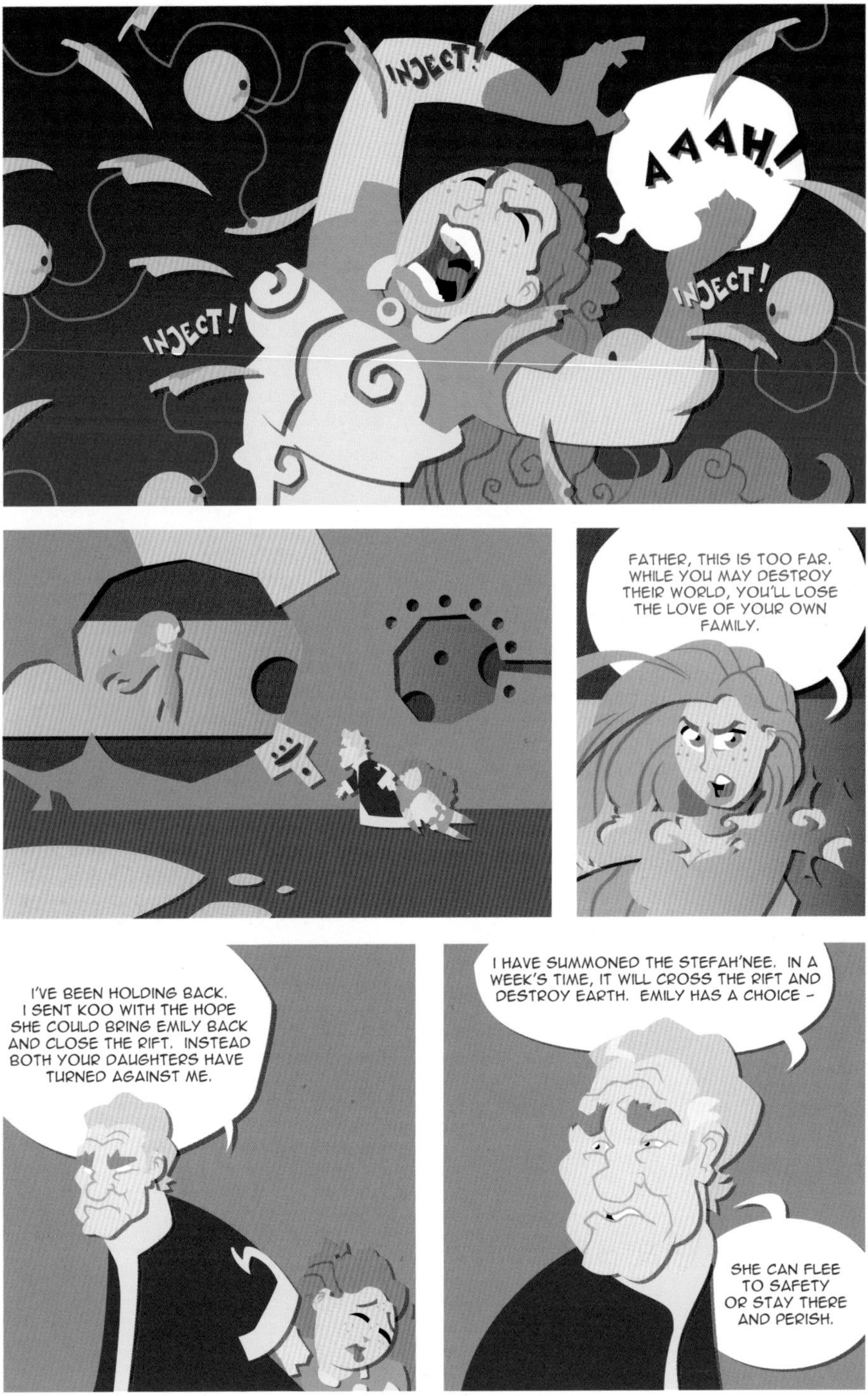
INJECT!
AAAH!
INJECT!
INJECT!
FATHER, THIS IS TOO FAR. WHILE YOU MAY DESTROY THEIR WORLD, YOU'LL LOSE THE LOVE OF YOUR OWN FAMILY.
I'VE BEEN HOLDING BACK. I SENT KOO WITH THE HOPE SHE COULD BRING EMILY BACK AND CLOSE THE RIFT. INSTEAD BOTH YOUR DAUGHTERS HAVE TURNED AGAINST ME.
I HAVE SUMMONED THE STEFAH'NEE. IN A WEEK'S TIME, IT WILL CROSS THE RIFT AND DESTROY EARTH. EMILY HAS A CHOICE –
SHE CAN FLEE TO SAFETY OR STAY THERE AND PERISH.

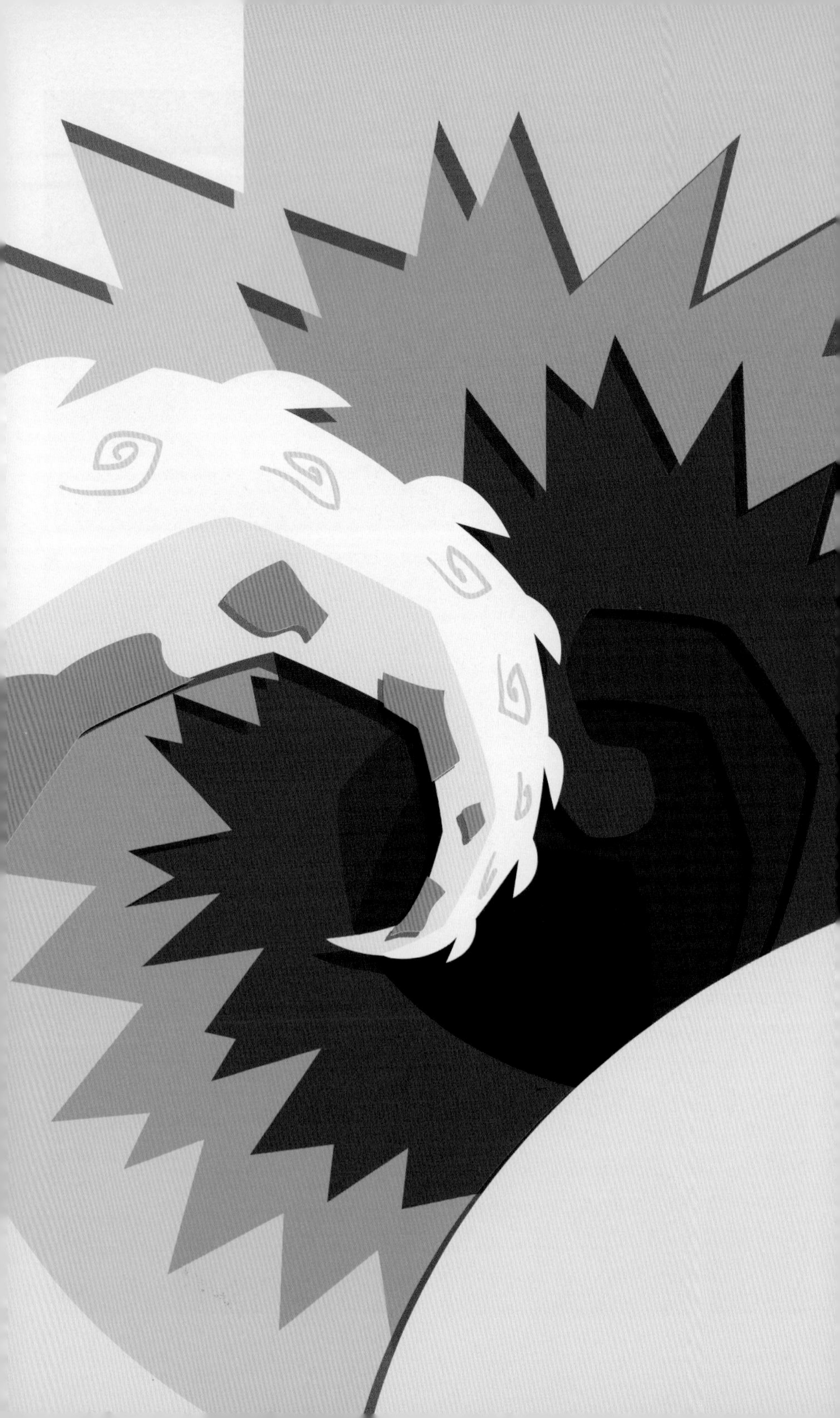

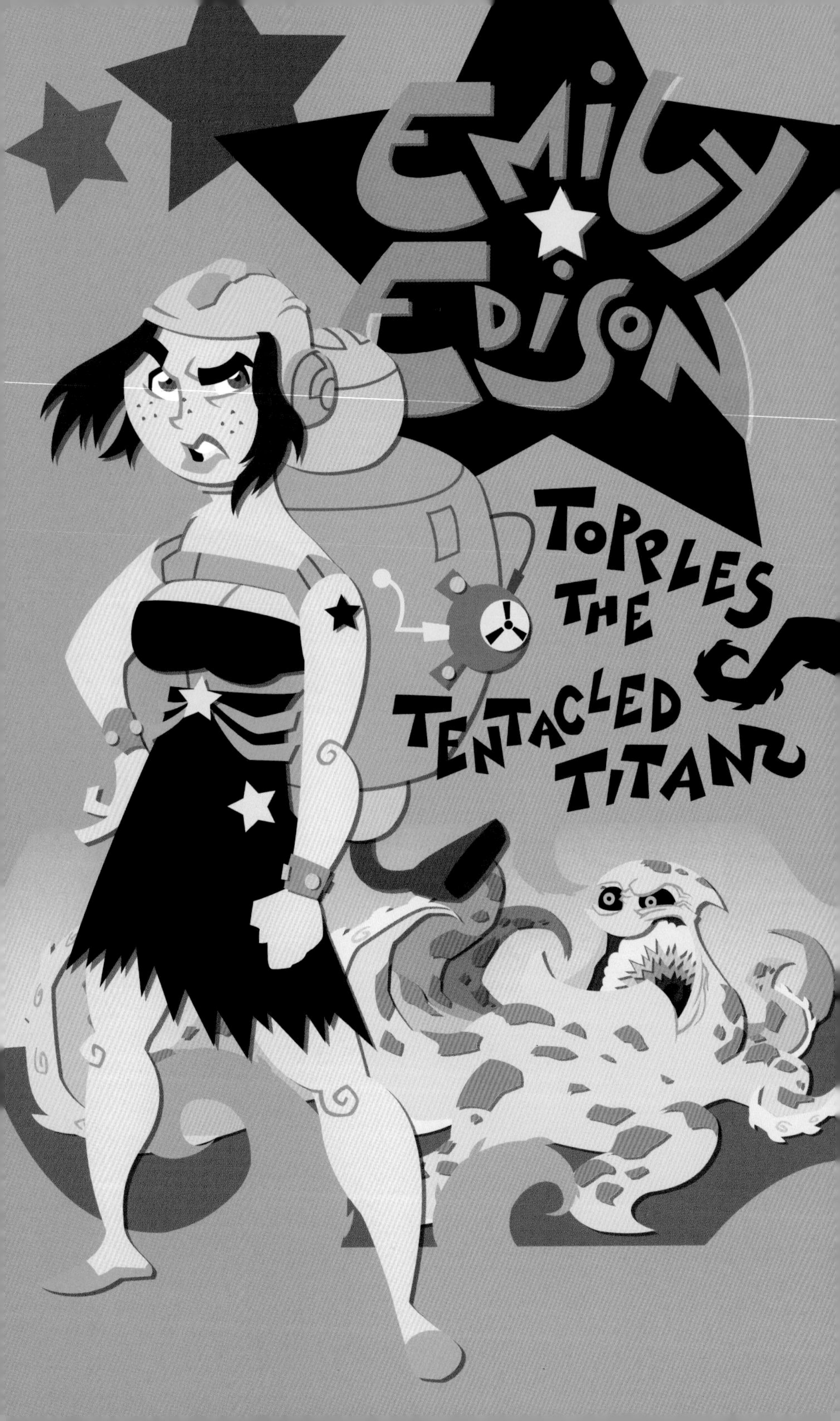
Emily Edison
Topples the Tentacled Titan

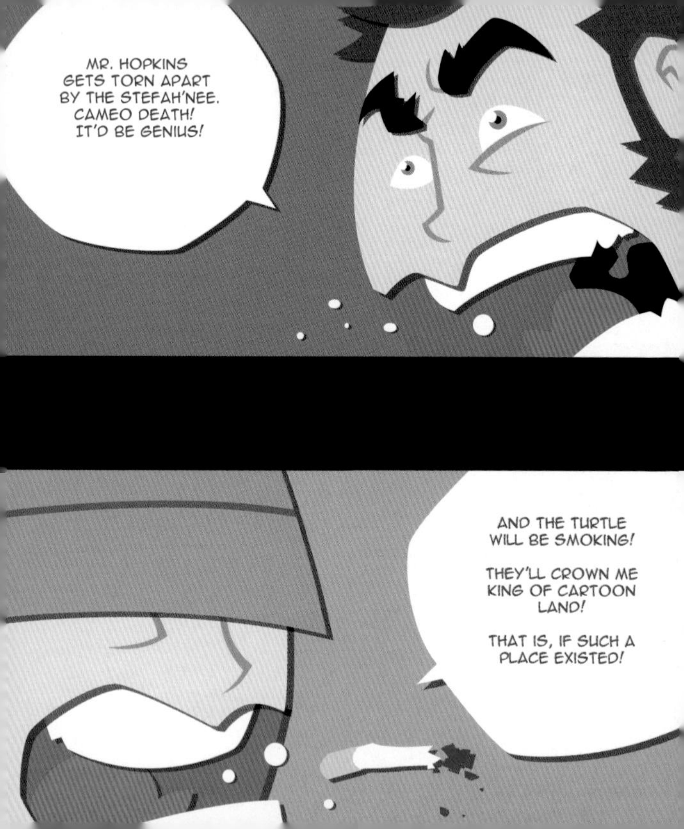
MR. HOPKINS GETS TORN APART BY THE STEFAH'NEE. CAMEO DEATH! IT'D BE GENIUS!
AND THE TURTLE WILL BE SMOKING!
THEY'LL CROWN ME KING OF CARTOON LAND!
THAT IS, IF SUCH A PLACE EXISTED!

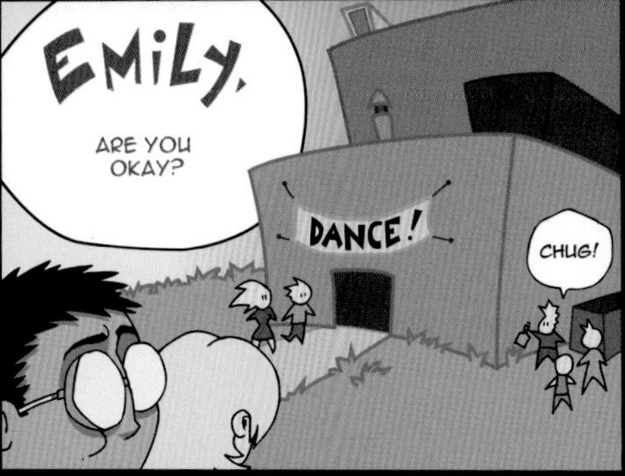
EMILY,
ARE YOU OKAY?
DANCE!
CHUG!

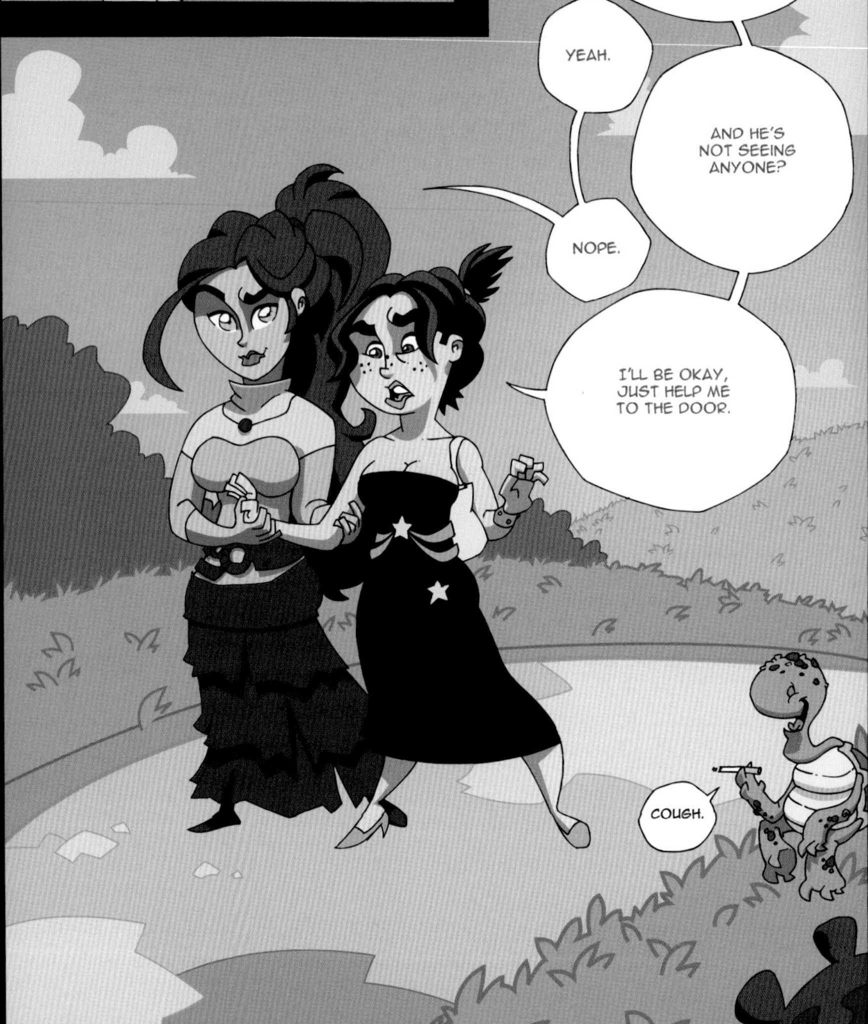
YOU HEARD TOM WOULD BE AT THE DANCE?
YEAH.
AND HE'S NOT SEEING ANYONE?
NOPE.
I'LL BE OKAY, JUST HELP ME TO THE DOOR.
COUGH.

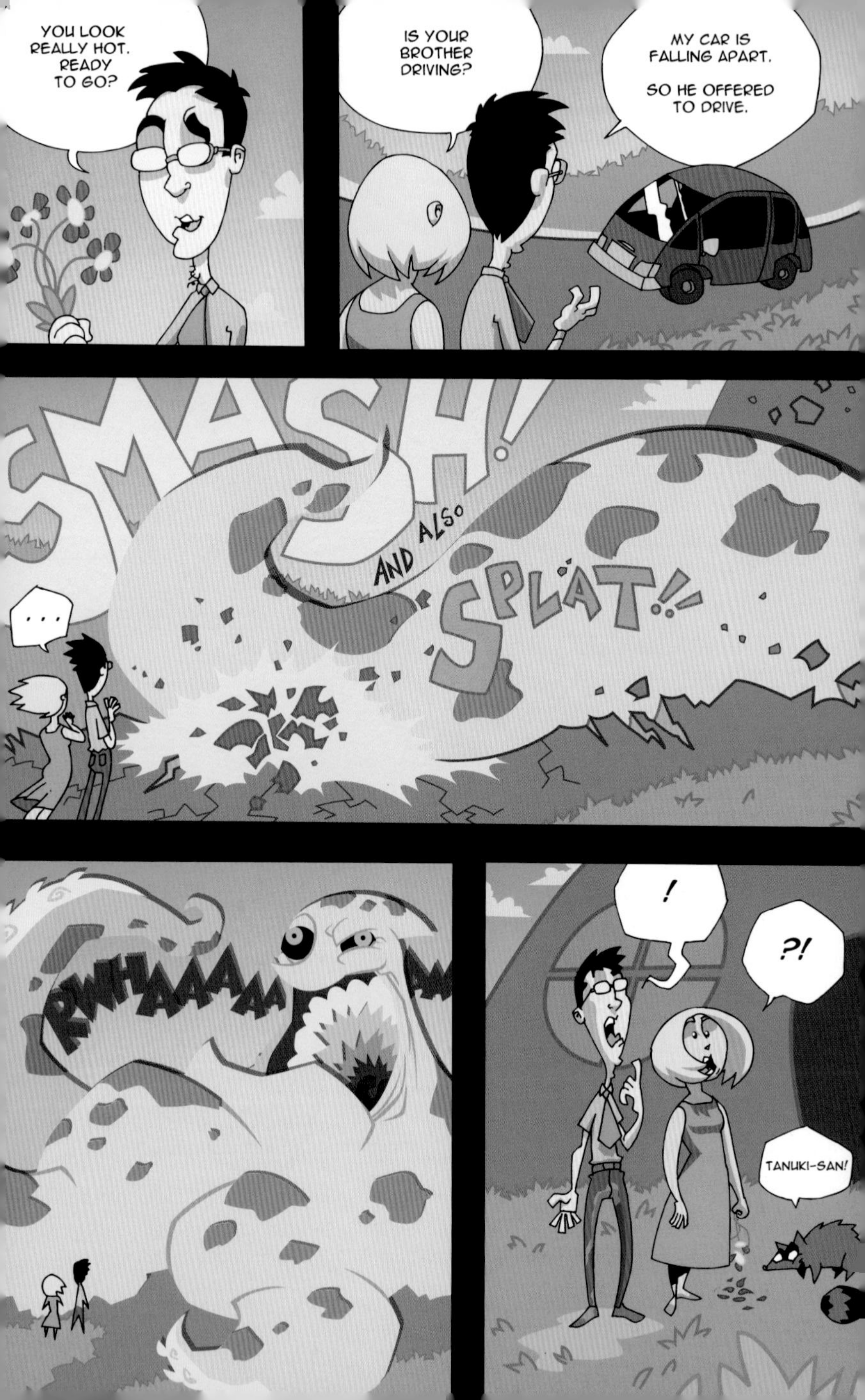
YOU LOOK REALLY HOT. READY TO GO?
IS YOUR BROTHER DRIVING?
MY CAR IS FALLING APART.
SO HE OFFERED TO DRIVE.
SMASH!
AND ALSO
SPLAT!!!
...
RWHAAAAA
!
?!
TANUKI-SAN!

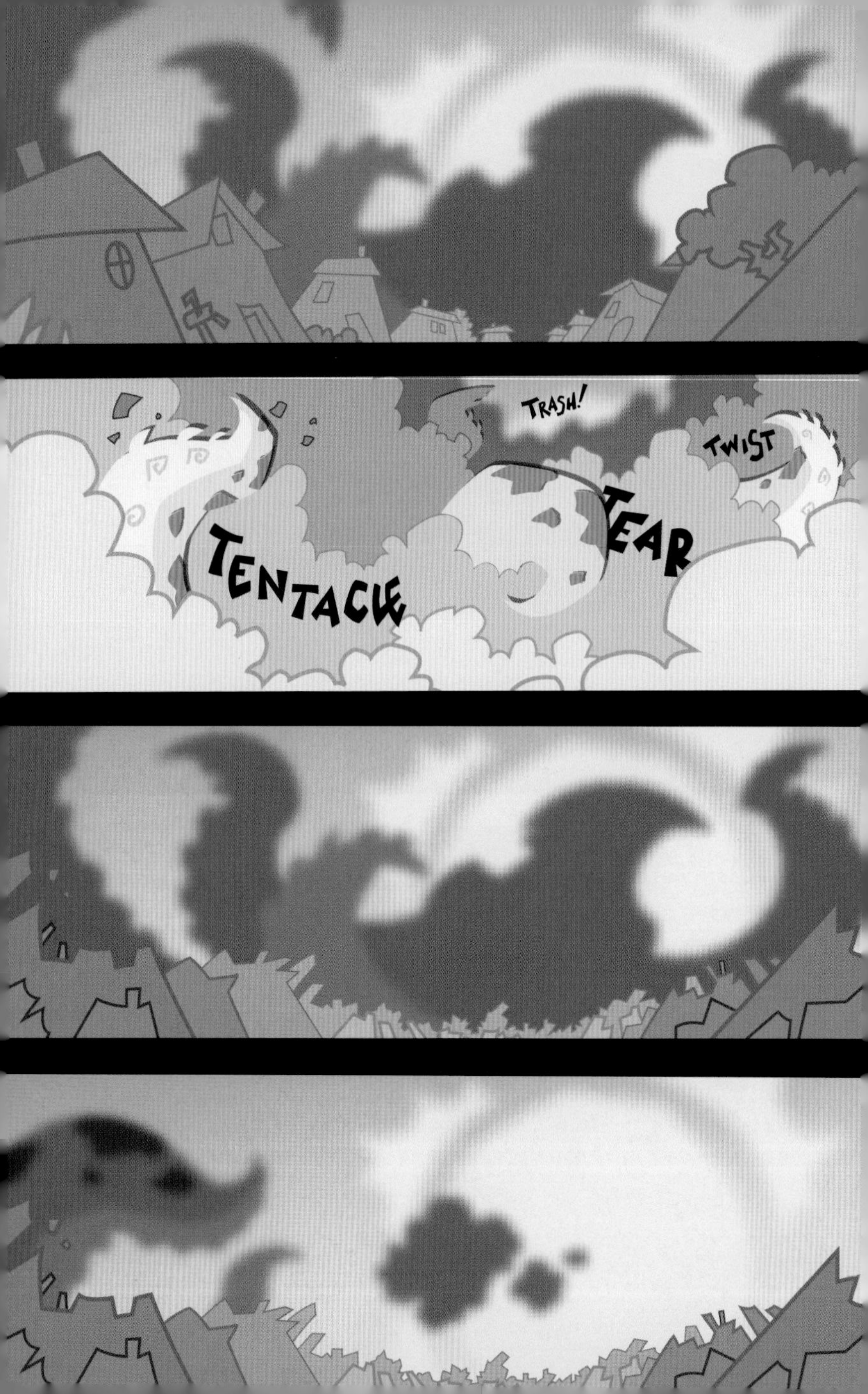
TENTACLE
TRASH!
TEAR
TWIST

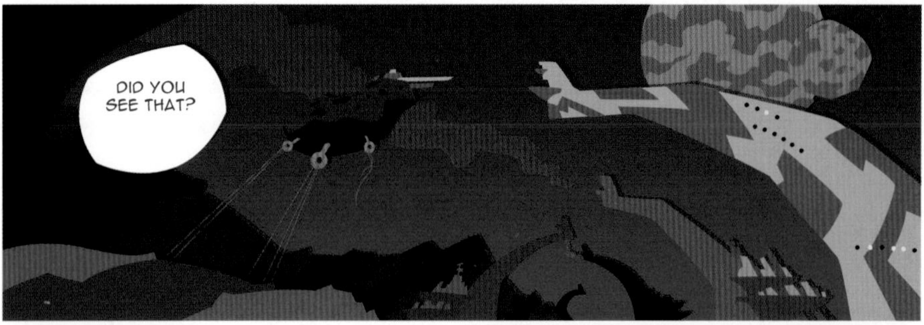
DID YOU SEE THAT?

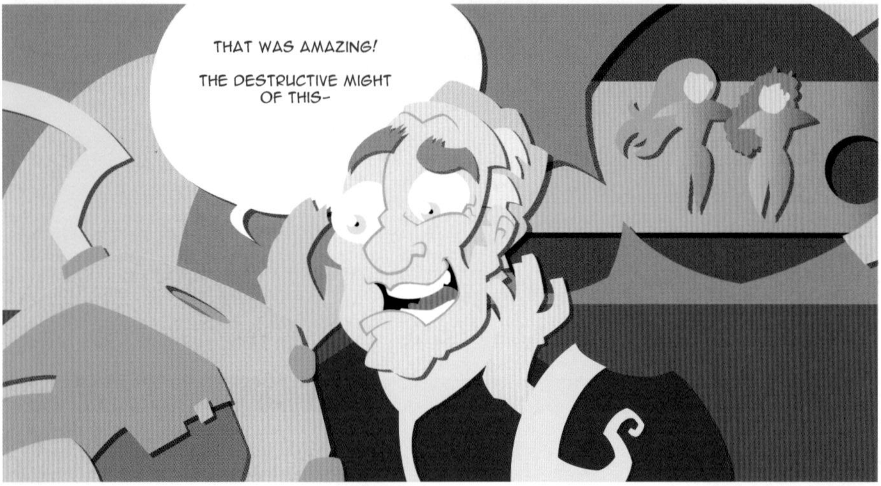
THAT WAS AMAZING!
THE DESTRUCTIVE MIGHT OF THIS-

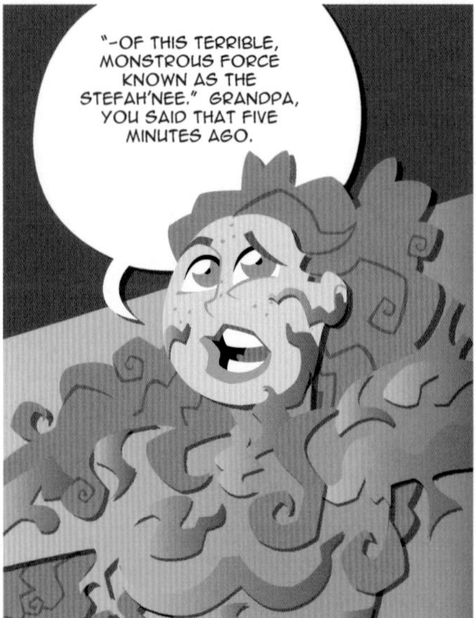
"-OF THIS TERRIBLE, MONSTROUS FORCE KNOWN AS THE STEFAH'NEE." GRANDPA, YOU SAID THAT FIVE MINUTES AGO.

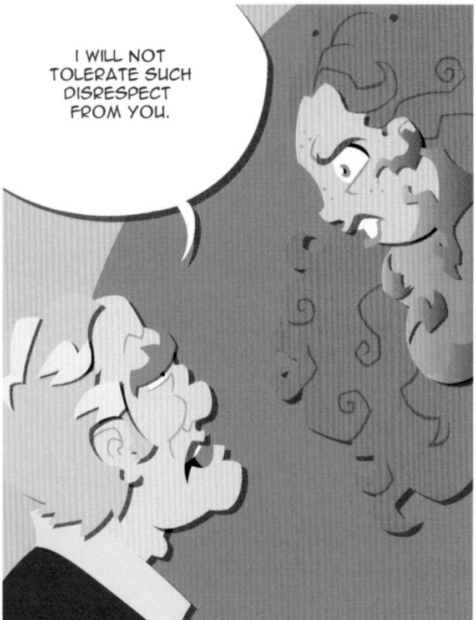
I WILL NOT TOLERATE SUCH DISRESPECT FROM YOU.

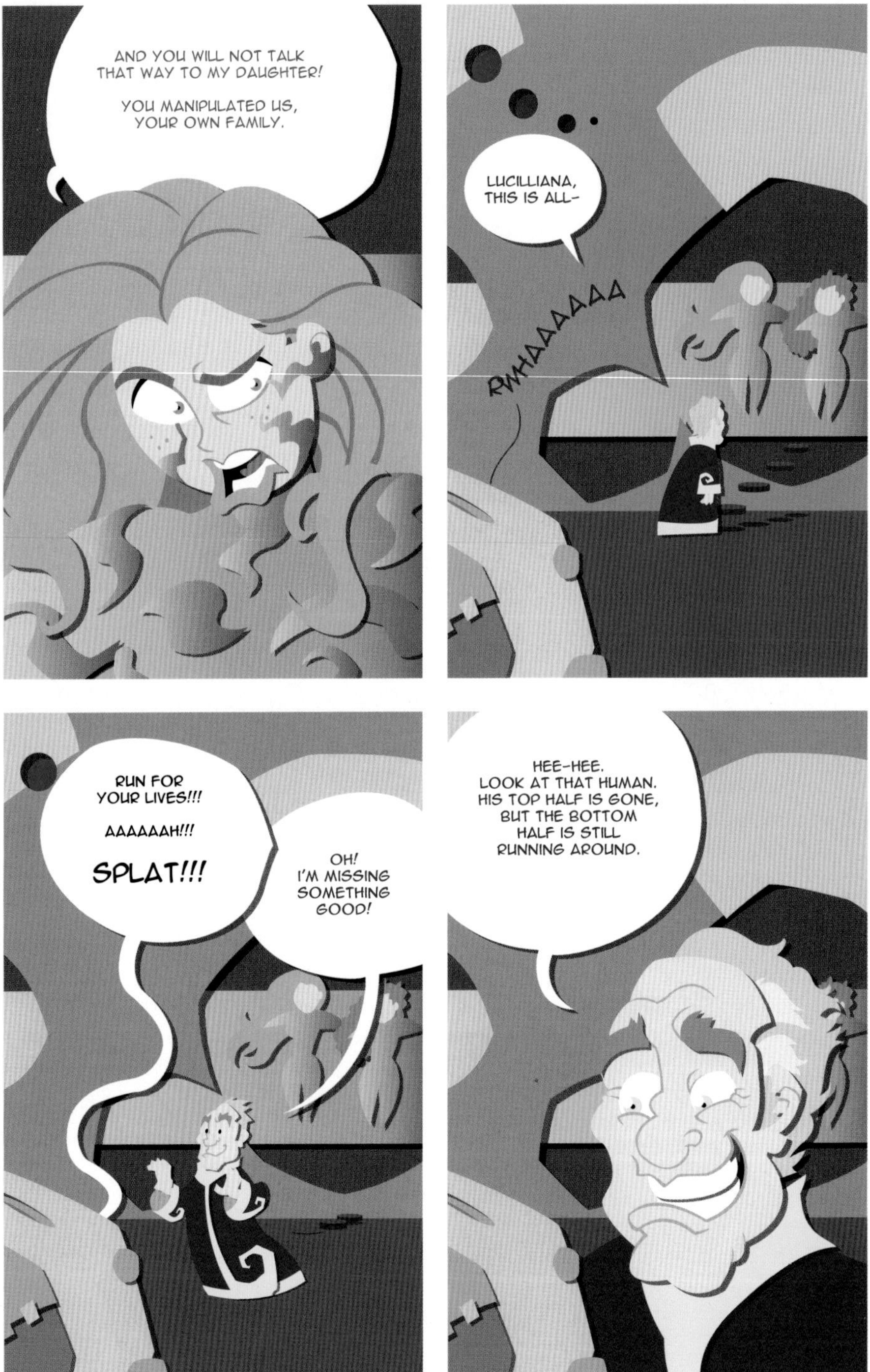
AND YOU WILL NOT TALK THAT WAY TO MY DAUGHTER!
YOU MANIPULATED US, YOUR OWN FAMILY.
LUCILLIANA, THIS IS ALL-
RWHAAAAAAA
RUN FOR YOUR LIVES!!!
AAAAAAH!!!
SPLAT!!!
OH! I'M MISSING SOMETHING GOOD!
HEE-HEE. LOOK AT THAT HUMAN. HIS TOP HALF IS GONE, BUT THE BOTTOM HALF IS STILL RUNNING AROUND.

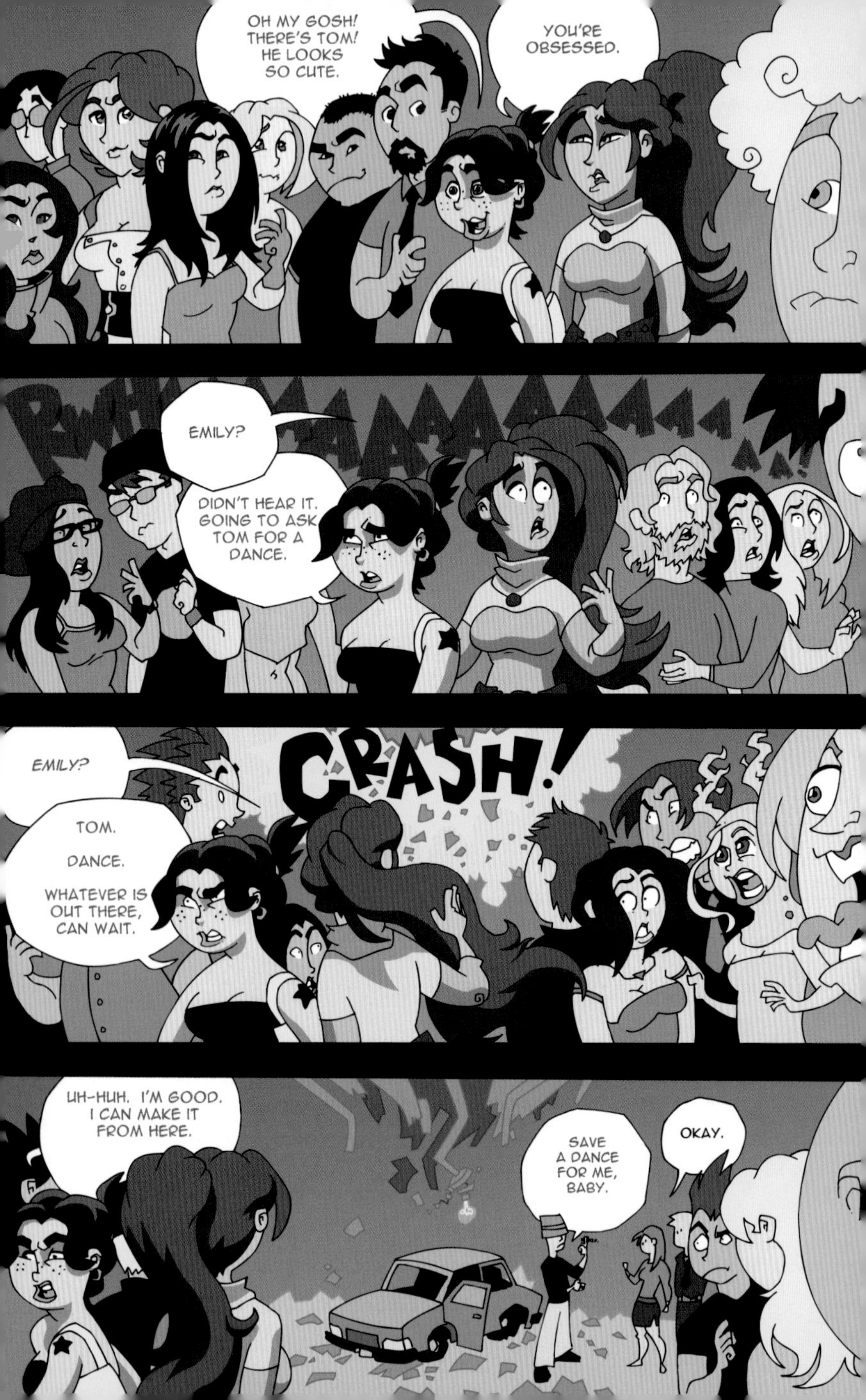

OH MY GOSH! THERE'S TOM! HE LOOKS SO CUTE.
YOU'RE OBSESSED.
EMILY?
DIDN'T HEAR IT. GOING TO ASK TOM FOR A DANCE.
EMILY?
CRASH!
TOM.
DANCE.
WHATEVER IS OUT THERE, CAN WAIT.
UH-HUH. I'M GOOD. I CAN MAKE IT FROM HERE.
SAVE A DANCE FOR ME, BABY.
OKAY.

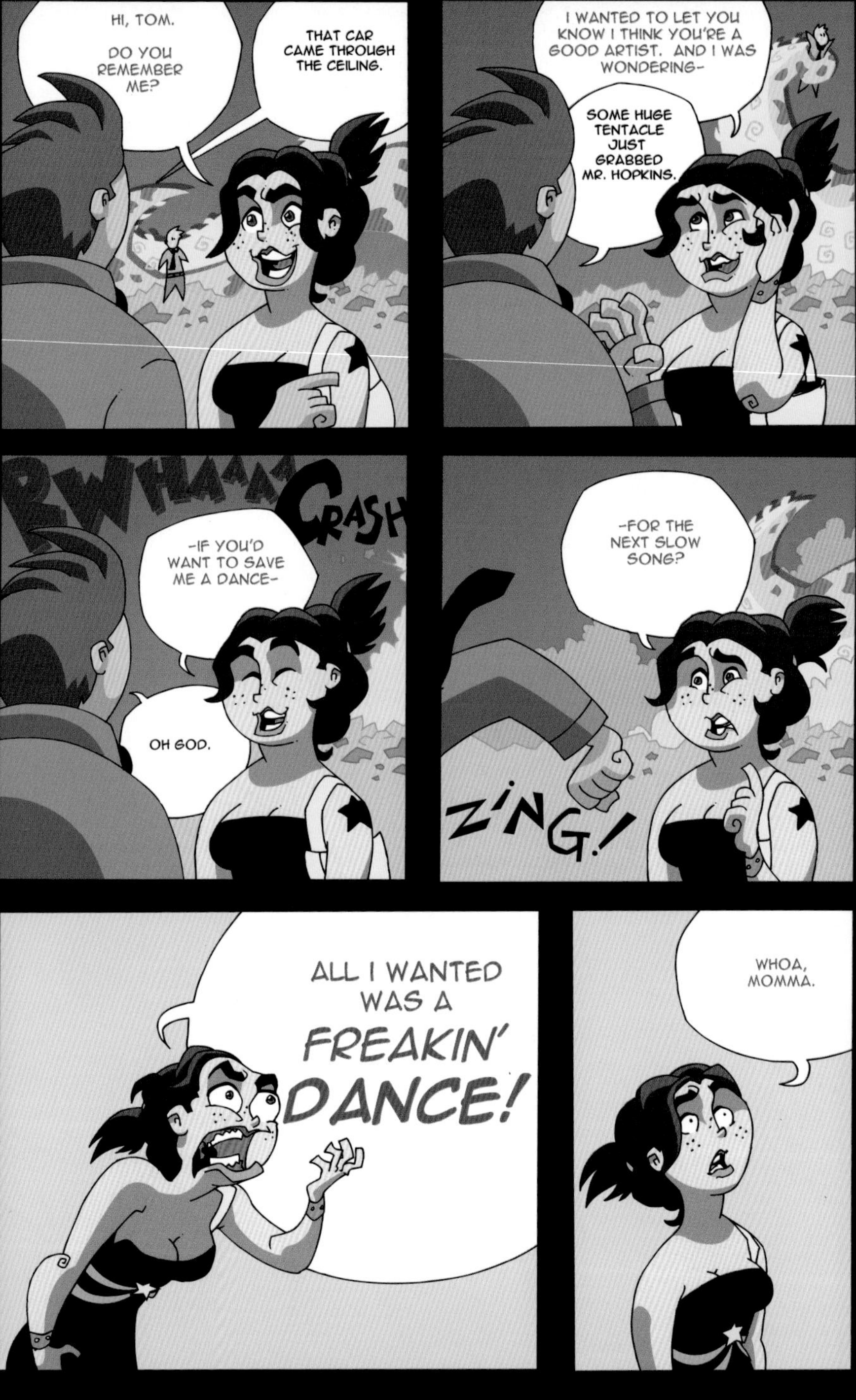

HI, TOM.
DO YOU REMEMBER ME?
THAT CAR CAME THROUGH THE CEILING.
I WANTED TO LET YOU KNOW I THINK YOU'RE A GOOD ARTIST. AND I WAS WONDERING-
SOME HUGE TENTACLE JUST GRABBED MR. HOPKINS.
RWHAAAA
CRASH
-IF YOU'D WANT TO SAVE ME A DANCE-
OH GOD.
-FOR THE NEXT SLOW SONG?
ZING!
ALL I WANTED WAS A FREAKIN' DANCE!
WHOA, MOMMA.

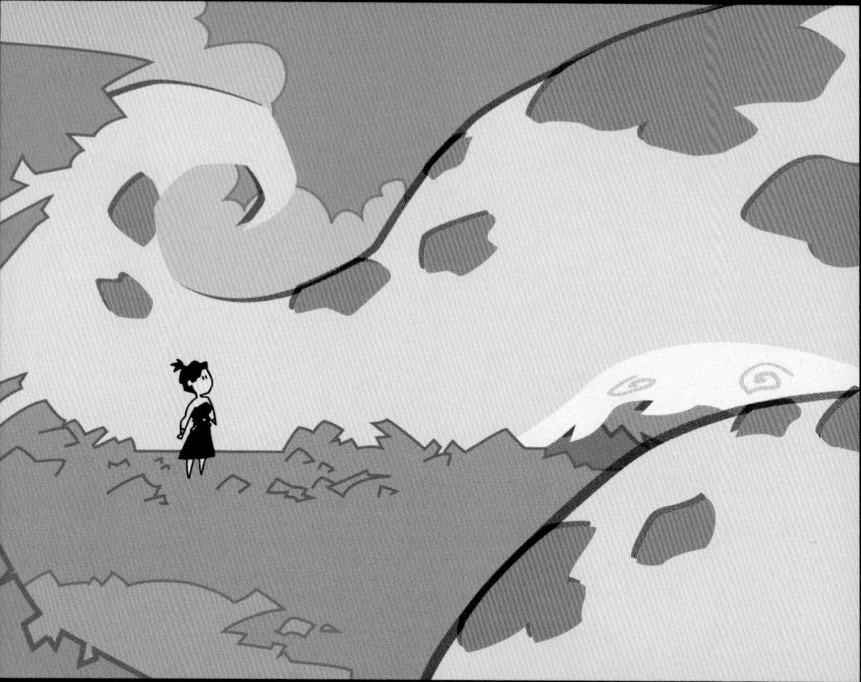

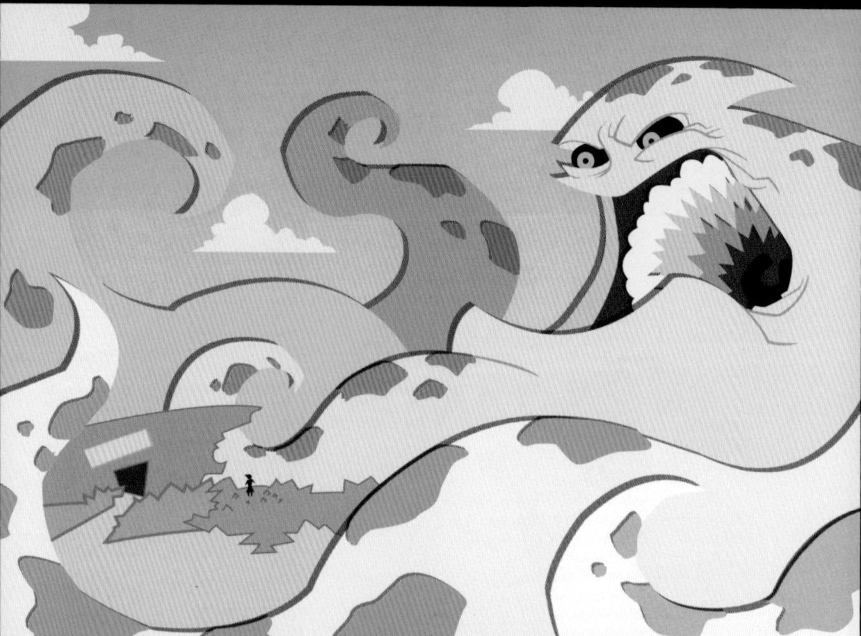

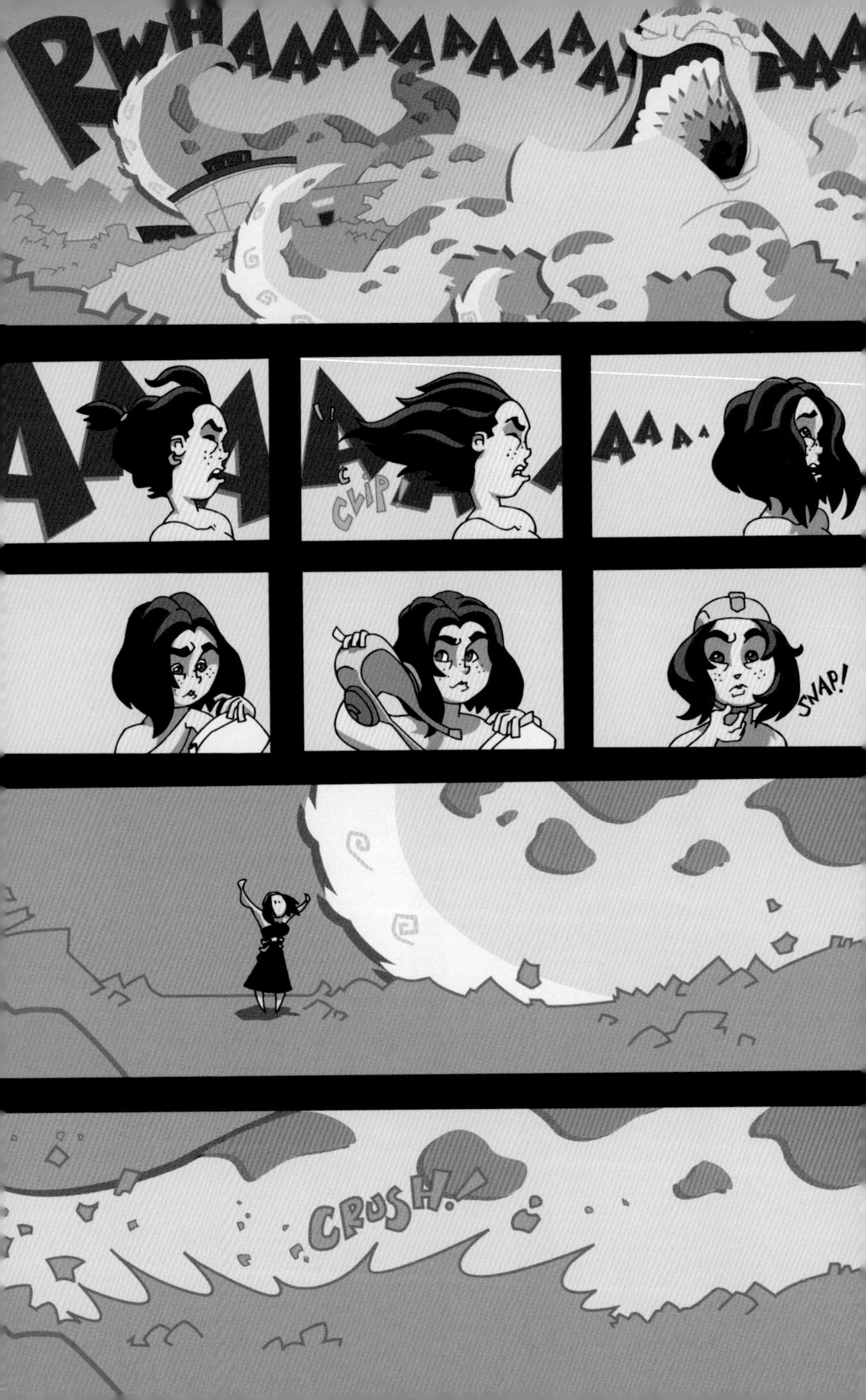
RWHAAAAAAAAAAAAAA
CLIP
SNAP!
CRUSH!

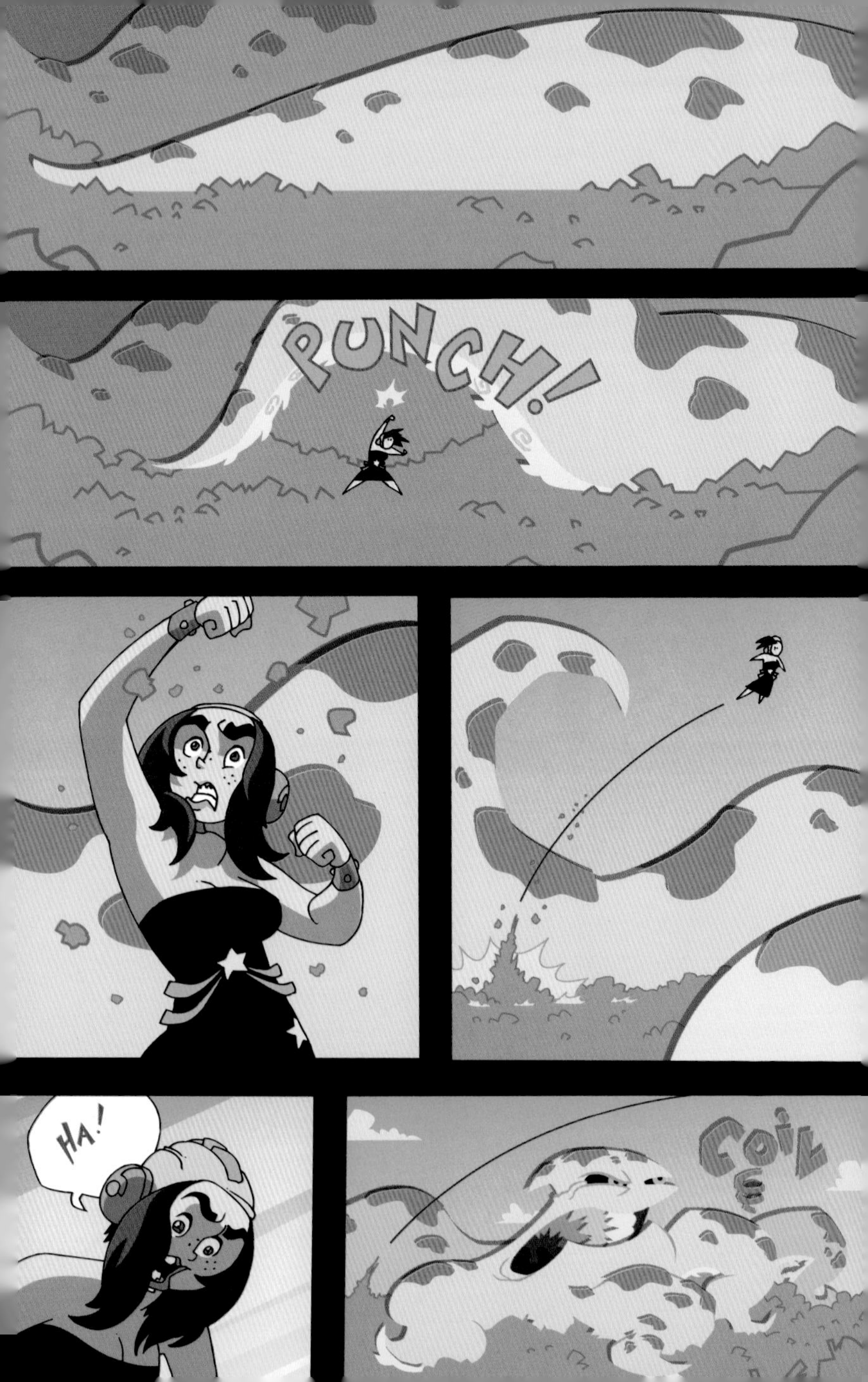
PUNCH!
HA!
COIL

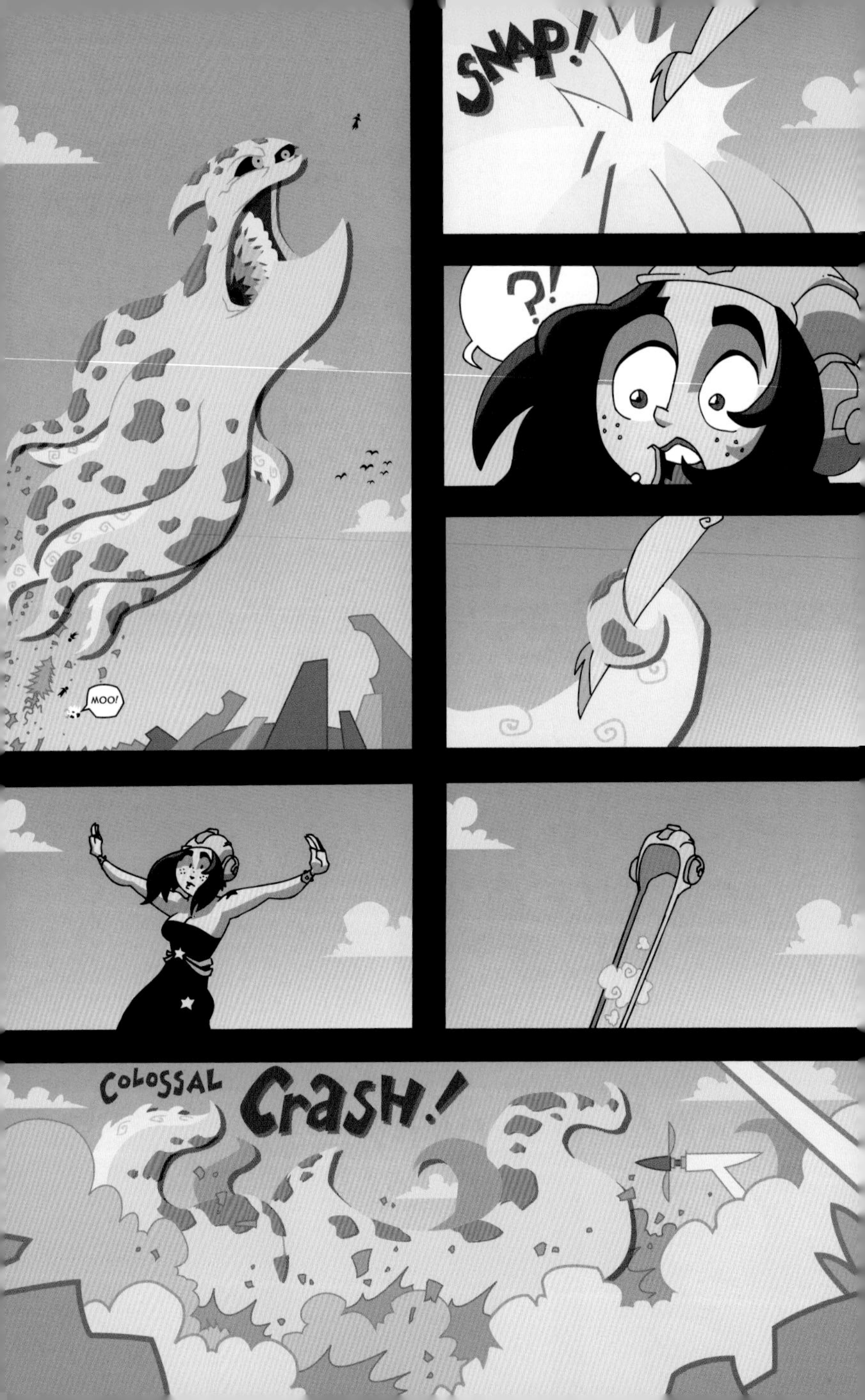
MOO!
SNAP!
?!
COLOSSAL CRASH!

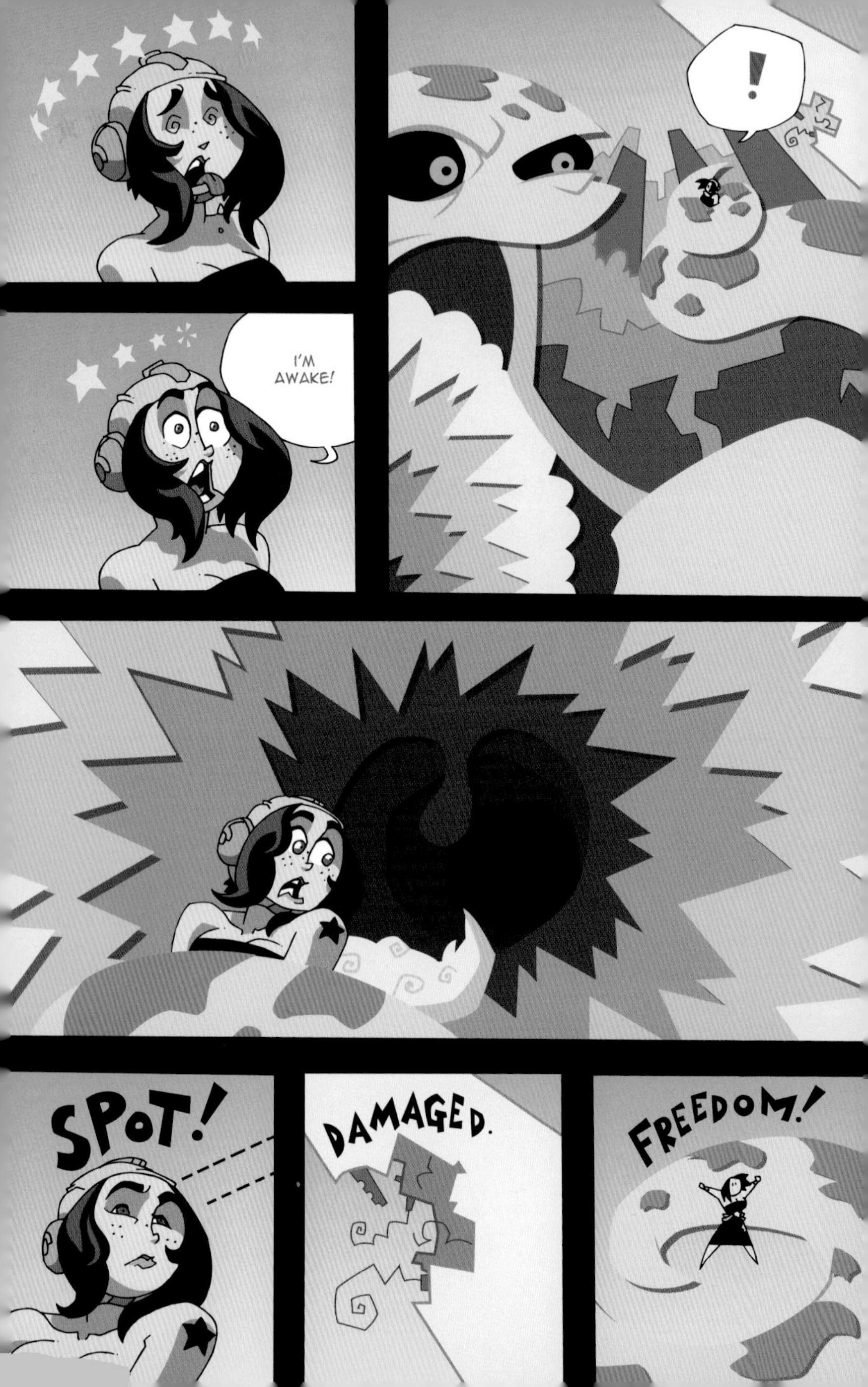
!
I'M AWAKE!
SPOT!
DAMAGED.
FREEDOM!

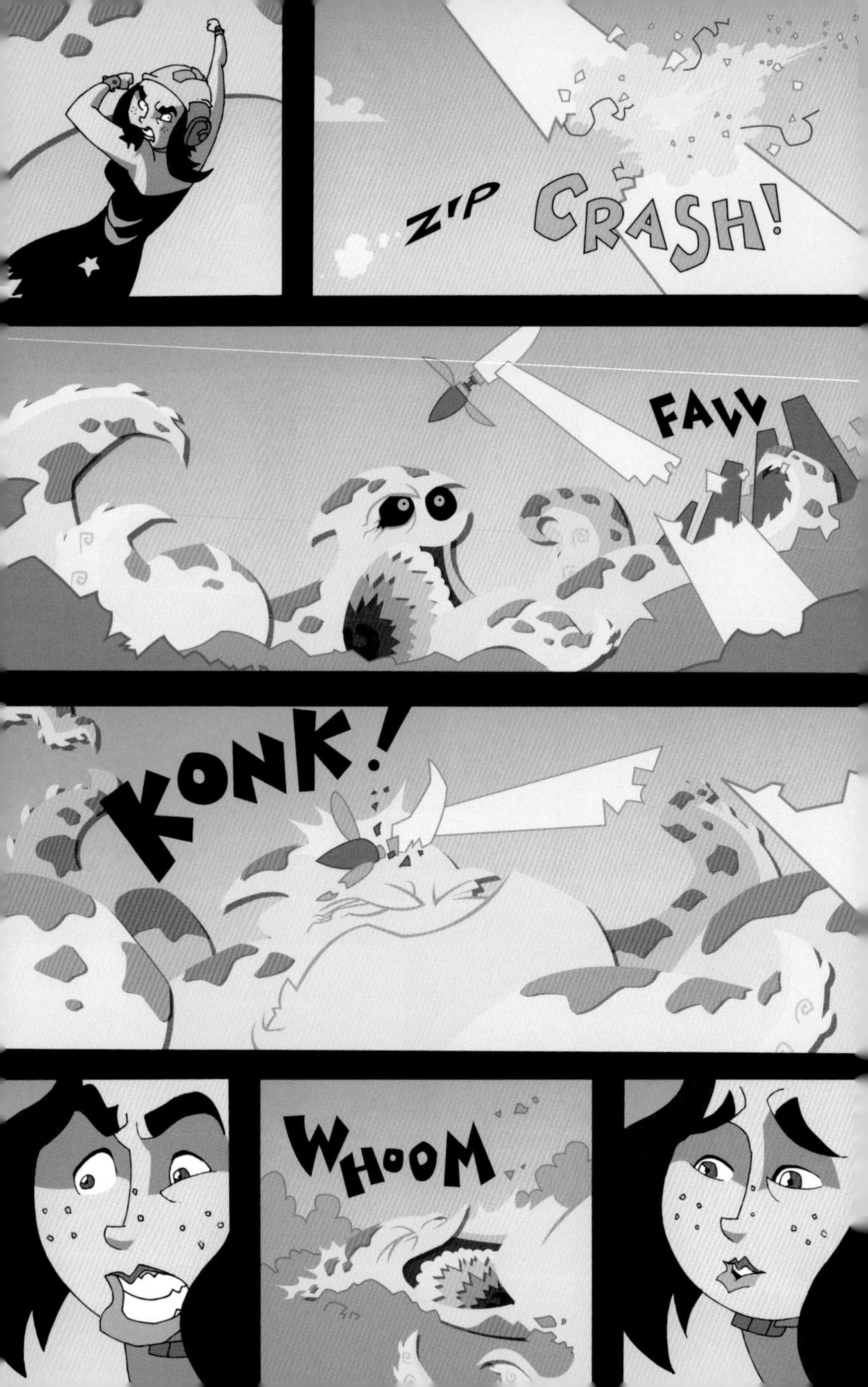
ZIP
CRASH!
FALL
KONK!
WHOOM

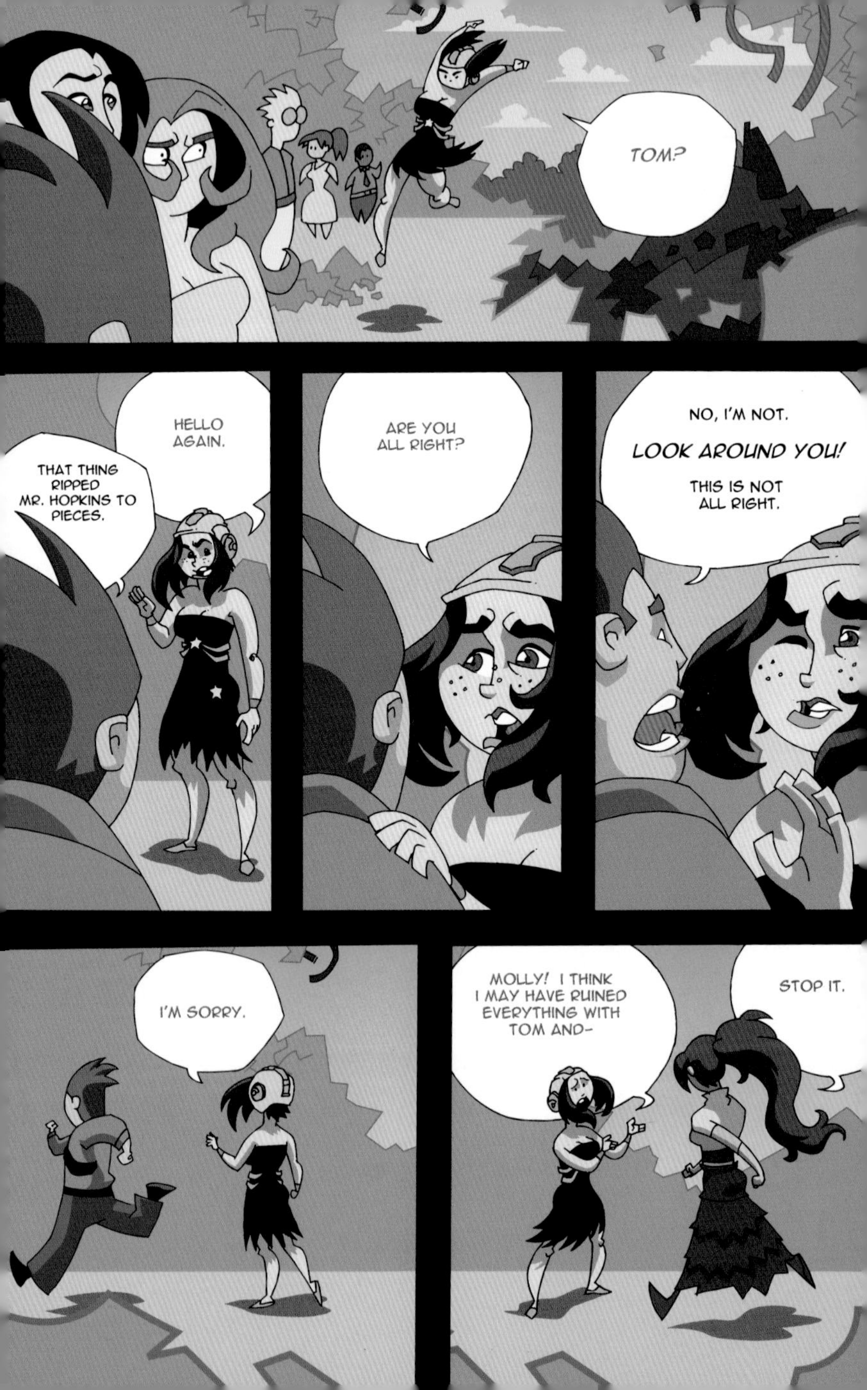
TOM?
HELLO AGAIN.
THAT THING RIPPED MR. HOPKINS TO PIECES.
ARE YOU ALL RIGHT?
NO, I'M NOT.
LOOK AROUND YOU!
THIS IS NOT ALL RIGHT.
I'M SORRY.
MOLLY! I THINK I MAY HAVE RUINED EVERYTHING WITH TOM AND-
STOP IT.

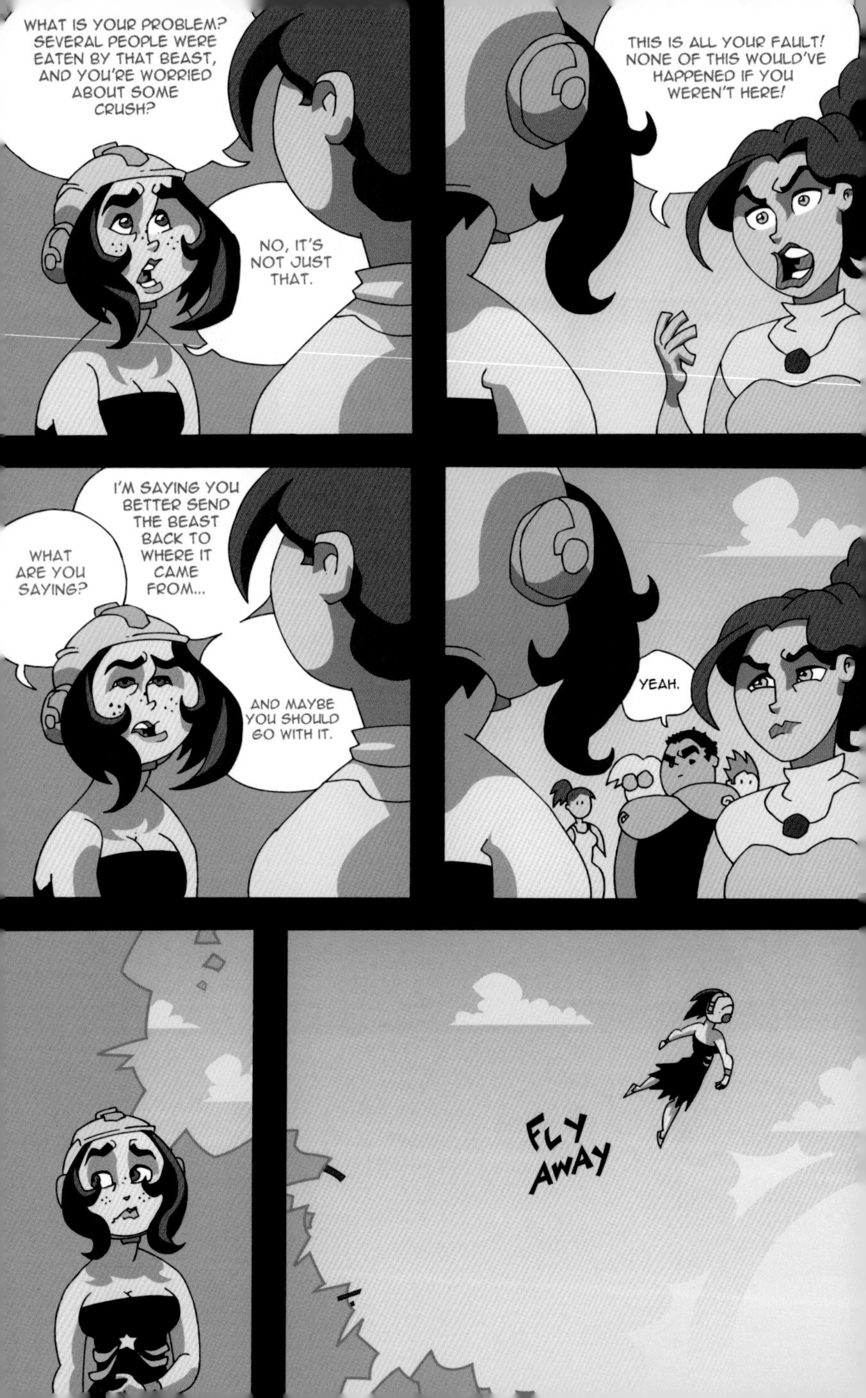
WHAT IS YOUR PROBLEM? SEVERAL PEOPLE WERE EATEN BY THAT BEAST, AND YOU'RE WORRIED ABOUT SOME CRUSH?
NO, IT'S NOT JUST THAT.
THIS IS ALL YOUR FAULT! NONE OF THIS WOULD'VE HAPPENED IF YOU WEREN'T HERE!
WHAT ARE YOU SAYING?
I'M SAYING YOU BETTER SEND THE BEAST BACK TO WHERE IT CAME FROM...
AND MAYBE YOU SHOULD GO WITH IT.
YEAH.
FLY AWAY

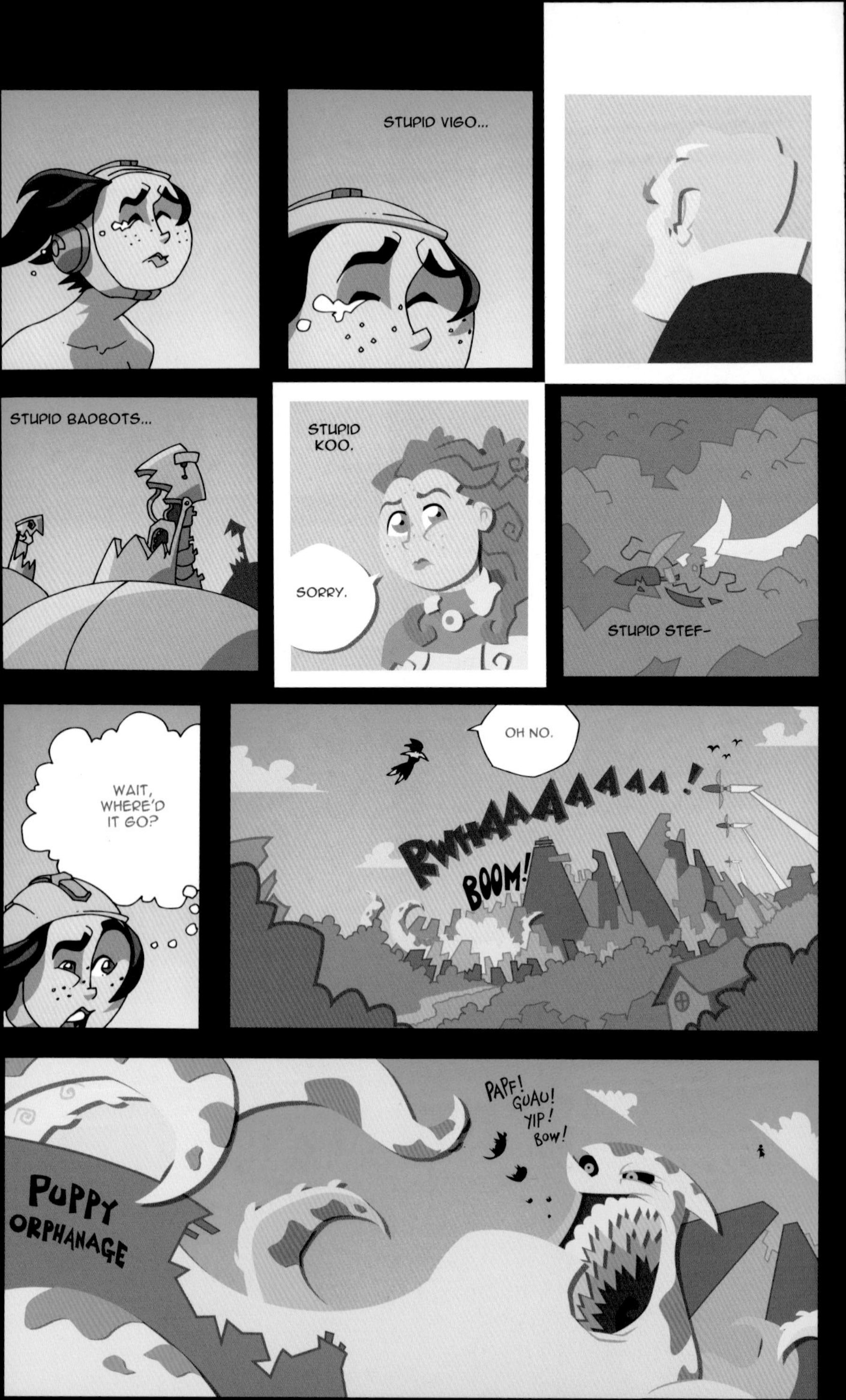
STUPID VIGO...
STUPID BADBOTS...
STUPID KOO.
SORRY.
STUPID STEF-
WAIT, WHERE'D IT GO?
OH NO.
RWHAAAAAAAA!
BOOM!
PAPF! GUAU! YIP! BOW!
PUPPY ORPHANAGE

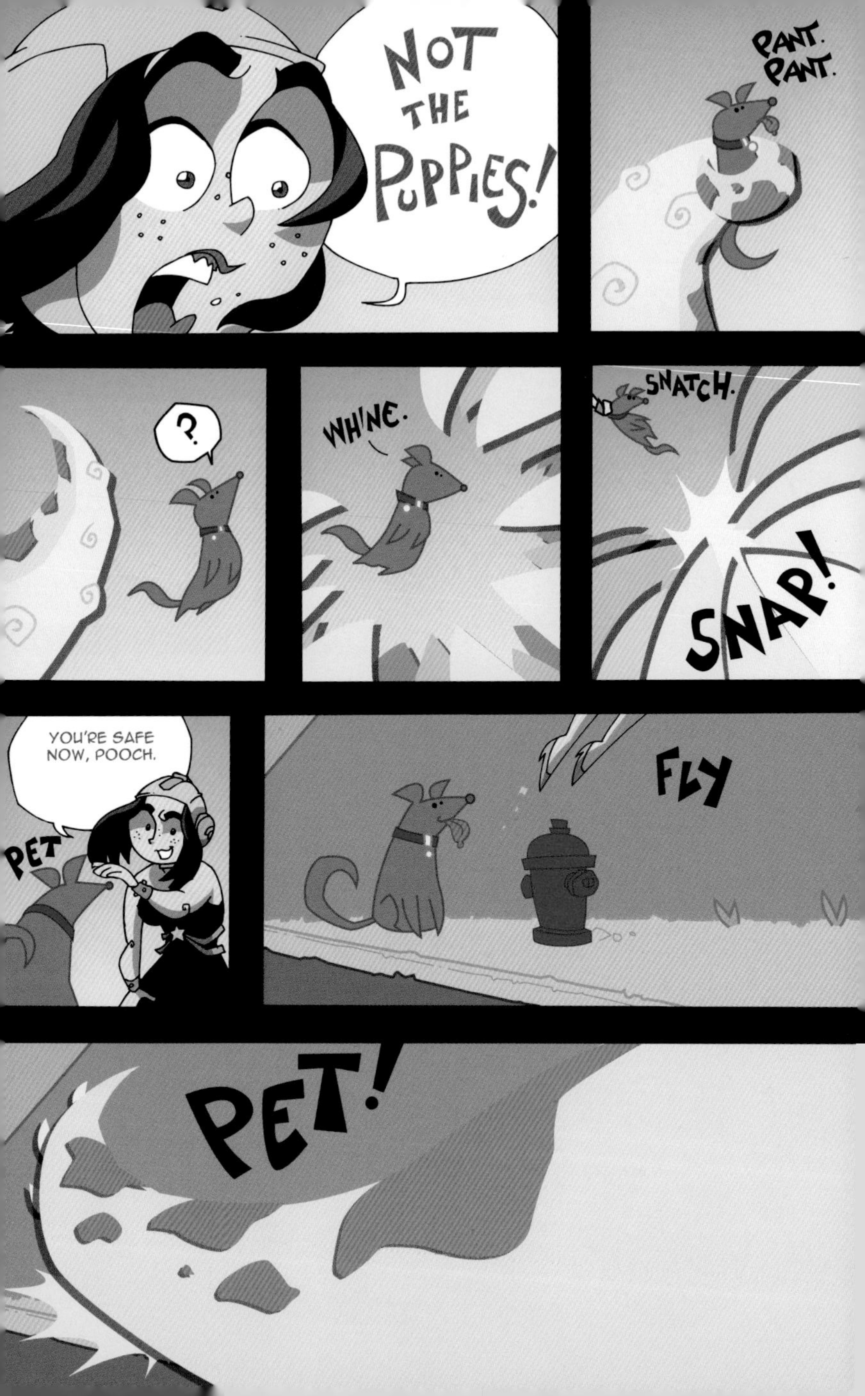
NOT THE PUPPIES!
PANT. PANT.
?
WHINE.
SNATCH.
SNAP!
YOU'RE SAFE NOW, POOCH.
PET
FLY
PET!

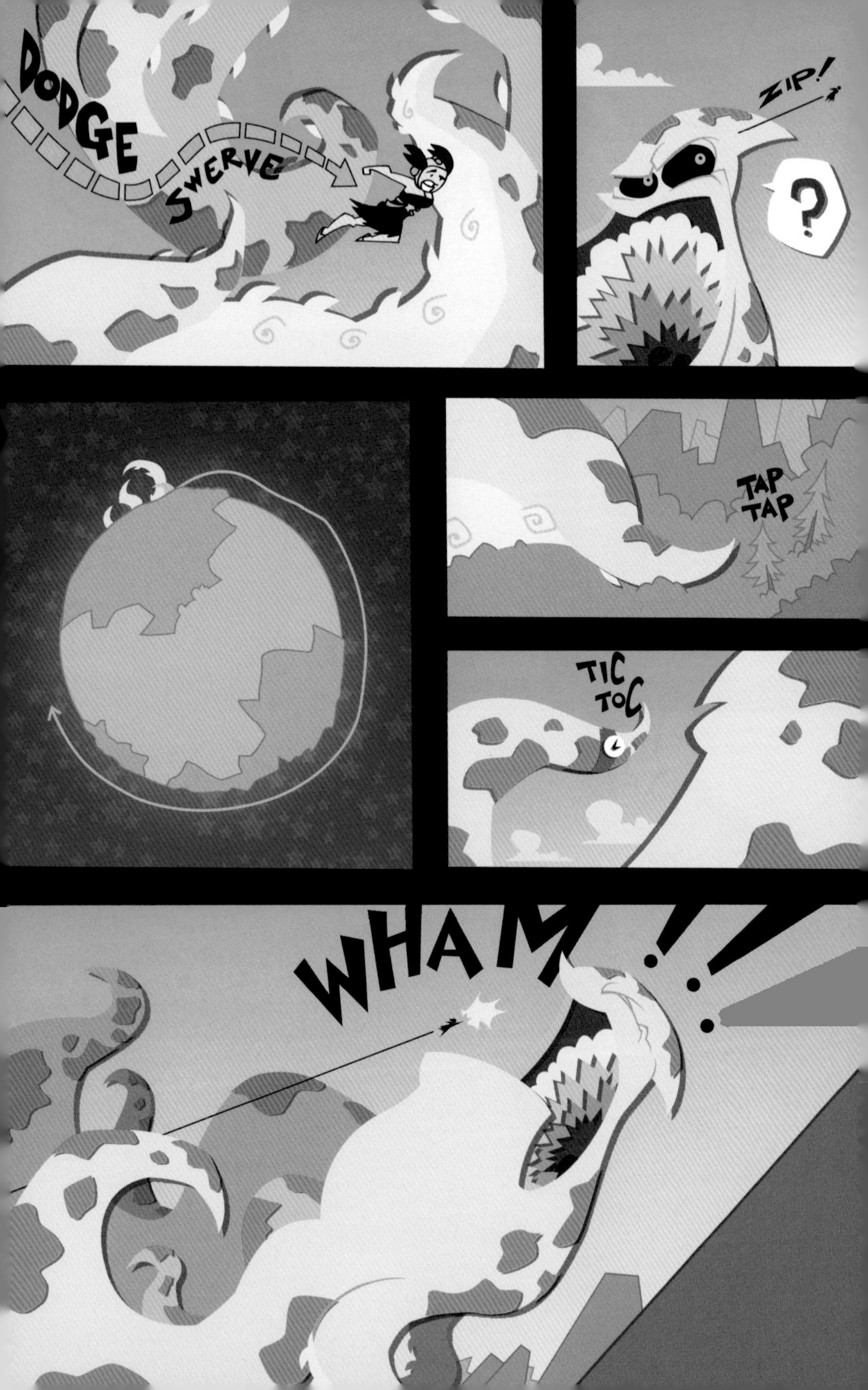
DODGE
SWERVE
ZIP!
?
TAP
TAP
TIC
TOC
WHAM!!

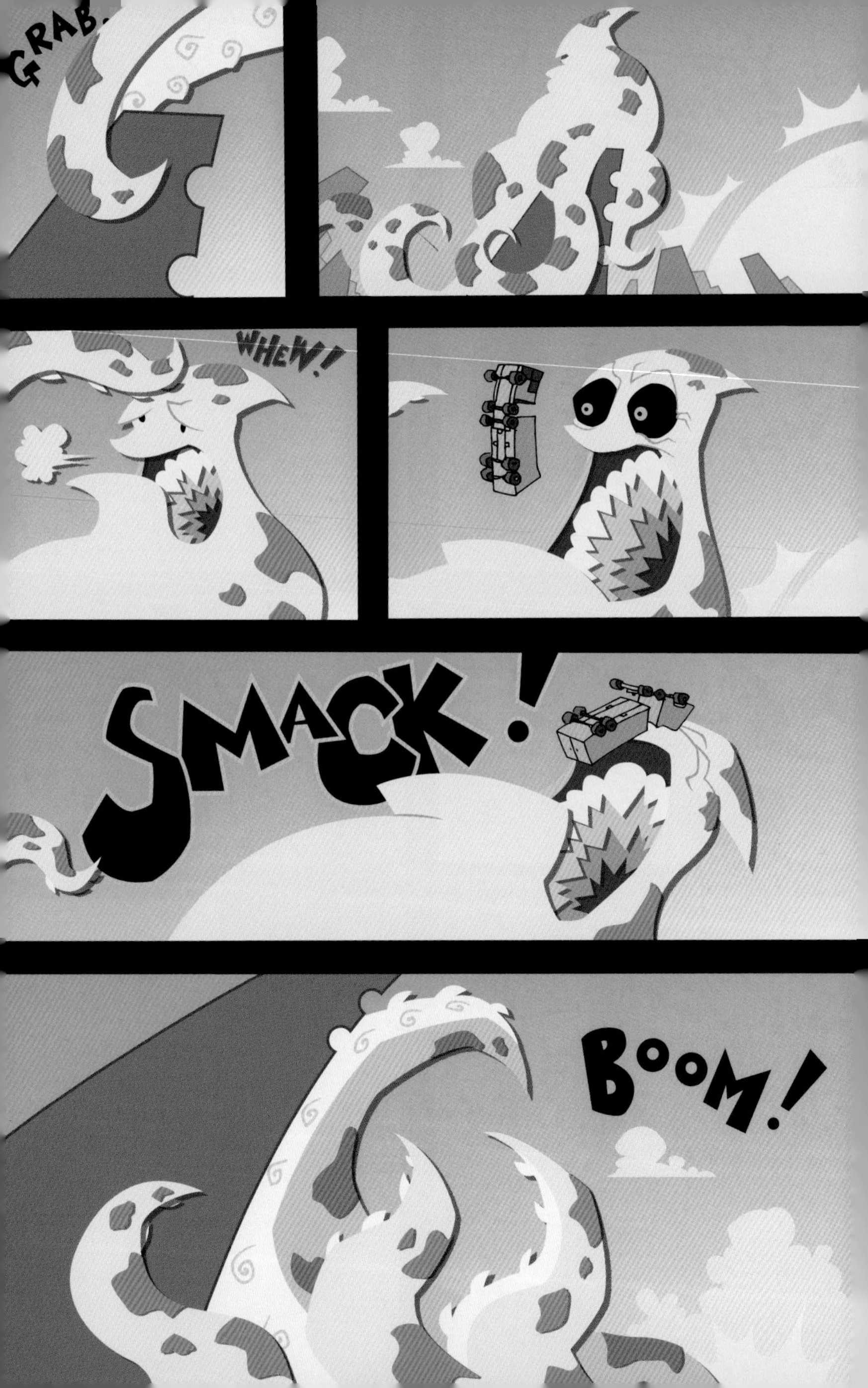
GRAB.
WHEW!
SMACK!
BOOM!

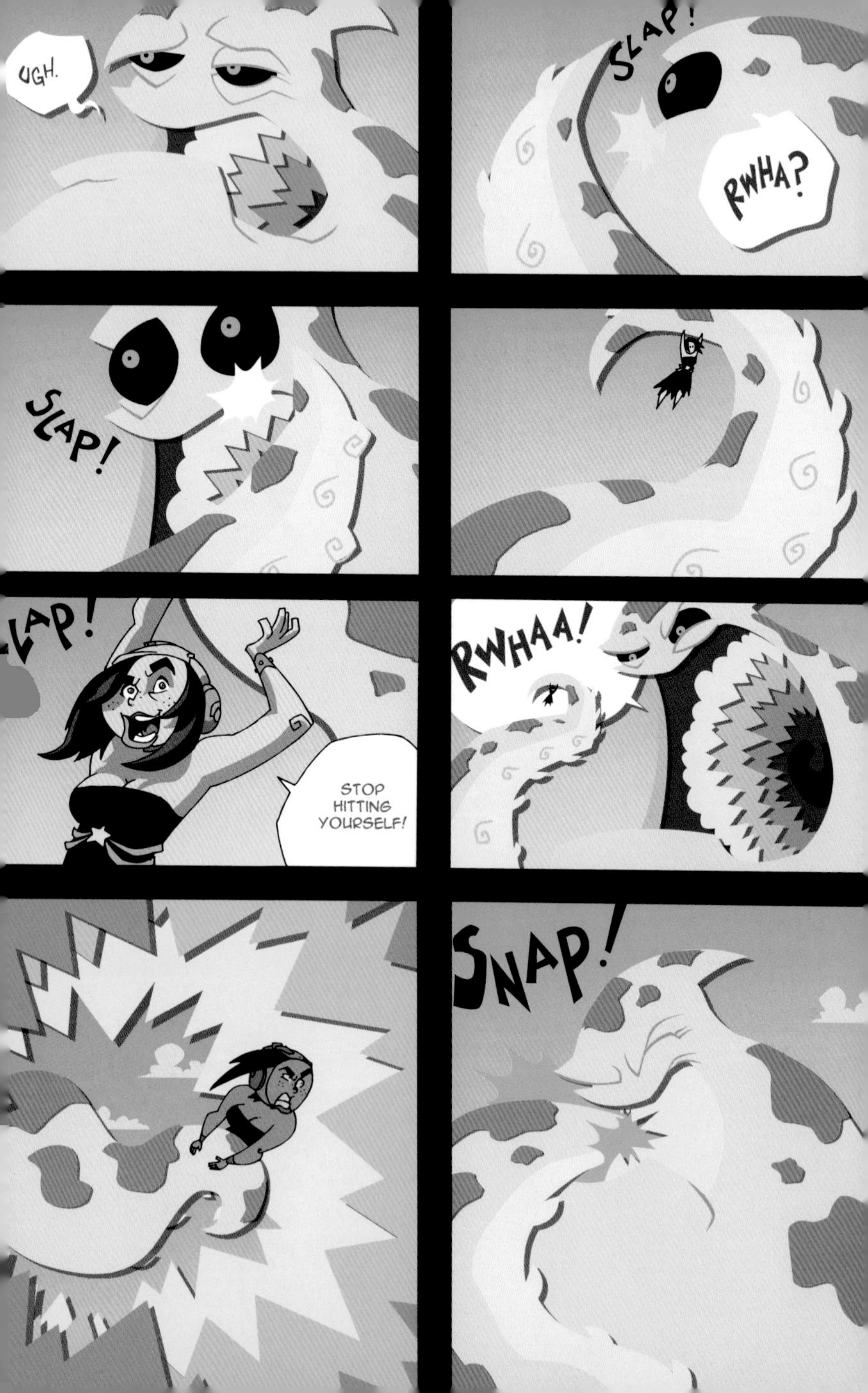
UGH.
SLAP!
RWHA?
SLAP!
LAP!
STOP HITTING YOURSELF!
RWHAA!
SNAP!

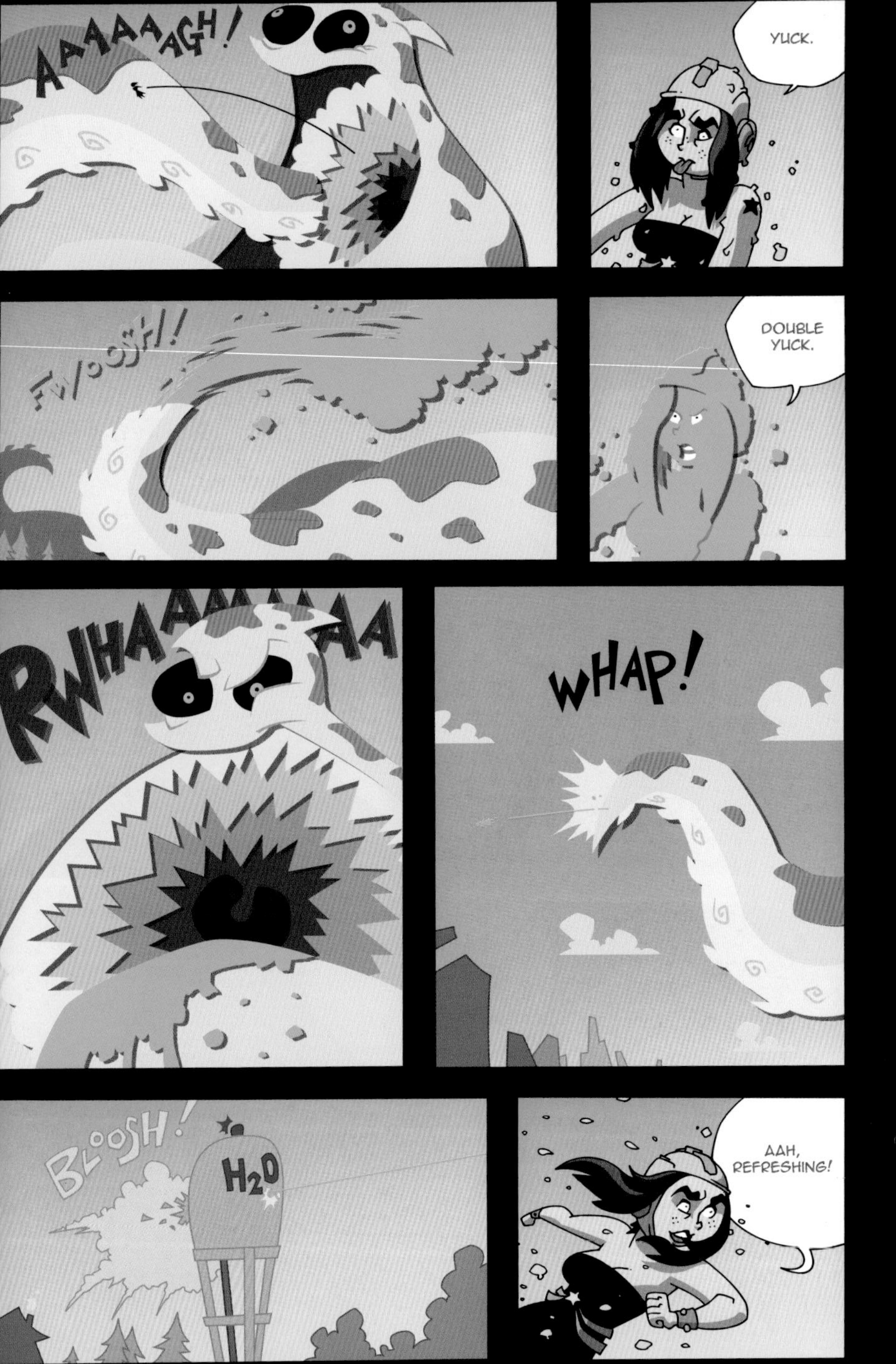
AAAAAAGH!
YUCK.
FWOOSH!!
DOUBLE YUCK.
RWHAAAAAAAA
WHAP!
BLOOSH!
H2O
AAH, REFRESHING!

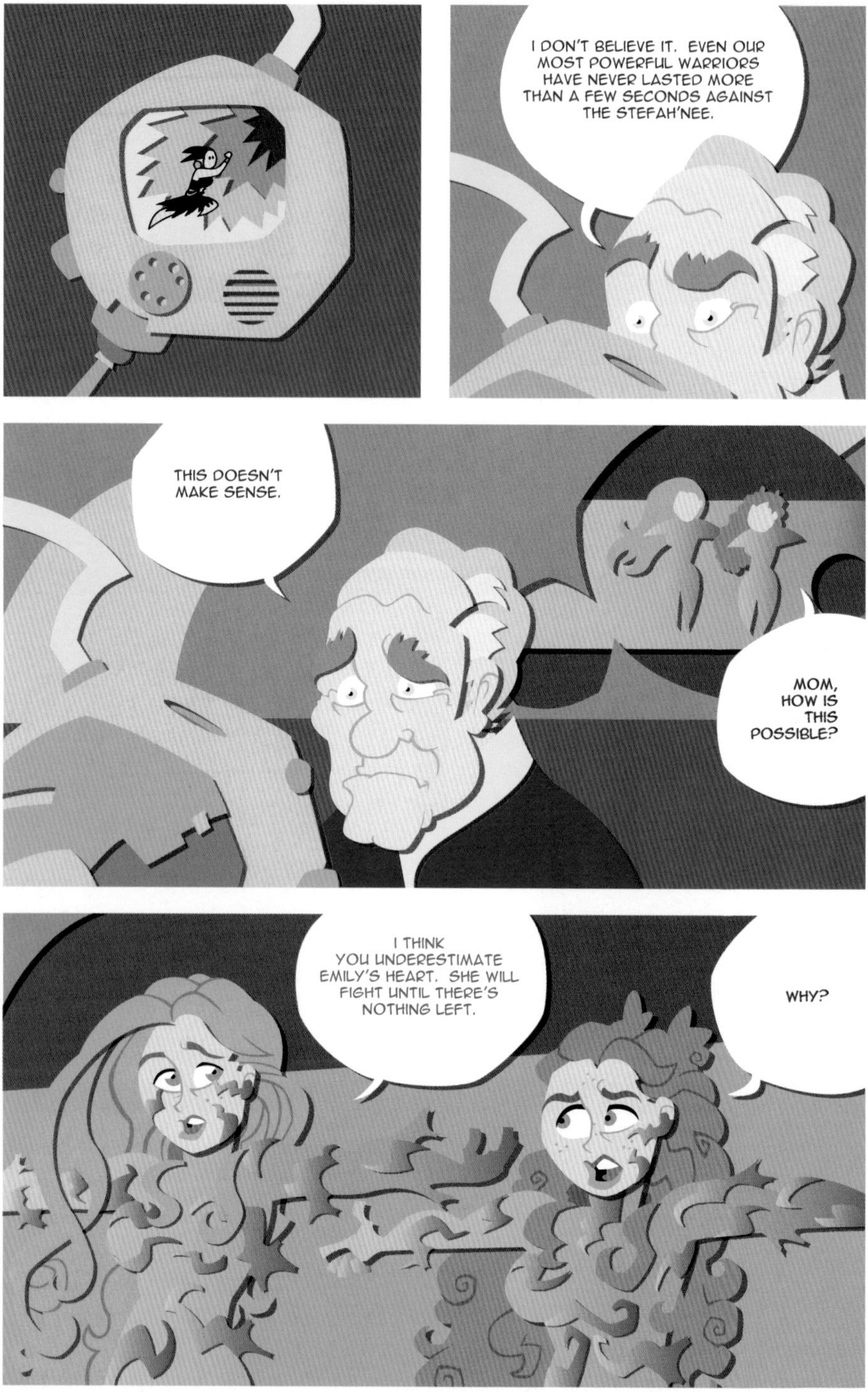
I DON'T BELIEVE IT. EVEN OUR MOST POWERFUL WARRIORS HAVE NEVER LASTED MORE THAN A FEW SECONDS AGAINST THE STEFAH'NEE.
THIS DOESN'T MAKE SENSE.
MOM, HOW IS THIS POSSIBLE?
I THINK YOU UNDERESTIMATE EMILY'S HEART. SHE WILL FIGHT UNTIL THERE'S NOTHING LEFT.
WHY?

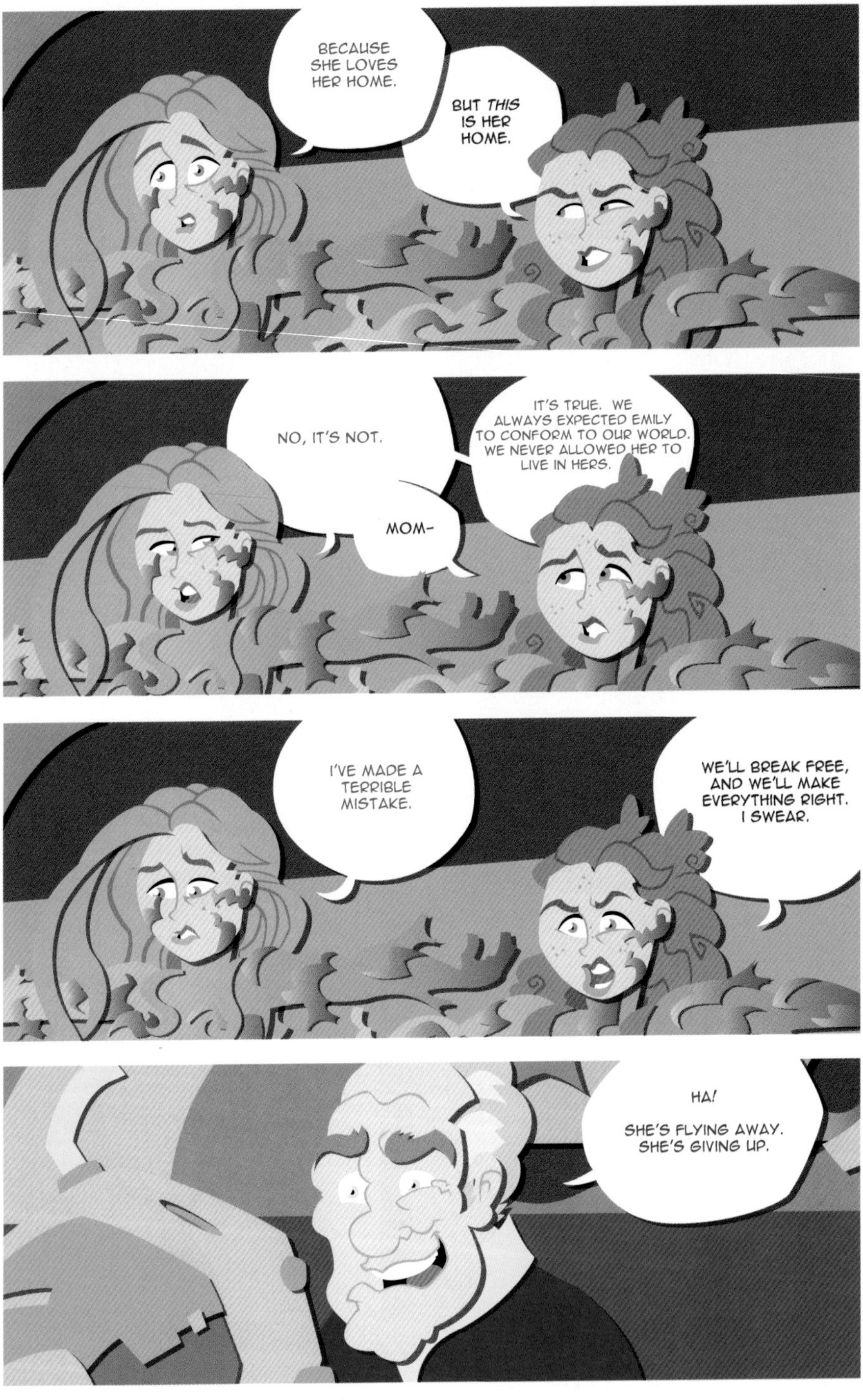

BECAUSE SHE LOVES HER HOME.
BUT *THIS* IS HER HOME.
NO, IT'S NOT.
MOM-
IT'S TRUE. WE ALWAYS EXPECTED EMILY TO CONFORM TO OUR WORLD. WE NEVER ALLOWED HER TO LIVE IN HERS.
I'VE MADE A TERRIBLE MISTAKE.
WE'LL BREAK FREE, AND WE'LL MAKE EVERYTHING RIGHT. I SWEAR.
HA!
SHE'S FLYING AWAY. SHE'S GIVING UP.

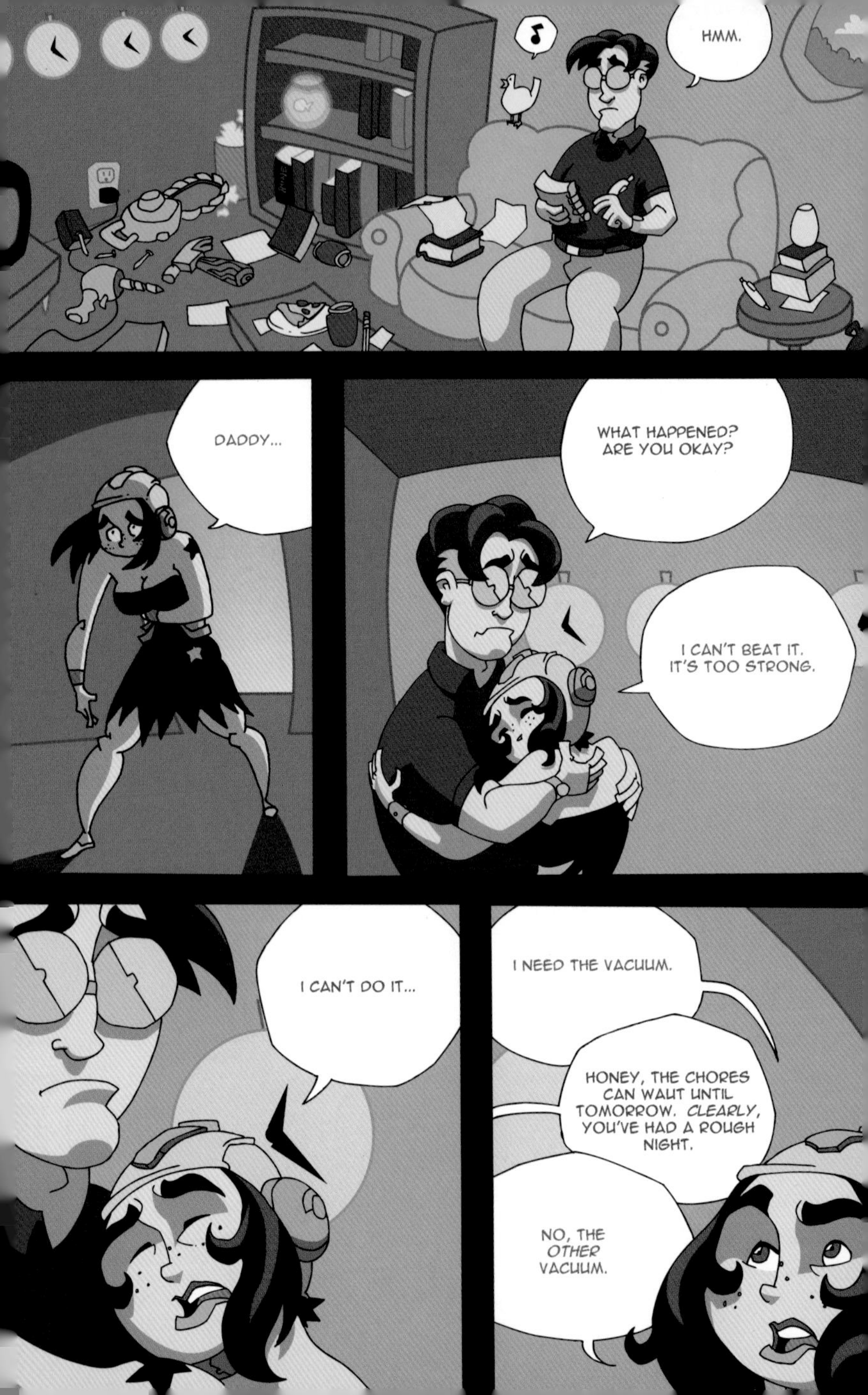
HMM.
DADDY...
WHAT HAPPENED? ARE YOU OKAY?
I CAN'T BEAT IT. IT'S TOO STRONG.
I CAN'T DO IT...
I NEED THE VACUUM.
HONEY, THE CHORES CAN WAIT UNTIL TOMORROW. *CLEARLY*, YOU'VE HAD A ROUGH NIGHT.
NO, THE *OTHER* VACUUM.

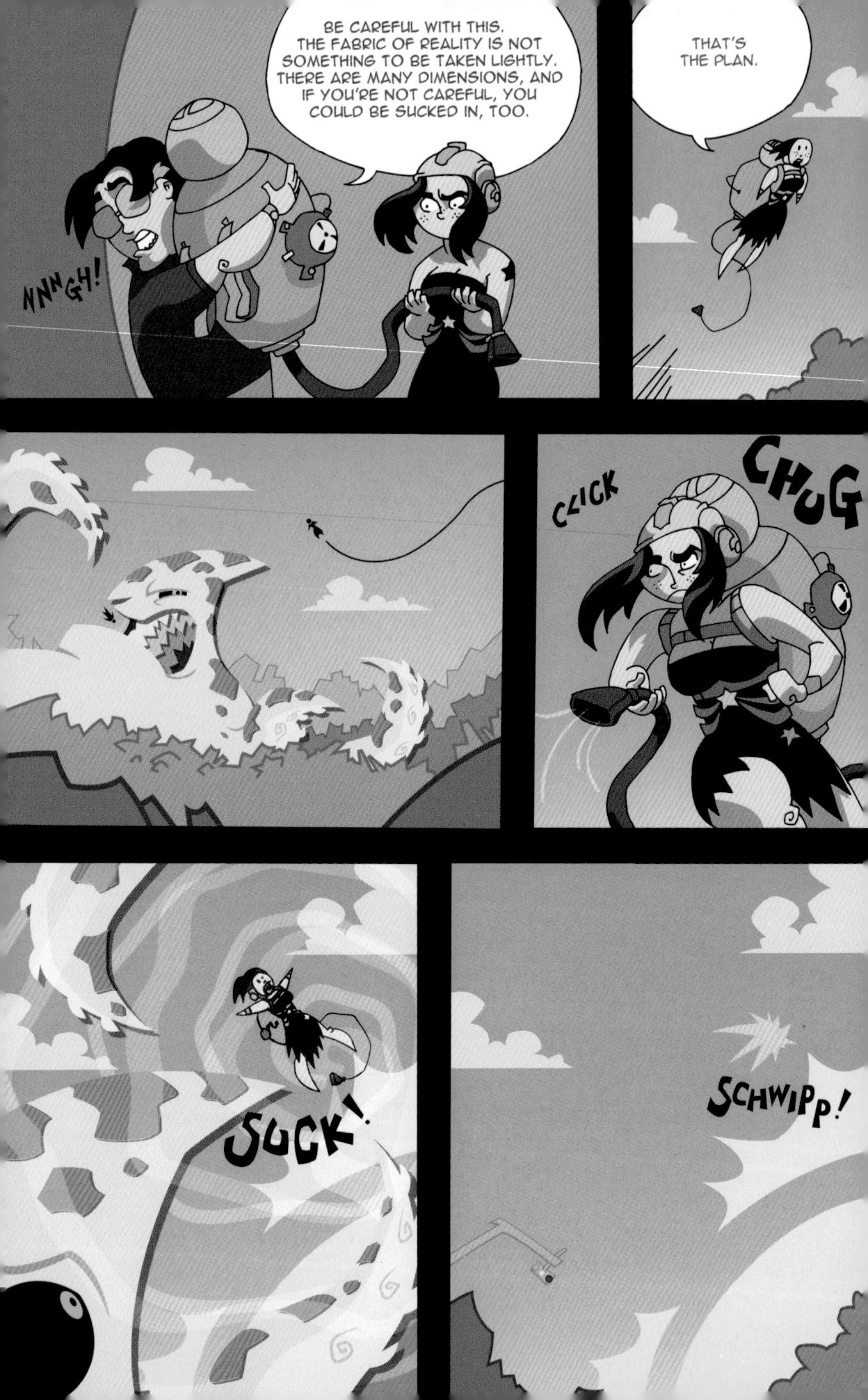
BE CAREFUL WITH THIS. THE FABRIC OF REALITY IS NOT SOMETHING TO BE TAKEN LIGHTLY. THERE ARE MANY DIMENSIONS, AND IF YOU'RE NOT CAREFUL, YOU COULD BE SUCKED IN, TOO.
NNNGH!
THAT'S THE PLAN.
CLICK
CHUG
SUCK!
SCHWIPP!

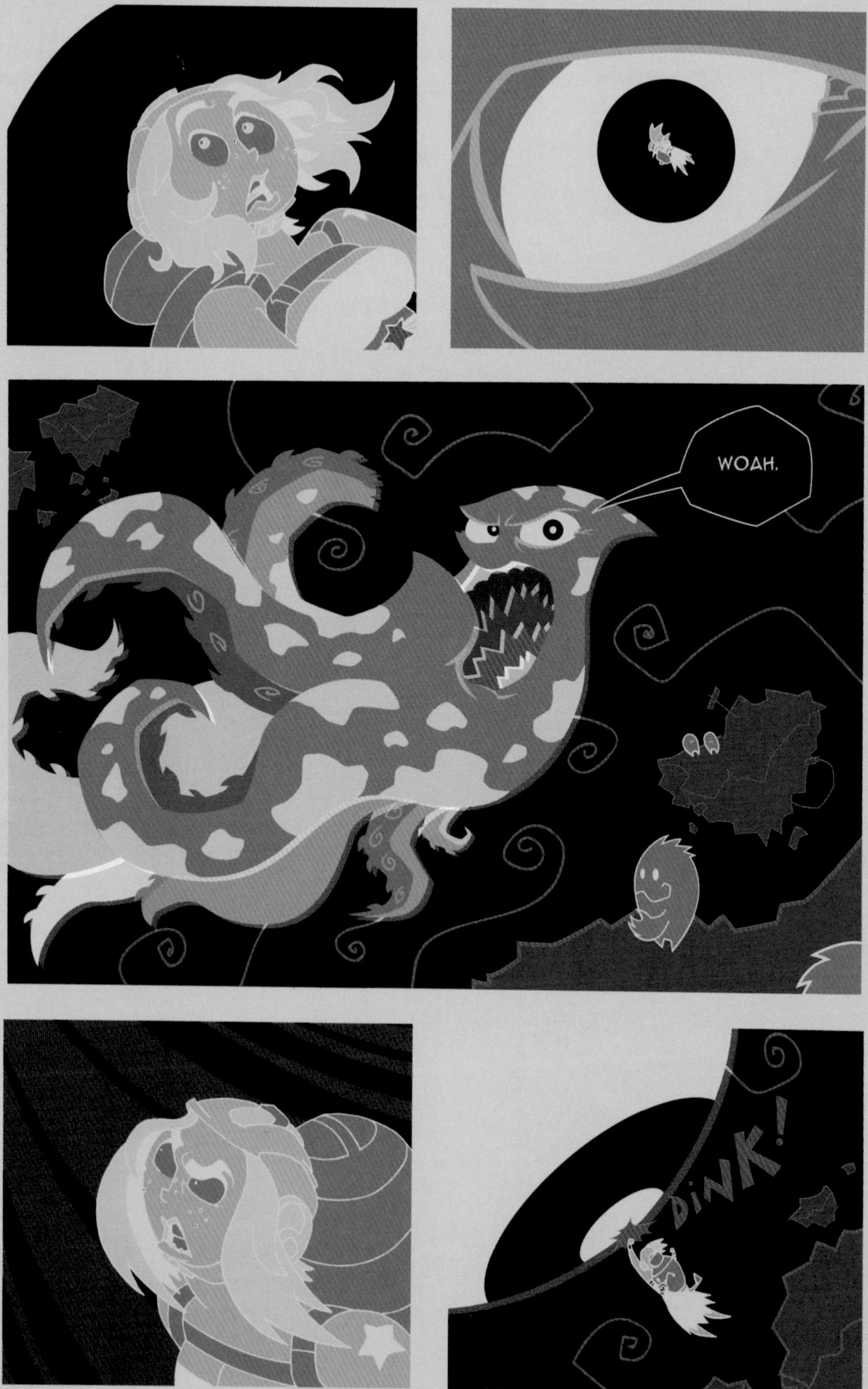
WOAH.
DINK!

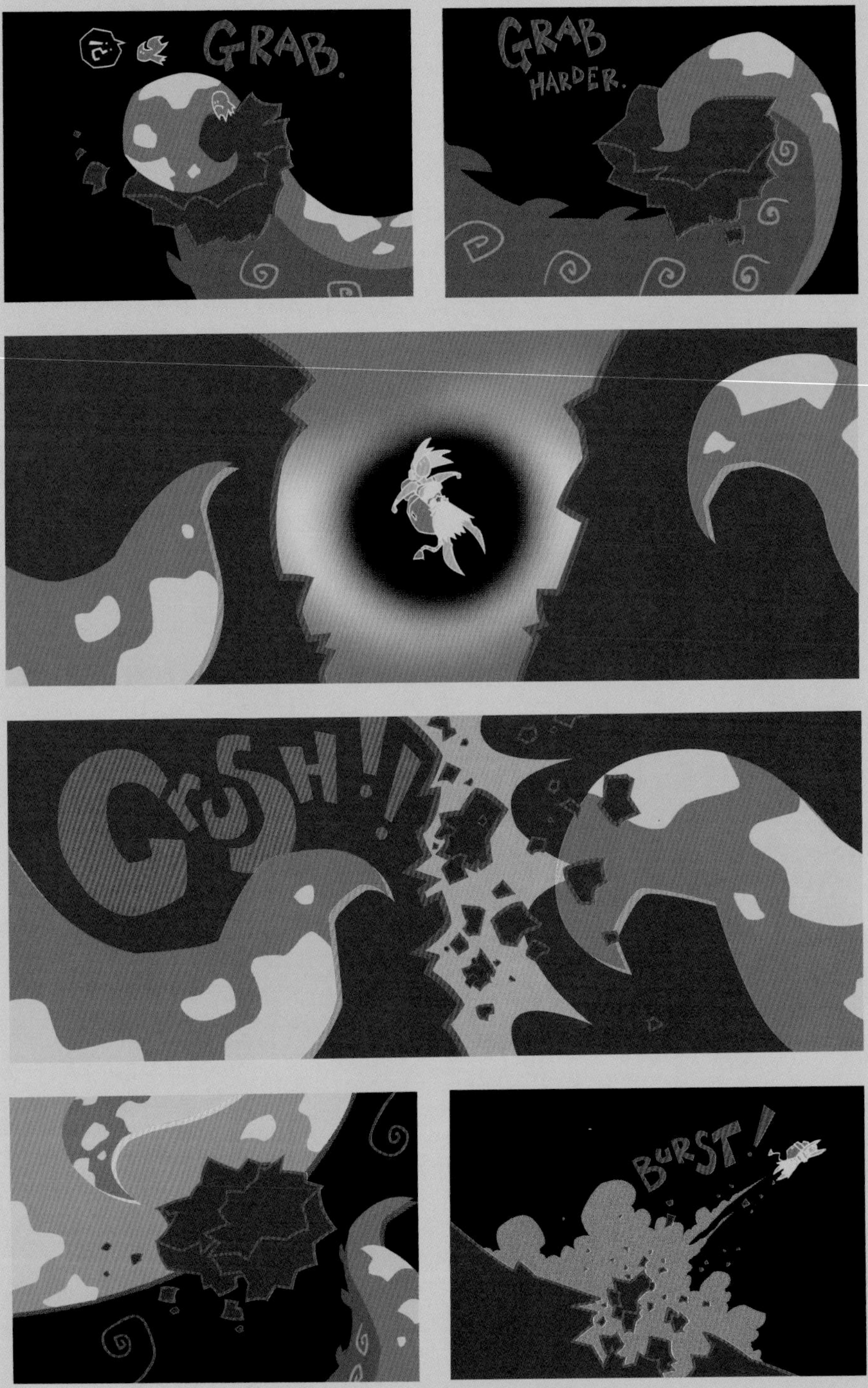
?!
GRAB.
GRAB
HARDER.
CRUSH!!
BURST!

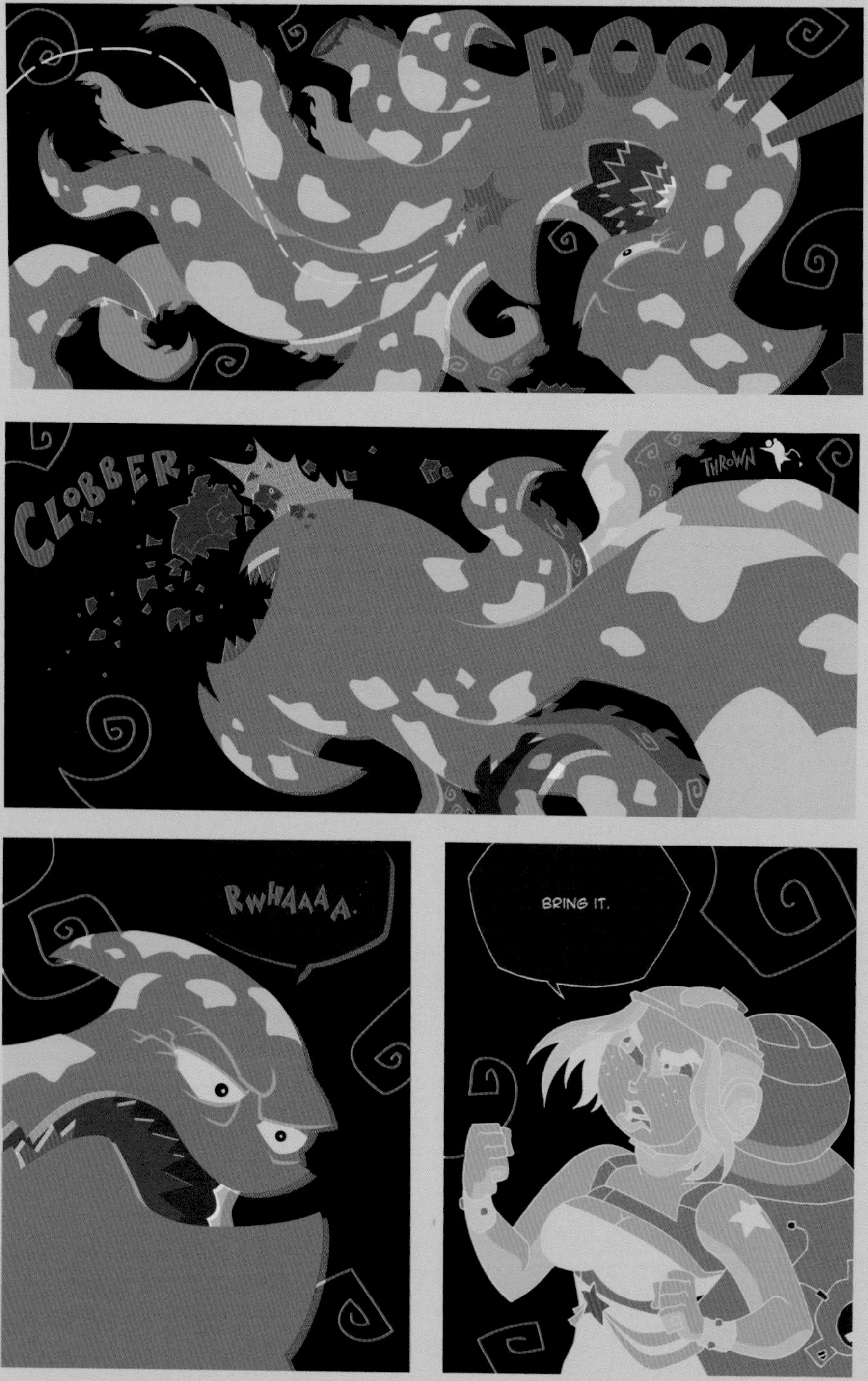
BOOM!
CLOBBER.
THROWN
RWHAAAA.
BRING IT.

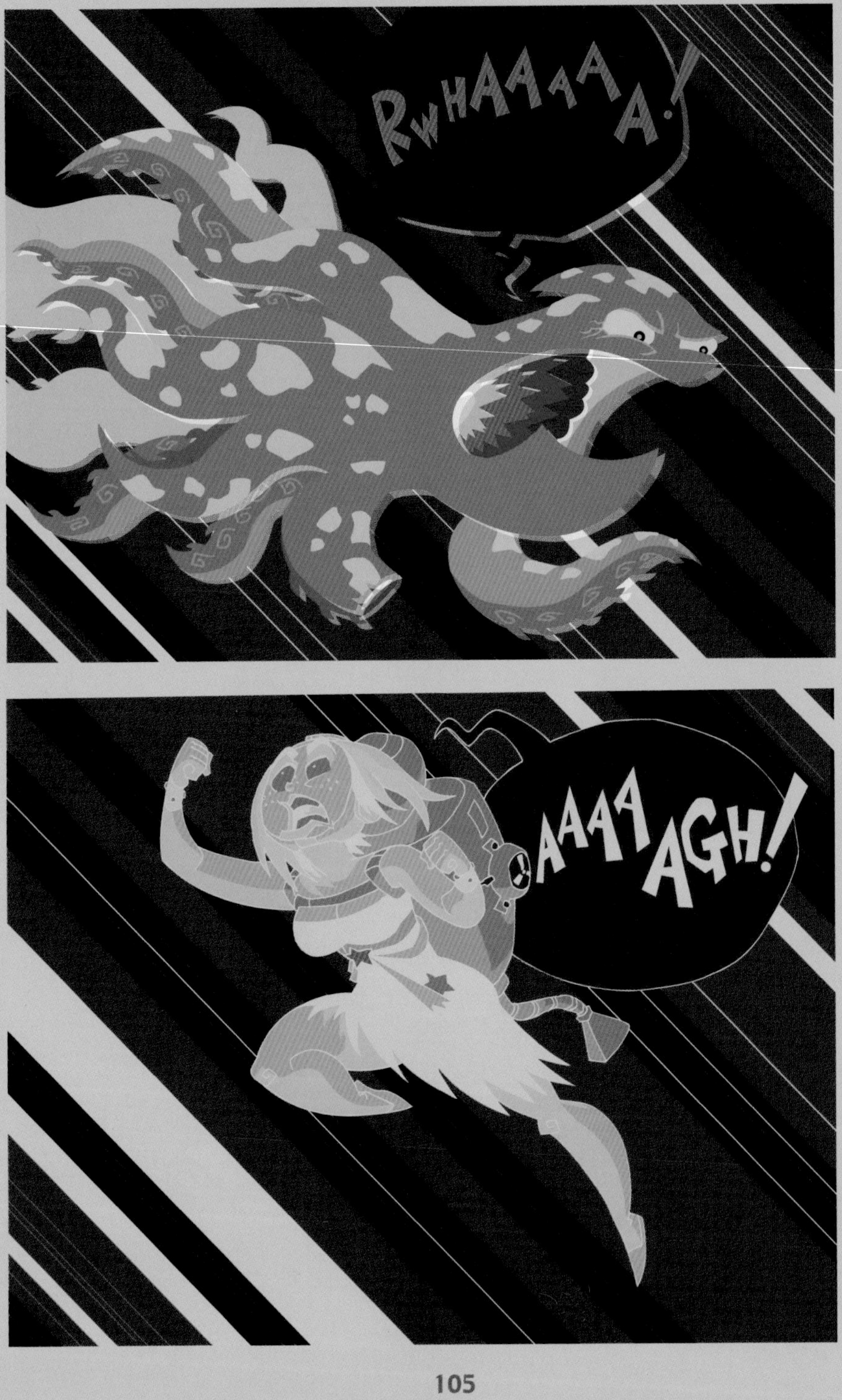
RWHAAAAAA!
AAAAAGH!

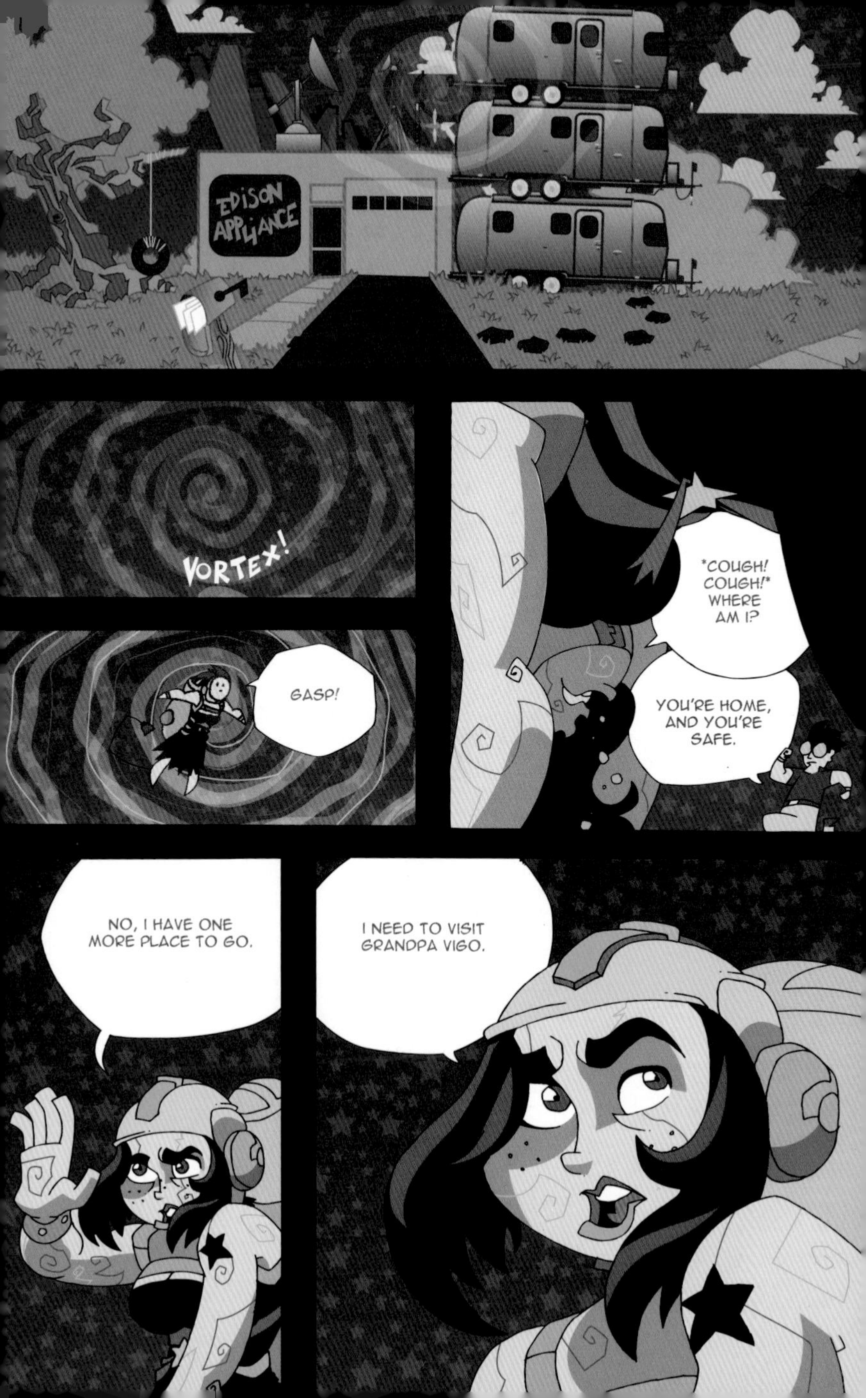
EDISON APPLIANCE
VORTEX!
GASP!
COUGH! COUGH! WHERE AM I?
YOU'RE HOME, AND YOU'RE SAFE.
NO, I HAVE ONE MORE PLACE TO GO.
I NEED TO VISIT GRANDPA VIGO.

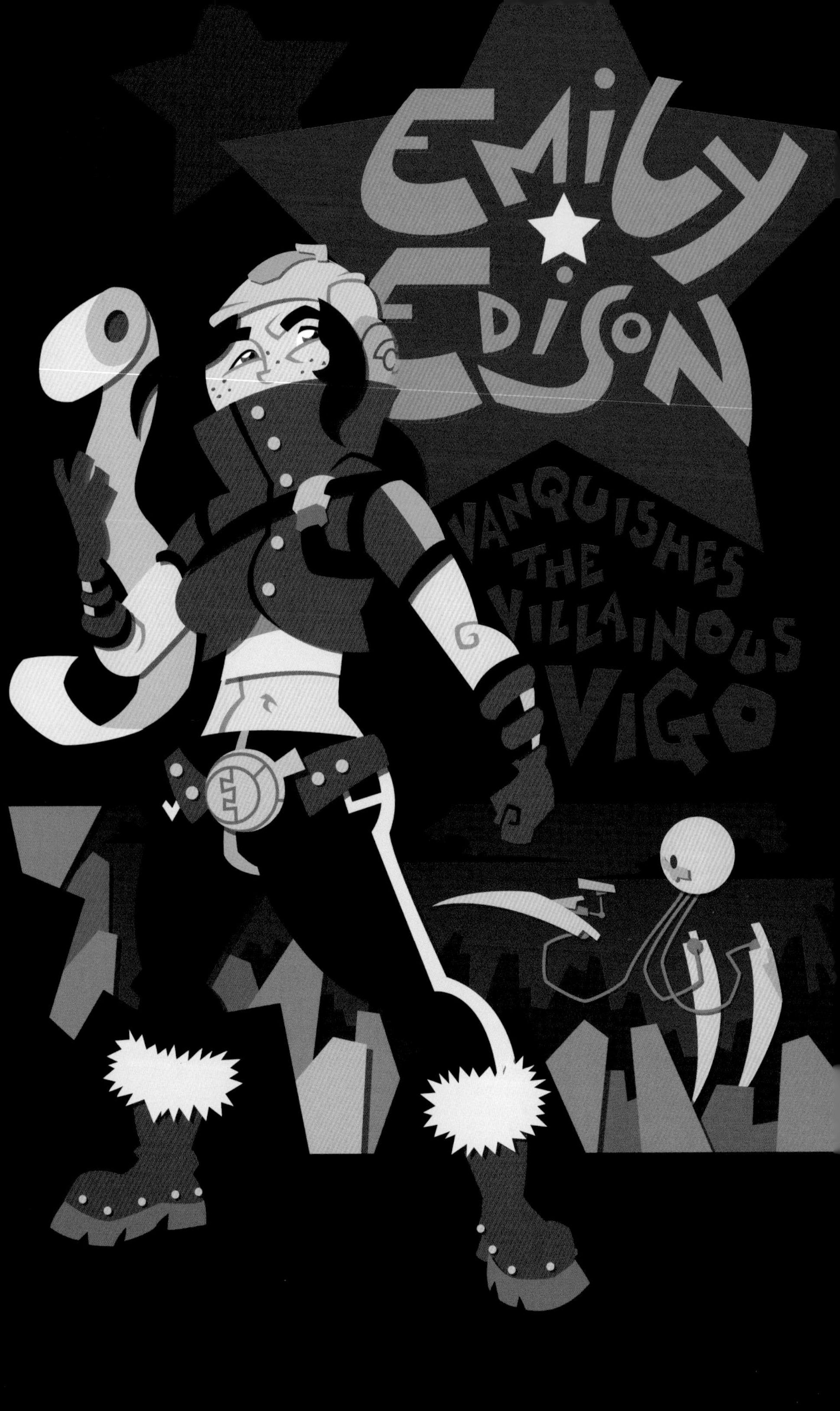
EMILY EDISON
VANQUISHES THE VILLAINOUS VIGO

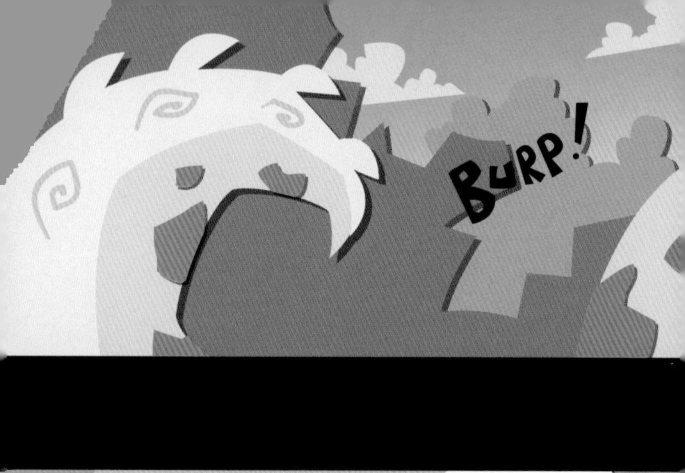
BURP!

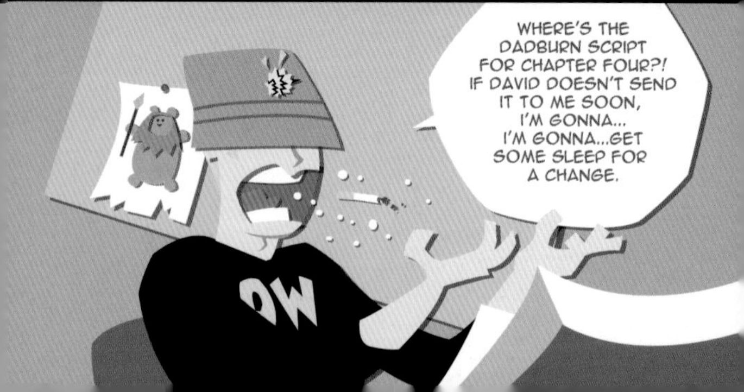
WHERE'S THE DADBURN SCRIPT FOR CHAPTER FOUR?! IF DAVID DOESN'T SEND IT TO ME SOON, I'M GONNA... I'M GONNA...GET SOME SLEEP FOR A CHANGE.
DW

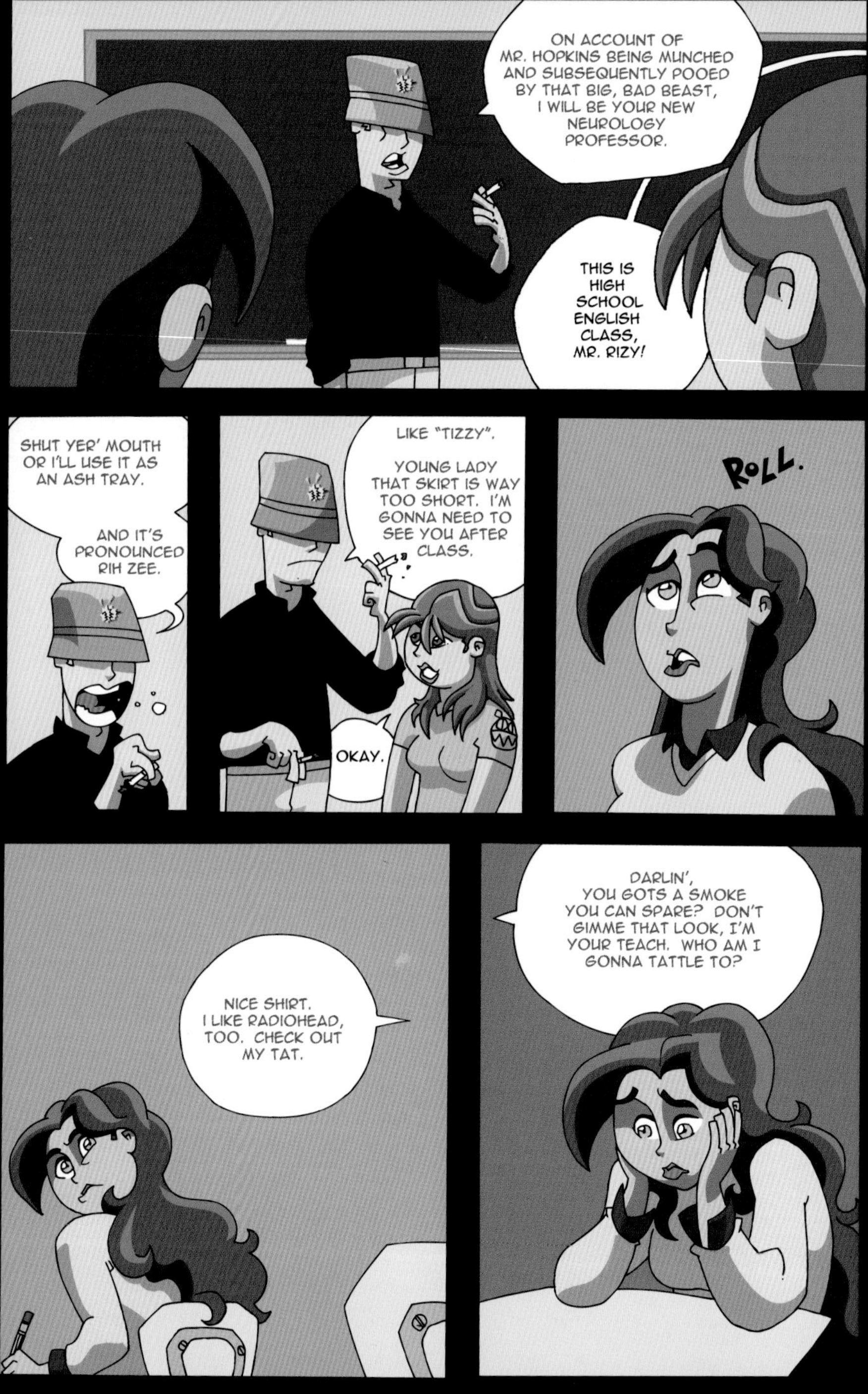
ON ACCOUNT OF MR. HOPKINS BEING MUNCHED AND SUBSEQUENTLY POOED BY THAT BIG, BAD BEAST, I WILL BE YOUR NEW NEUROLOGY PROFESSOR.
THIS IS HIGH SCHOOL ENGLISH CLASS, MR. RIZY!
SHUT YER' MOUTH OR I'LL USE IT AS AN ASH TRAY.
AND IT'S PRONOUNCED RIH ZEE.
LIKE "TIZZY".
YOUNG LADY THAT SKIRT IS WAY TOO SHORT. I'M GONNA NEED TO SEE YOU AFTER CLASS.
OKAY.
ROLL.
NICE SHIRT. I LIKE RADIOHEAD, TOO. CHECK OUT MY TAT.
DARLIN', YOU GOTS A SMOKE YOU CAN SPARE? DON'T GIMME THAT LOOK, I'M YOUR TEACH. WHO AM I GONNA TATTLE TO?

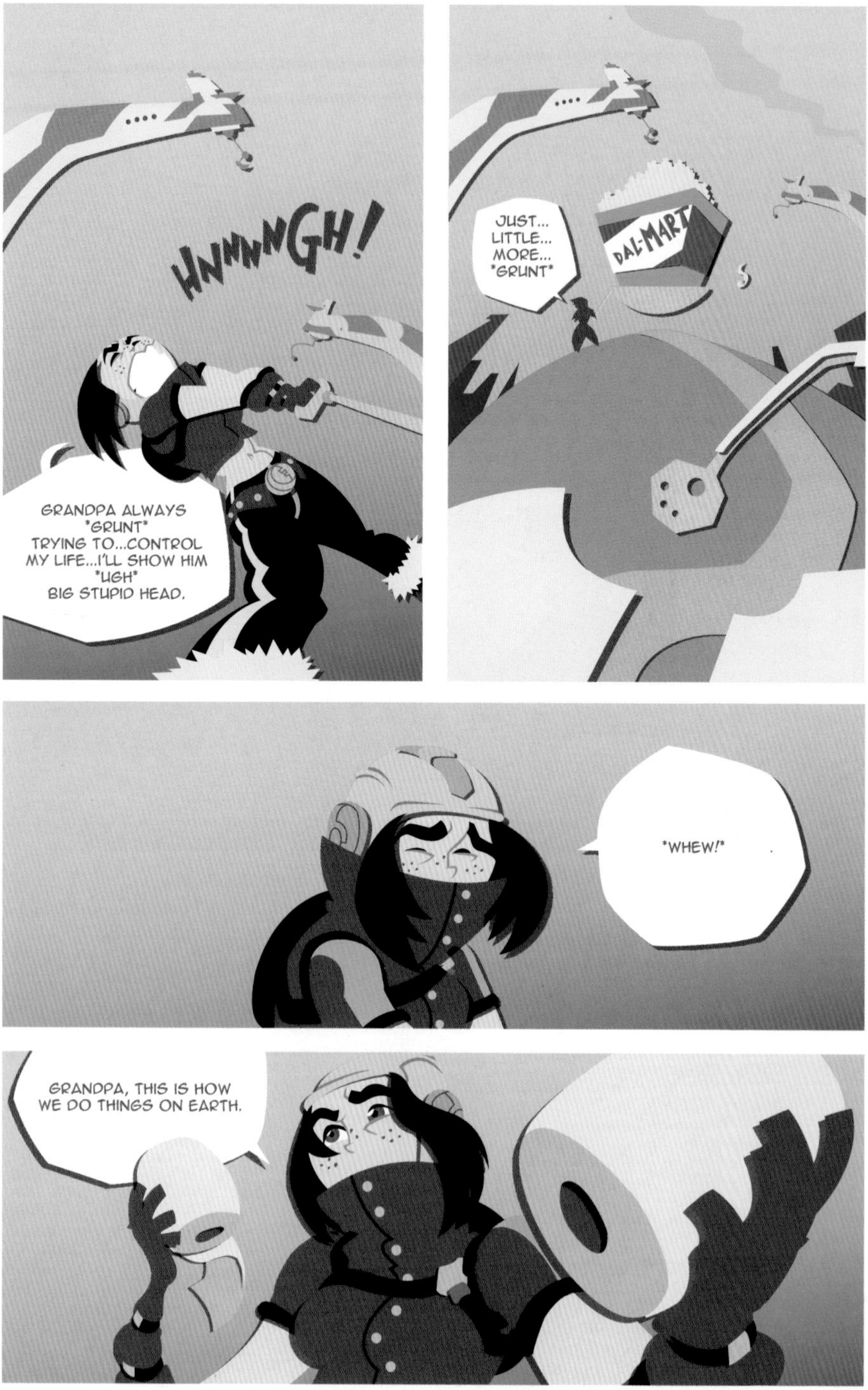
HNNNNGH!
GRANDPA ALWAYS *GRUNT* TRYING TO...CONTROL MY LIFE...I'LL SHOW HIM *UGH* BIG STUPID HEAD.
JUST... LITTLE... MORE... *GRUNT*
DAL-MART
WHEW!
GRANDPA, THIS IS HOW WE DO THINGS ON EARTH.

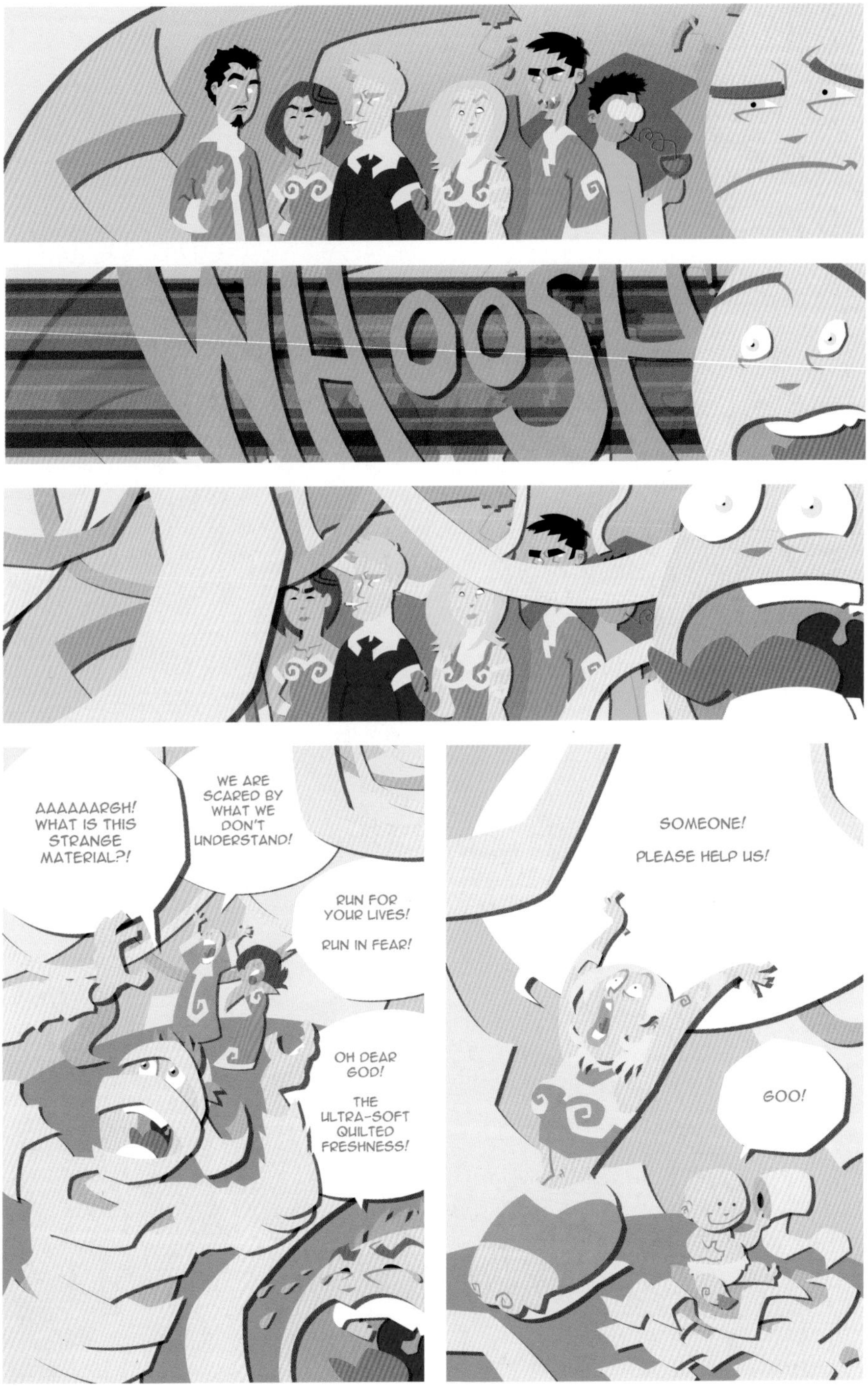
WHOOSH
AAAAAARGH! WHAT IS THIS STRANGE MATERIAL?!
WE ARE SCARED BY WHAT WE DON'T UNDERSTAND!
RUN FOR YOUR LIVES!
RUN IN FEAR!
OH DEAR GOD!
THE ULTRA-SOFT QUILTED FRESHNESS!
SOMEONE!
PLEASE HELP US!
GOO!

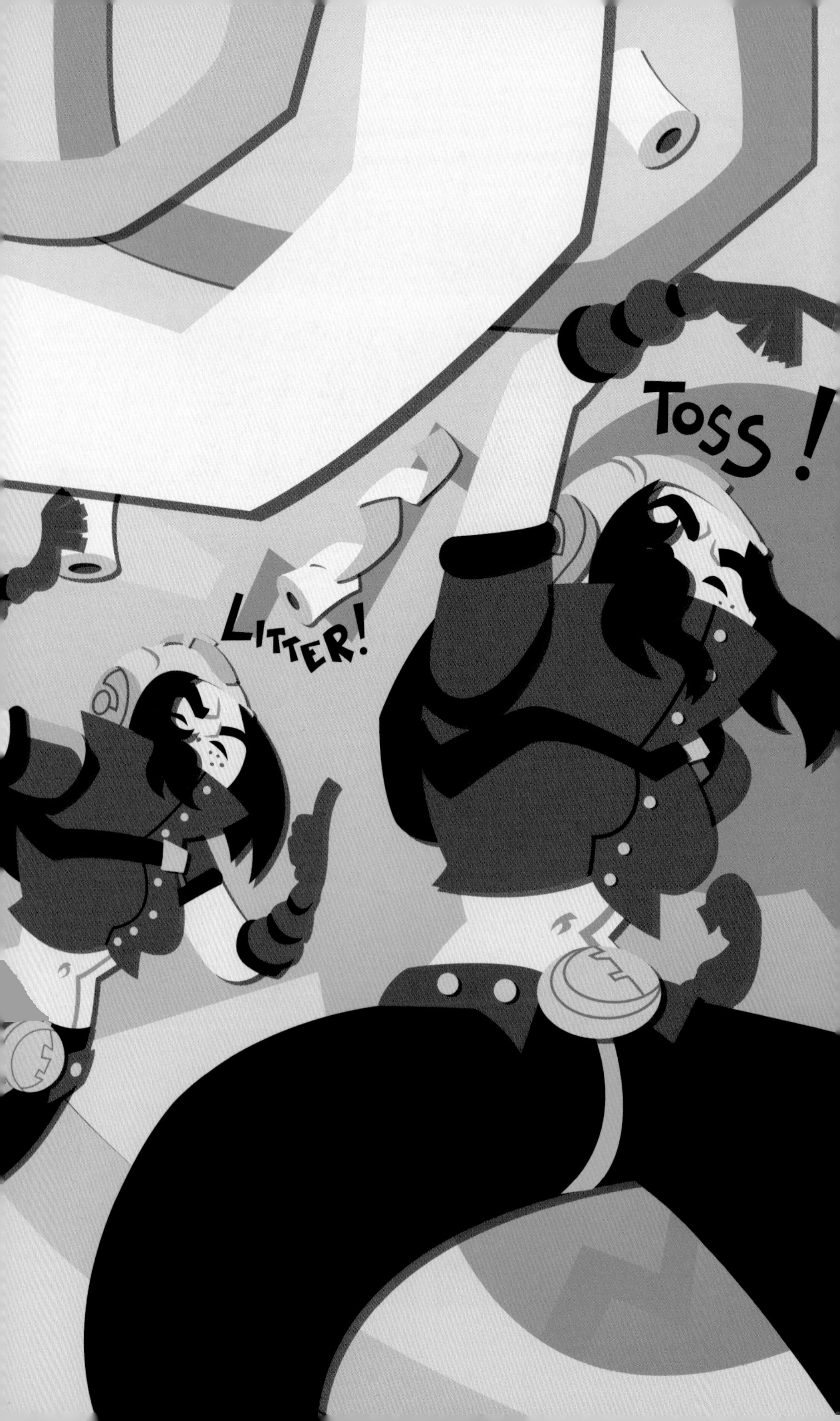
TOSS!
LITTER!

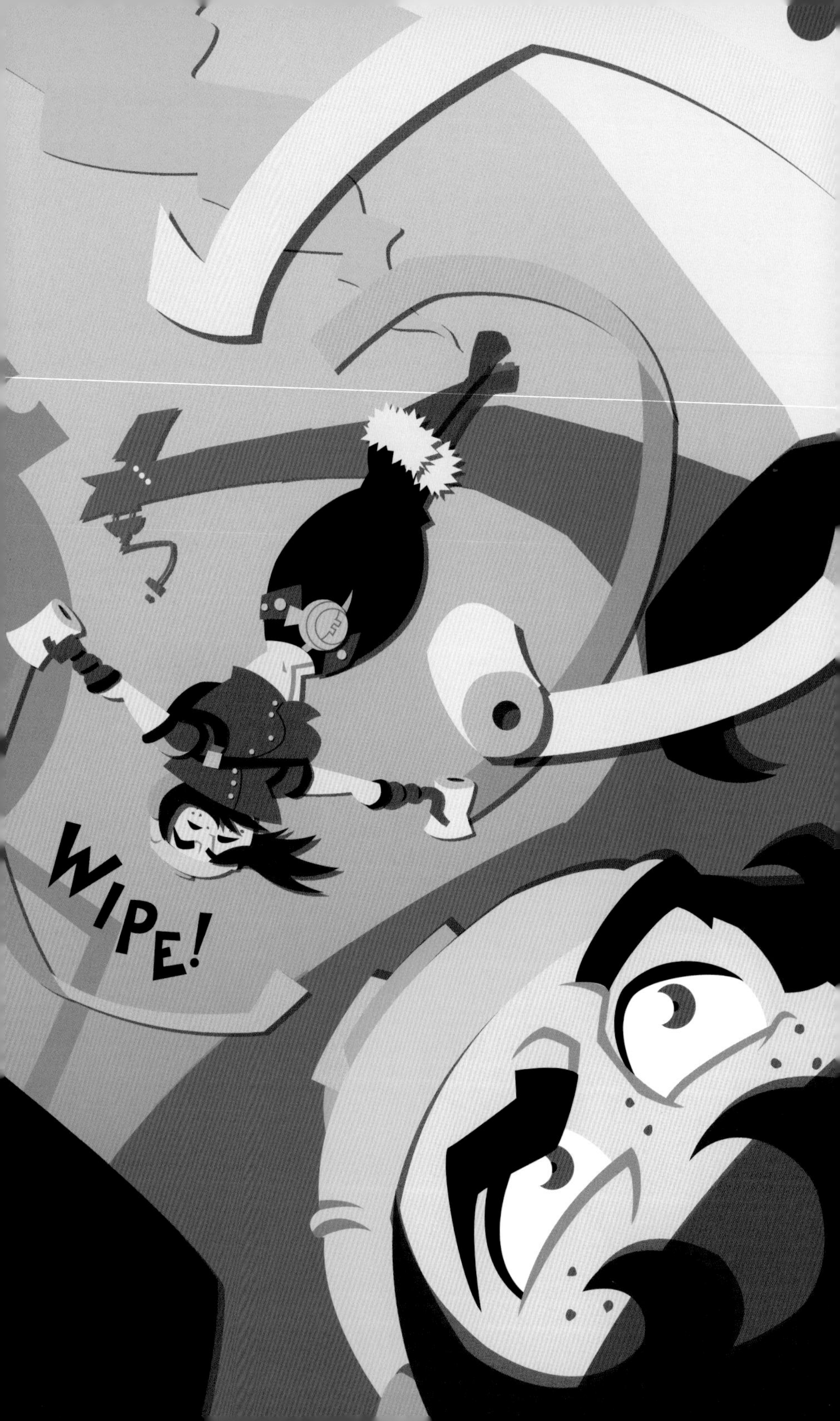
WIPE!

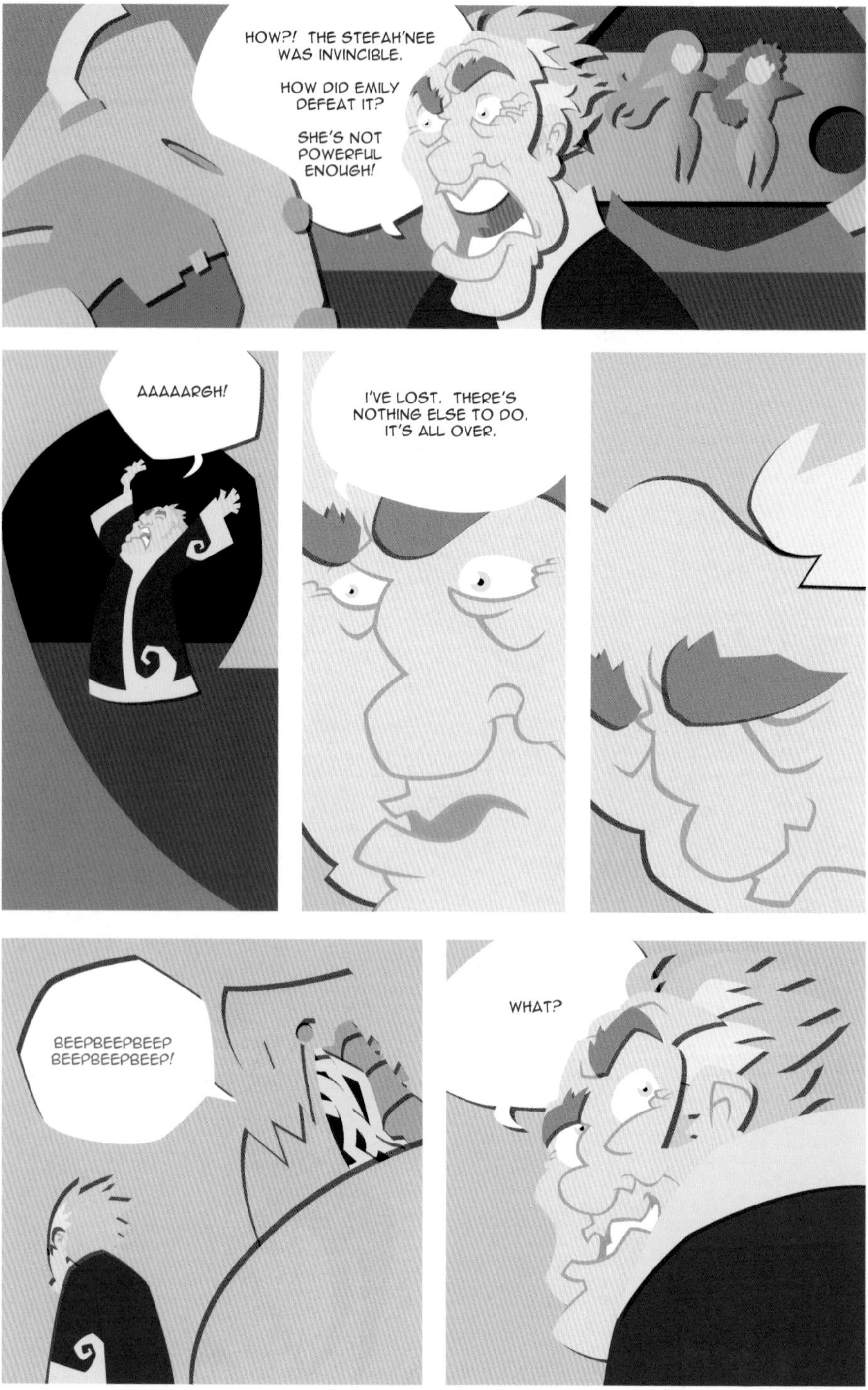
HOW?! THE STEFAH'NEE WAS INVINCIBLE.
HOW DID EMILY DEFEAT IT?
SHE'S NOT POWERFUL ENOUGH!
AAAAARGH!
I'VE LOST. THERE'S NOTHING ELSE TO DO. IT'S ALL OVER.
BEEPBEEPBEEP BEEPBEEPBEEP!
WHAT?

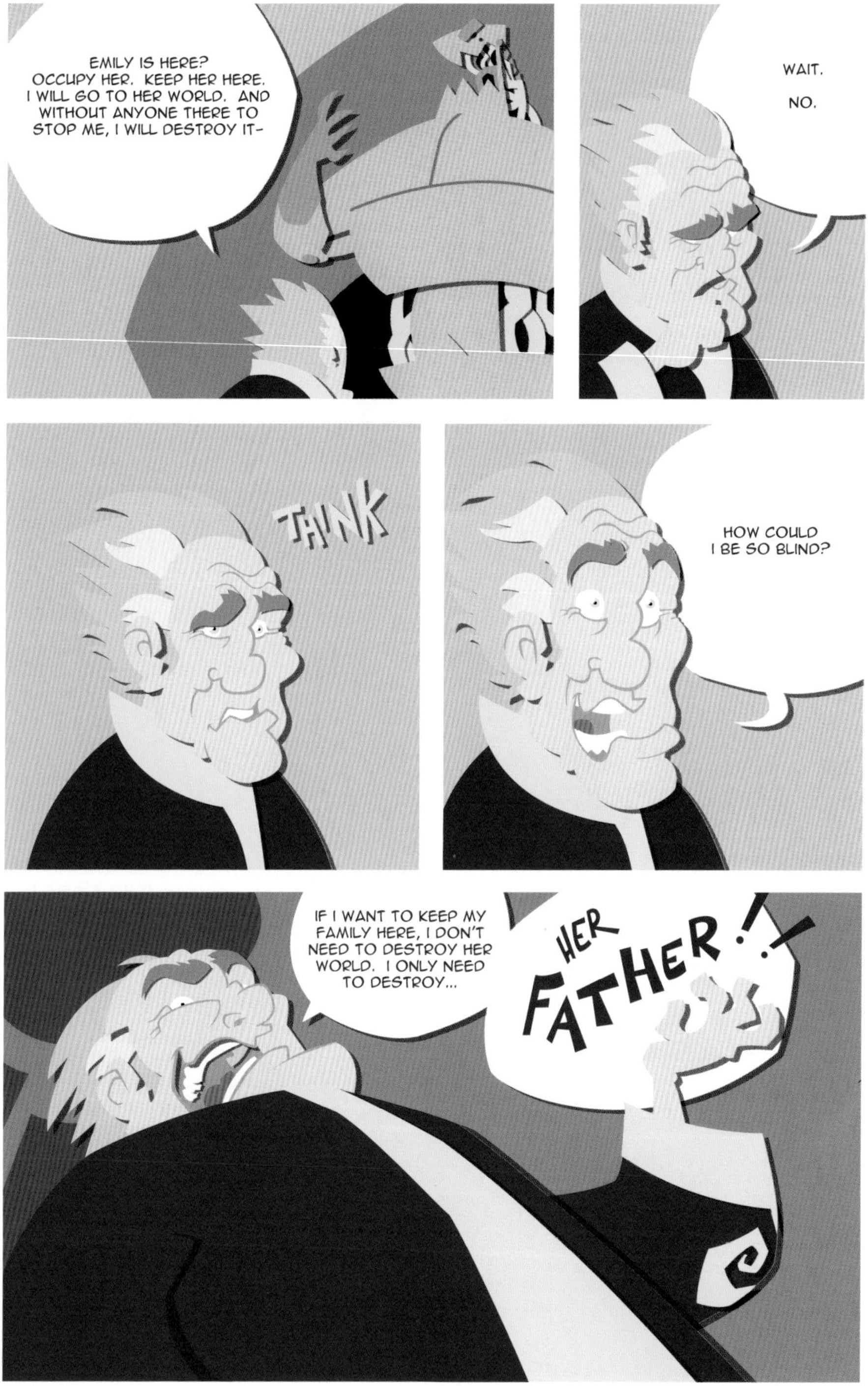
EMILY IS HERE? OCCUPY HER. KEEP HER HERE. I WILL GO TO HER WORLD. AND WITHOUT ANYONE THERE TO STOP ME, I WILL DESTROY IT-
WAIT.
NO.
THINK
HOW COULD I BE SO BLIND?
IF I WANT TO KEEP MY FAMILY HERE, I DON'T NEED TO DESTROY HER WORLD. I ONLY NEED TO DESTROY...
HER FATHER!!

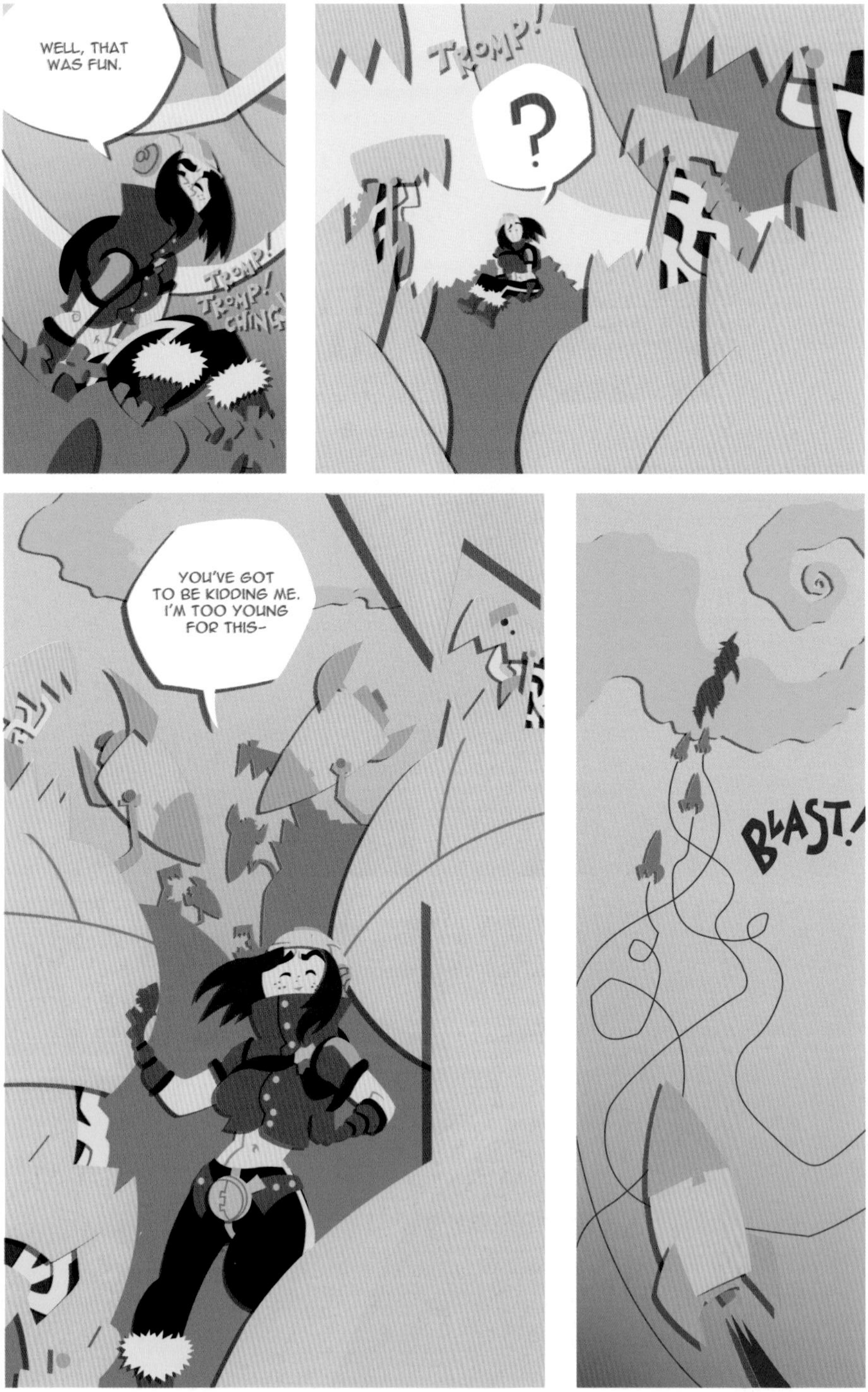
WELL, THAT WAS FUN.
TROMP!
TROMP!
CHING!
TROMP!
?
YOU'VE GOT TO BE KIDDING ME. I'M TOO YOUNG FOR THIS-
BLAST!

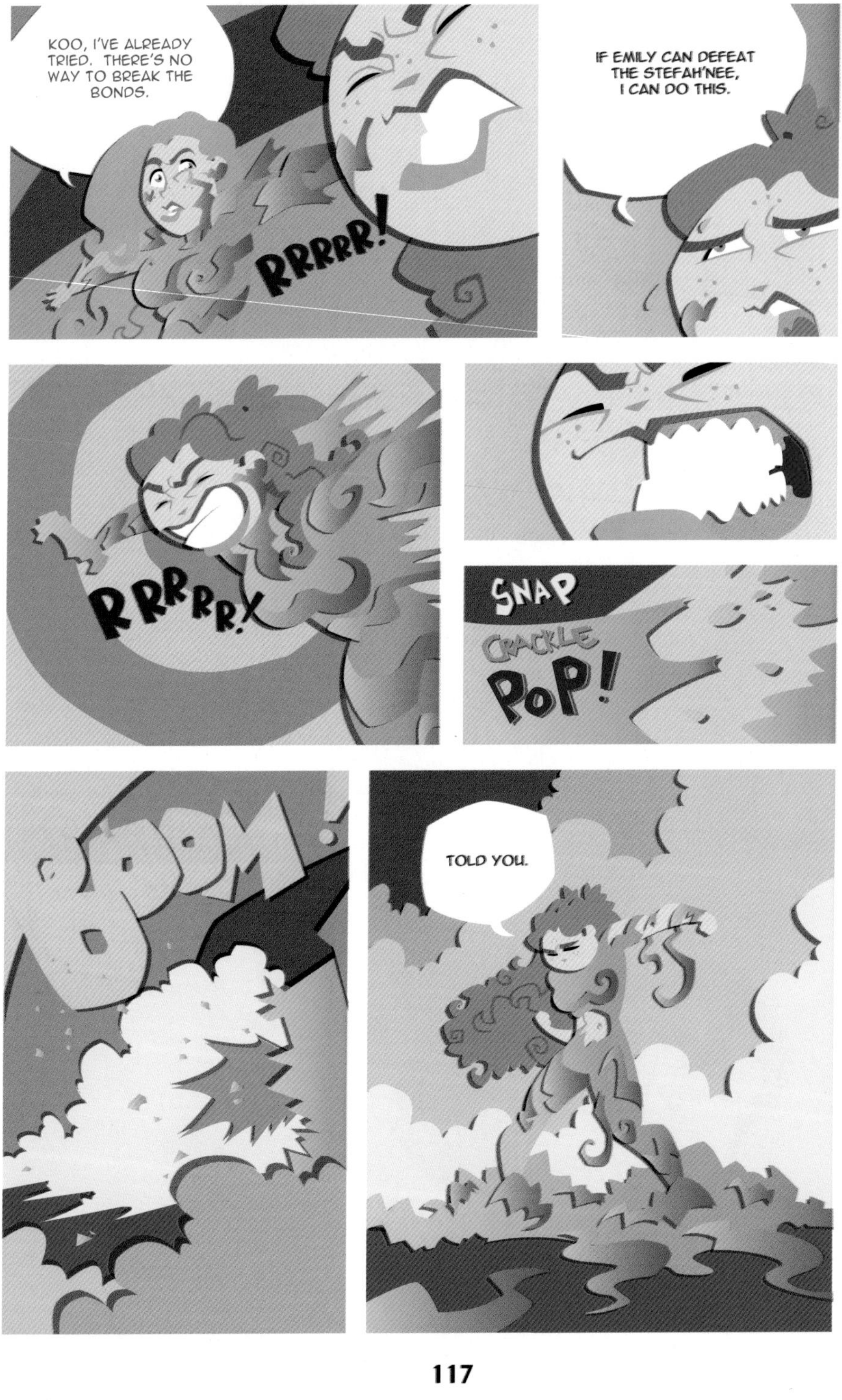
KOO, I'VE ALREADY TRIED. THERE'S NO WAY TO BREAK THE BONDS.
RRRRR!
IF EMILY CAN DEFEAT THE STEFAH'NEE, I CAN DO THIS.
RRRRRR!
SNAP
CRACKLE
POP!
BOOM!
TOLD YOU.

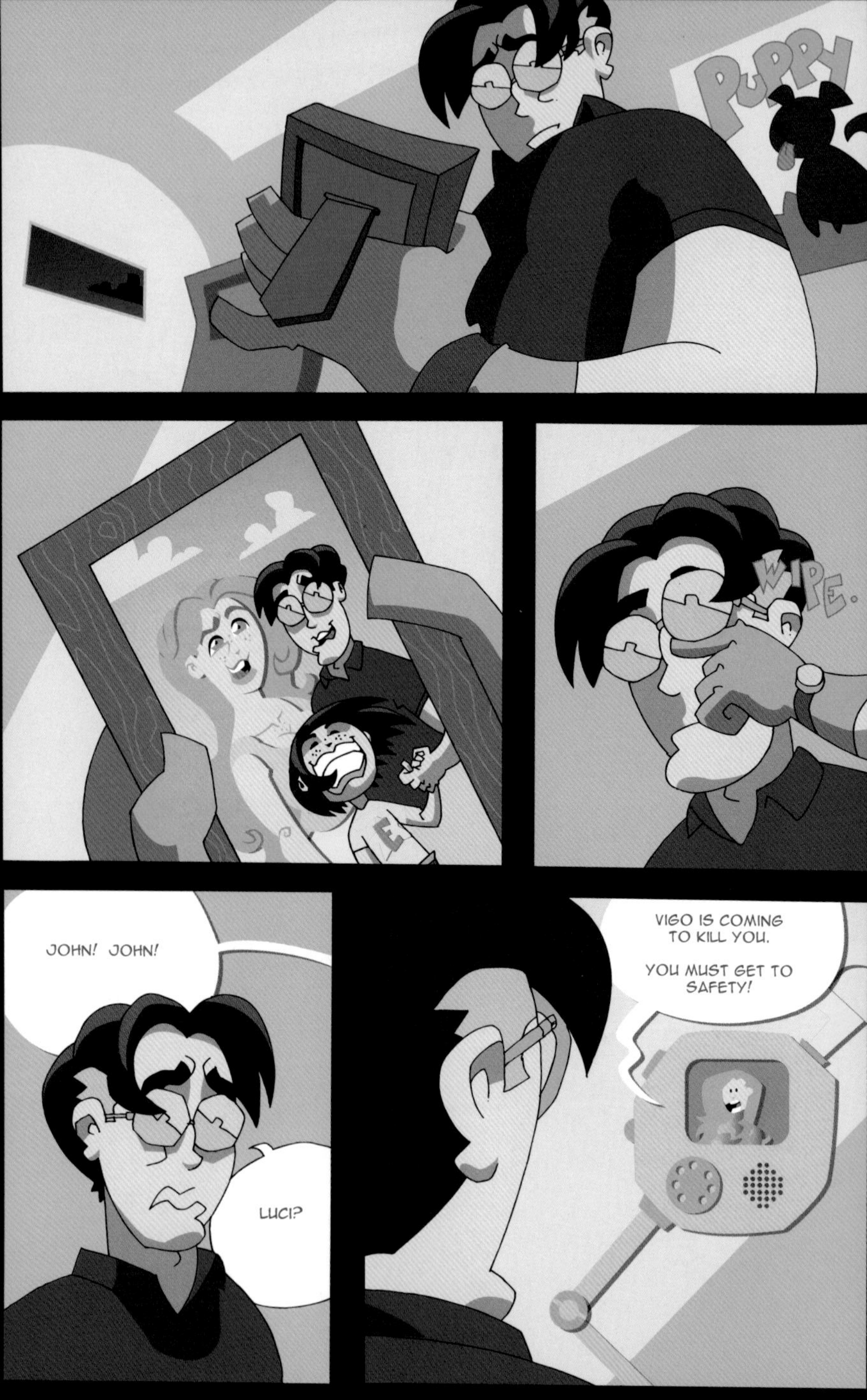
PUPPY
WIPE.
JOHN! JOHN!
LUCI?
VIGO IS COMING TO KILL YOU.
YOU MUST GET TO SAFETY!

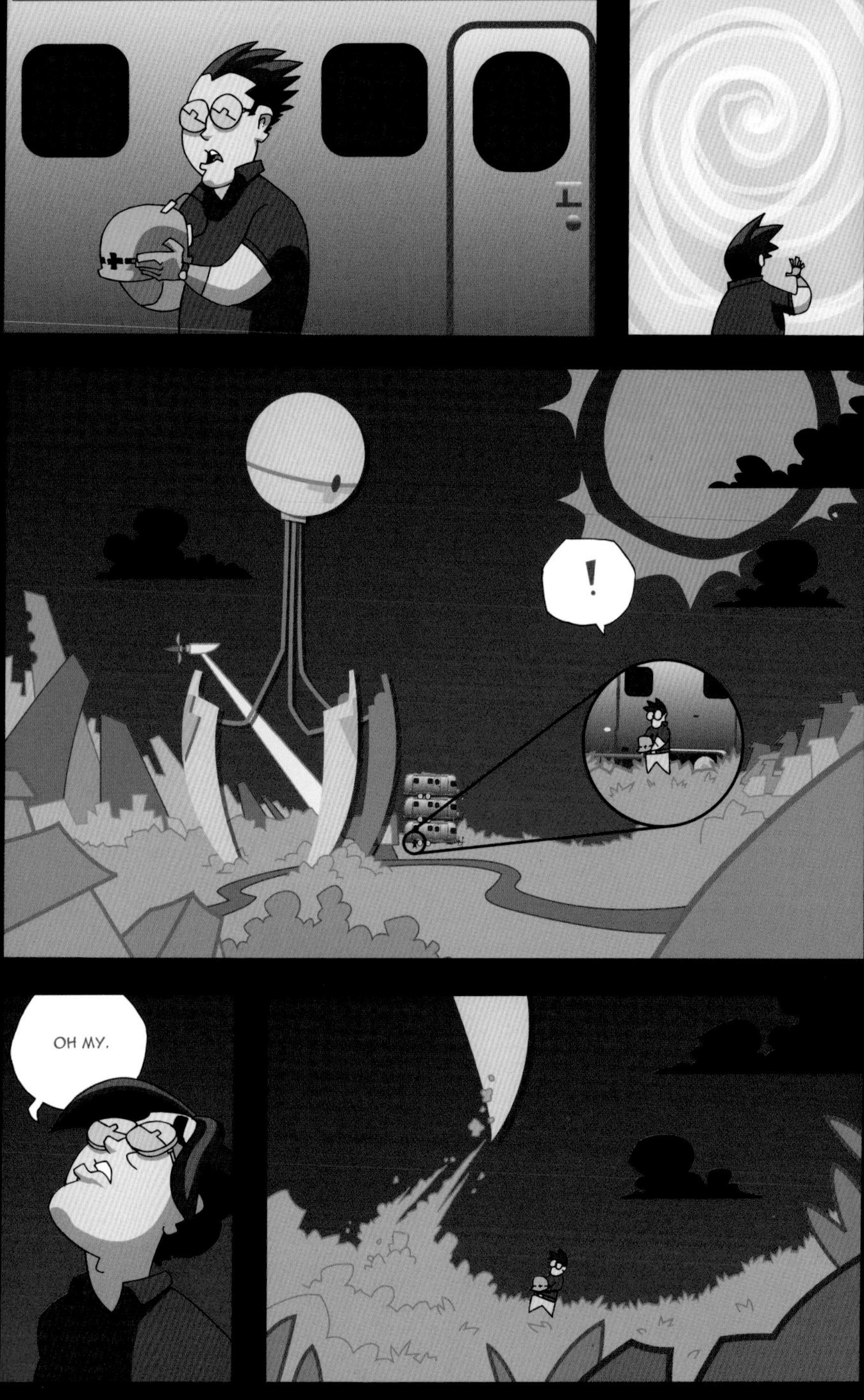
!
OH MY.

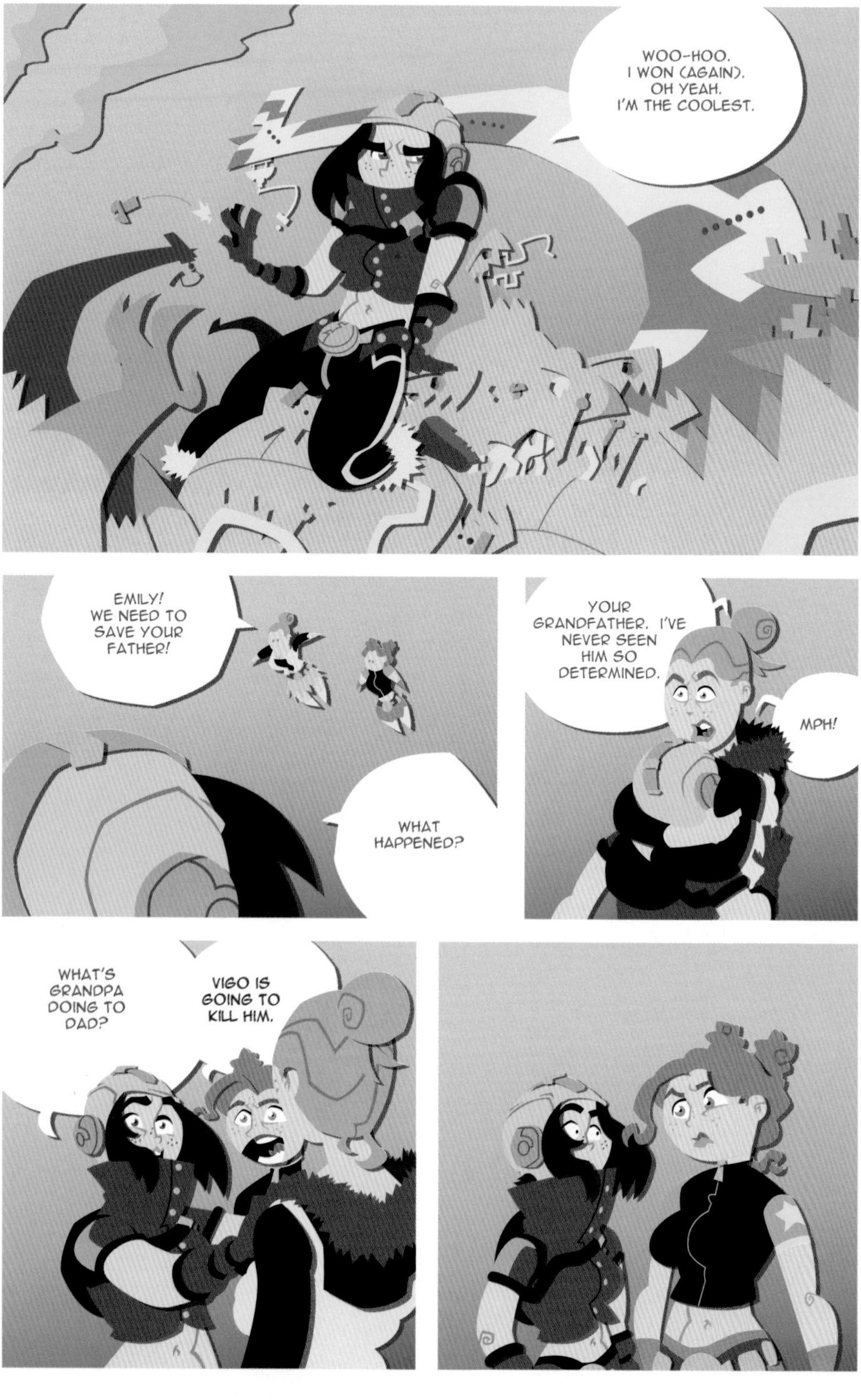
WOO-HOO. I WON (AGAIN). OH YEAH. I'M THE COOLEST.
EMILY! WE NEED TO SAVE YOUR FATHER!
WHAT HAPPENED?
YOUR GRANDFATHER. I'VE NEVER SEEN HIM SO DETERMINED.
MPH!
WHAT'S GRANDPA DOING TO DAD?
VIGO IS GOING TO KILL HIM.

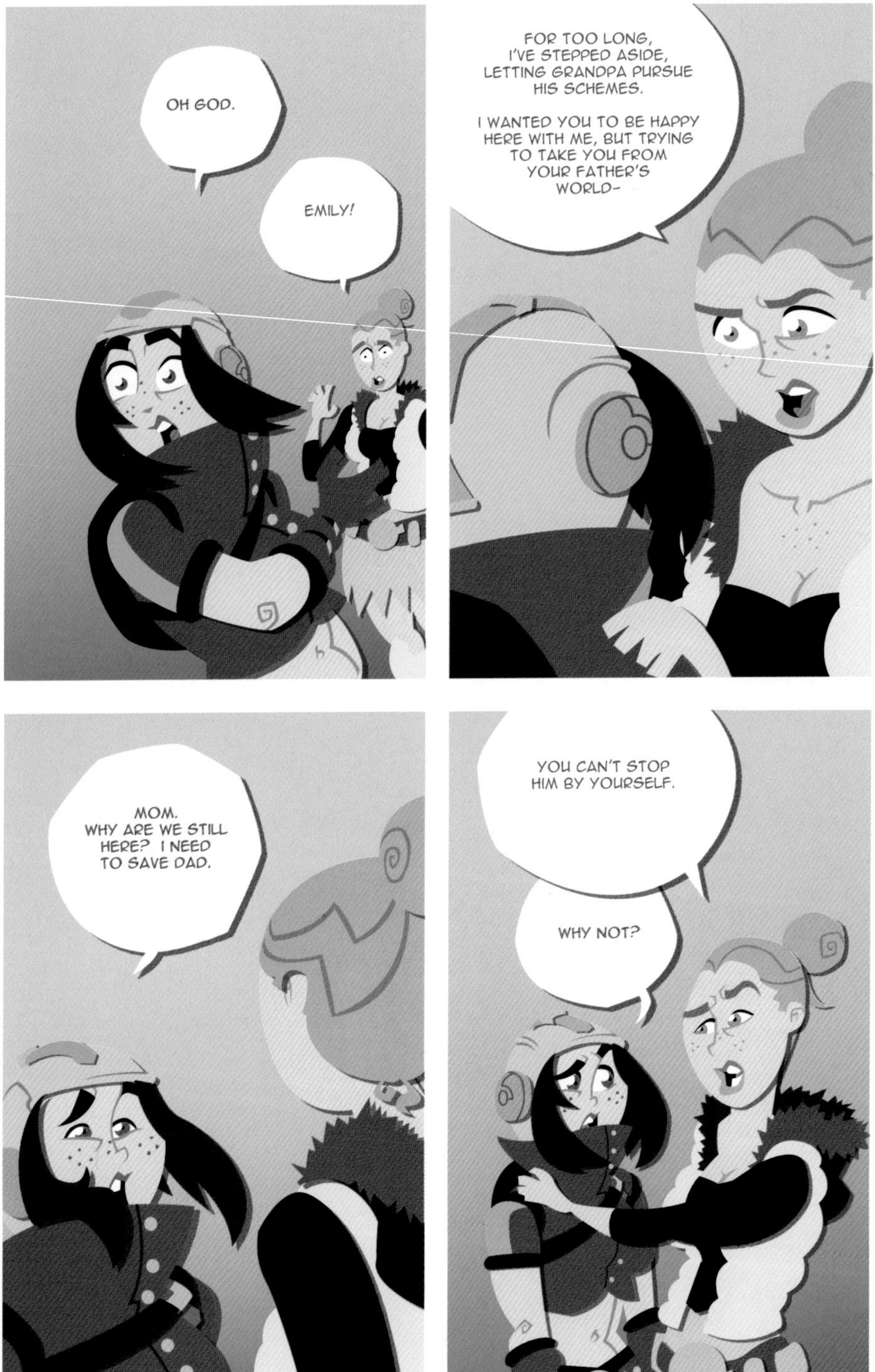
OH GOD.
EMILY!
FOR TOO LONG, I'VE STEPPED ASIDE, LETTING GRANDPA PURSUE HIS SCHEMES.
I WANTED YOU TO BE HAPPY HERE WITH ME, BUT TRYING TO TAKE YOU FROM YOUR FATHER'S WORLD-
MOM. WHY ARE WE STILL HERE? I NEED TO SAVE DAD.
YOU CAN'T STOP HIM BY YOURSELF.
WHY NOT?

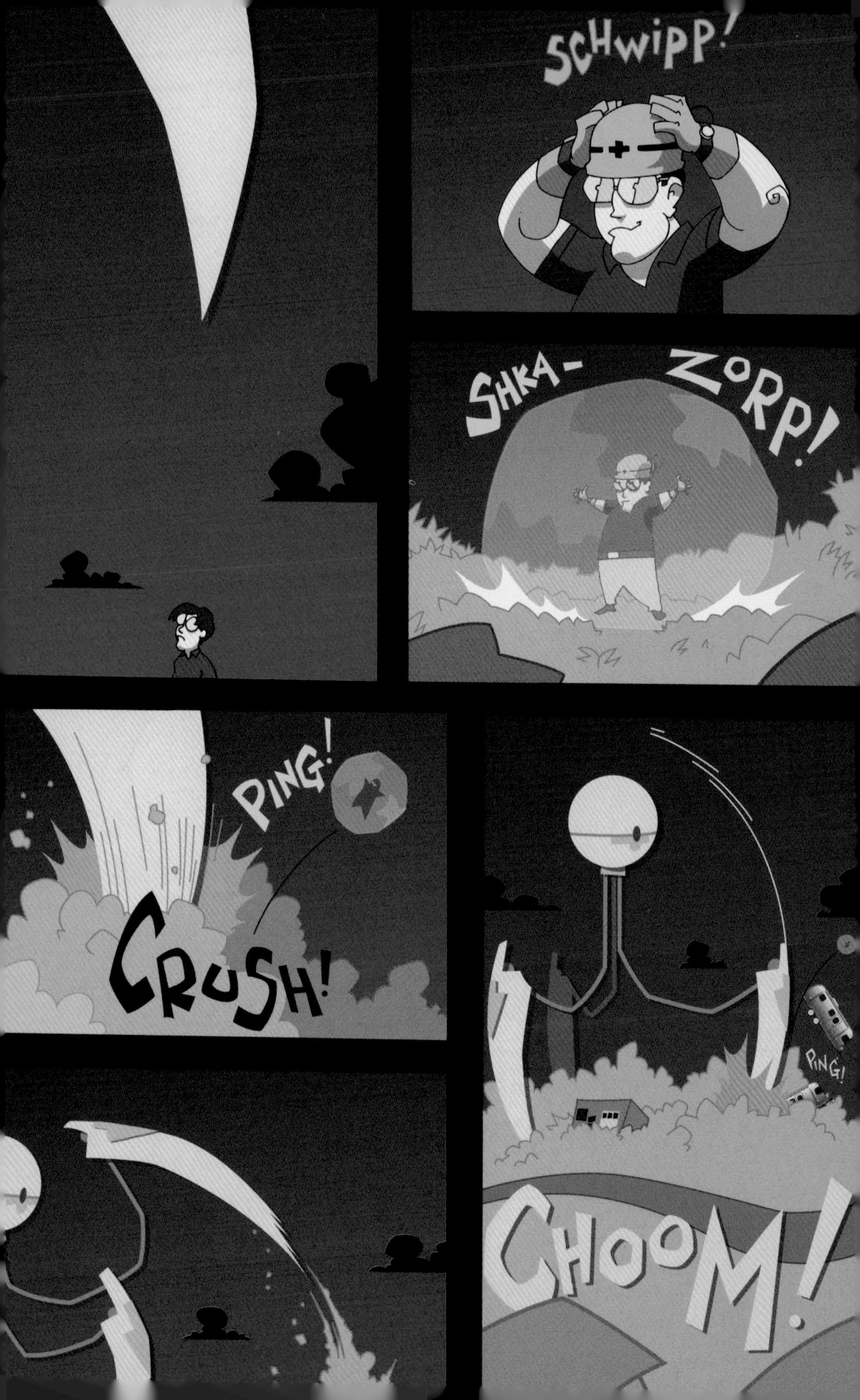
SCHWIPP!
SHKA-ZORP!
PING!
CRUSH!
PING!
CHOOM!

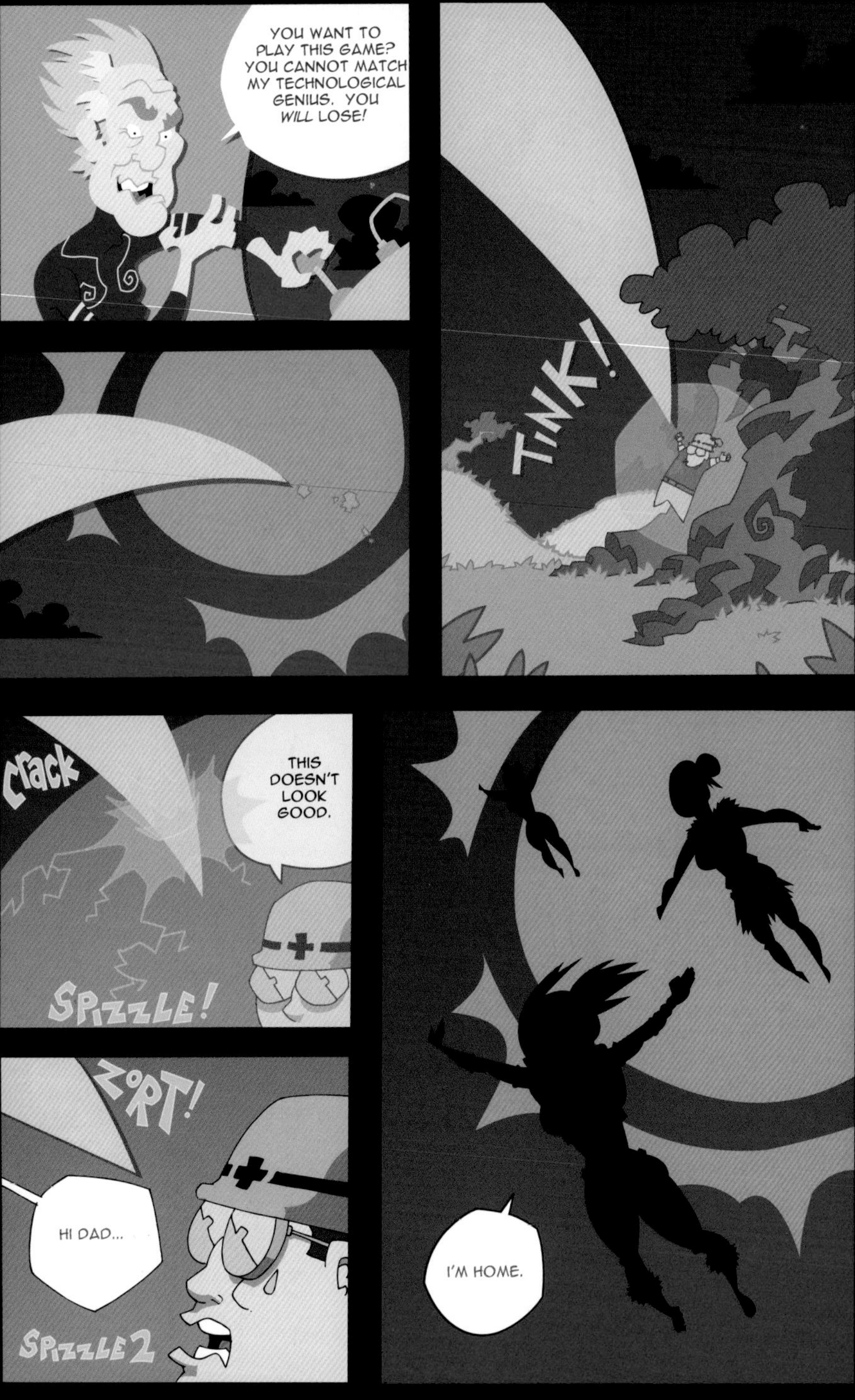

YOU WANT TO PLAY THIS GAME? YOU CANNOT MATCH MY TECHNOLOGICAL GENIUS. YOU WILL LOSE!
TINK!
crack
THIS DOESN'T LOOK GOOD.
SPIZZLE!
ZORT!
HI DAD...
SPIZZLE 2
I'M HOME.

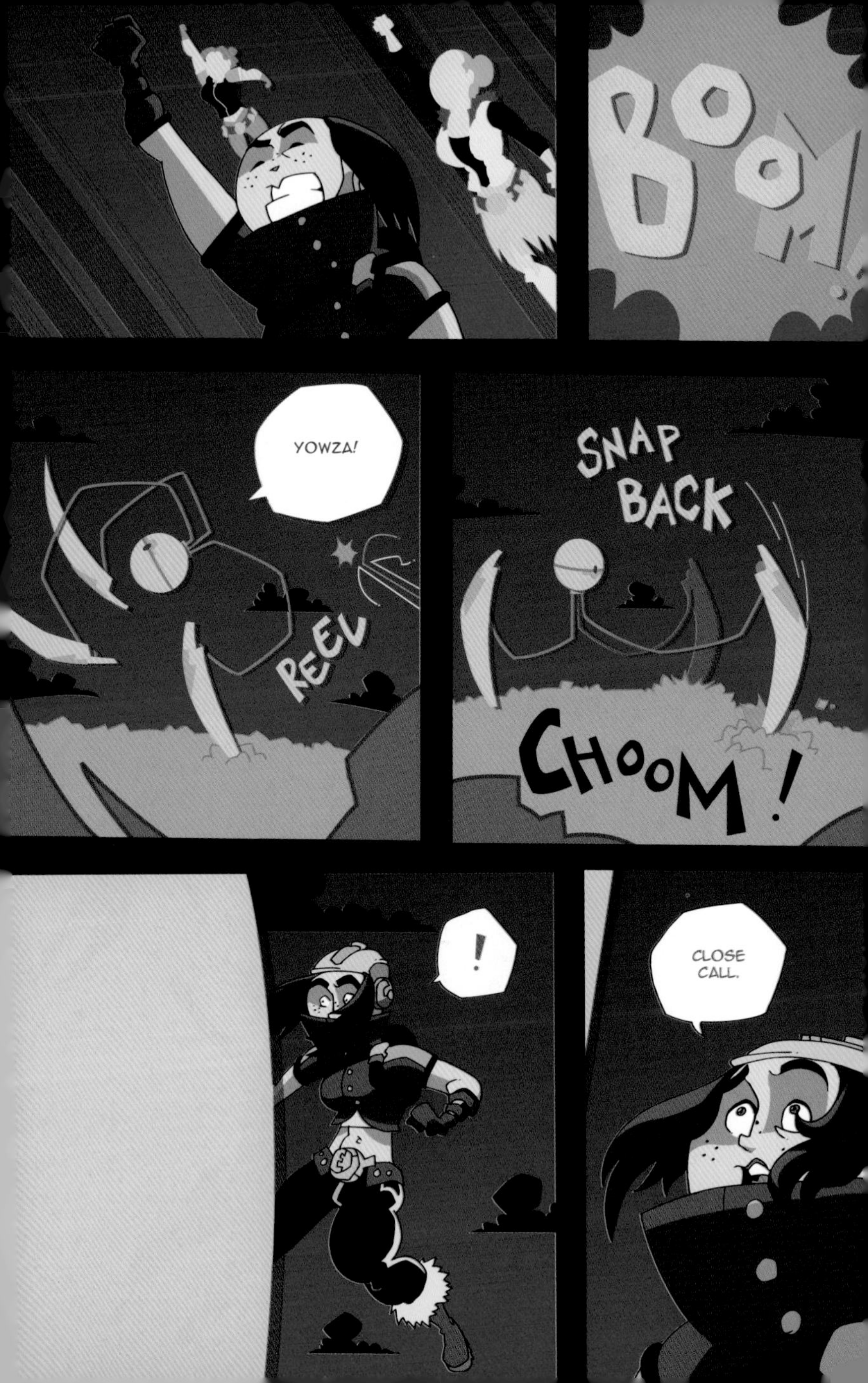
BOOM!
YOWZA!
REEL
SNAP BACK
CHOOM!
!
CLOSE CALL.

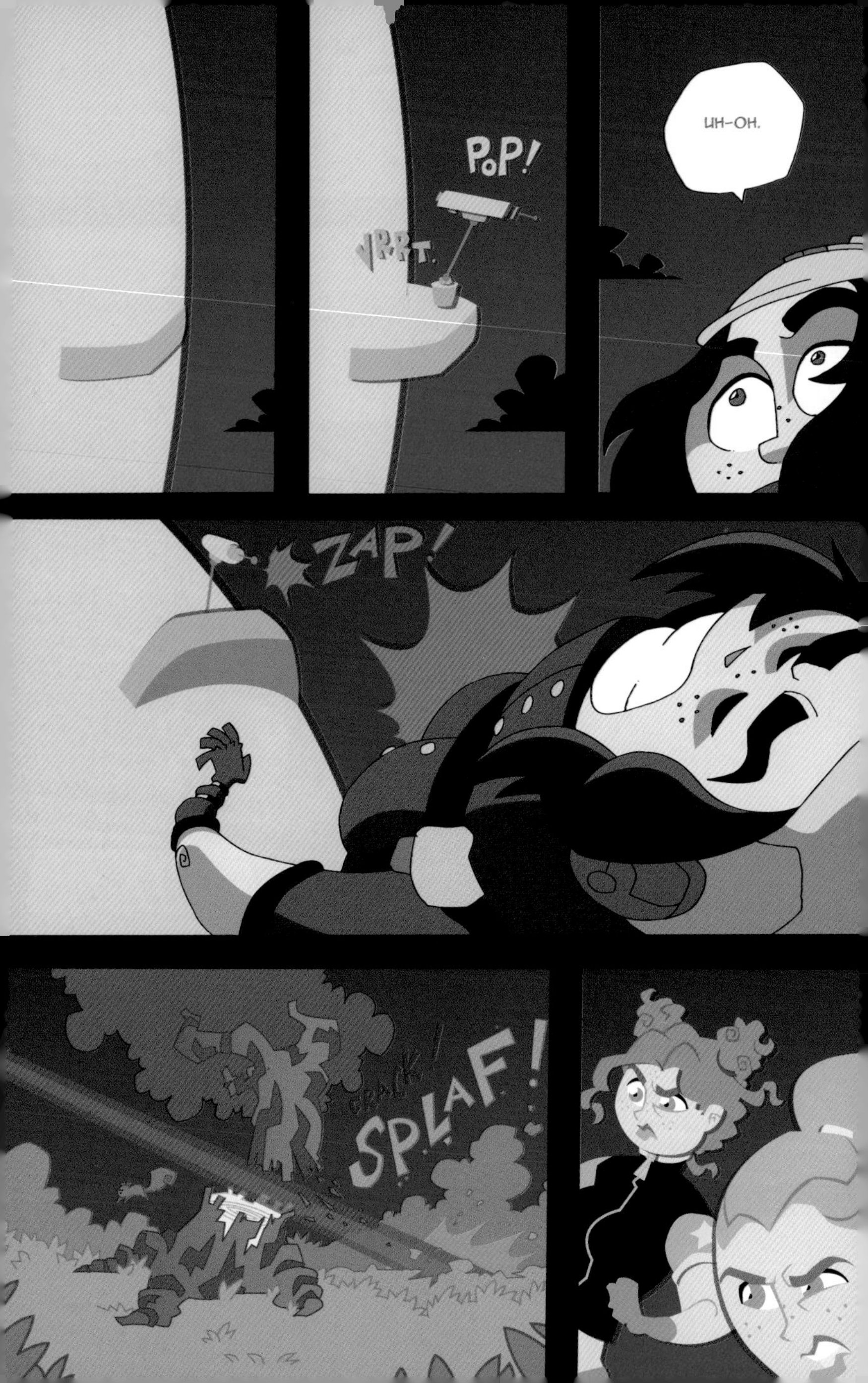
POP!
VRRT.
UH-OH.
ZAP!
SPLAF!

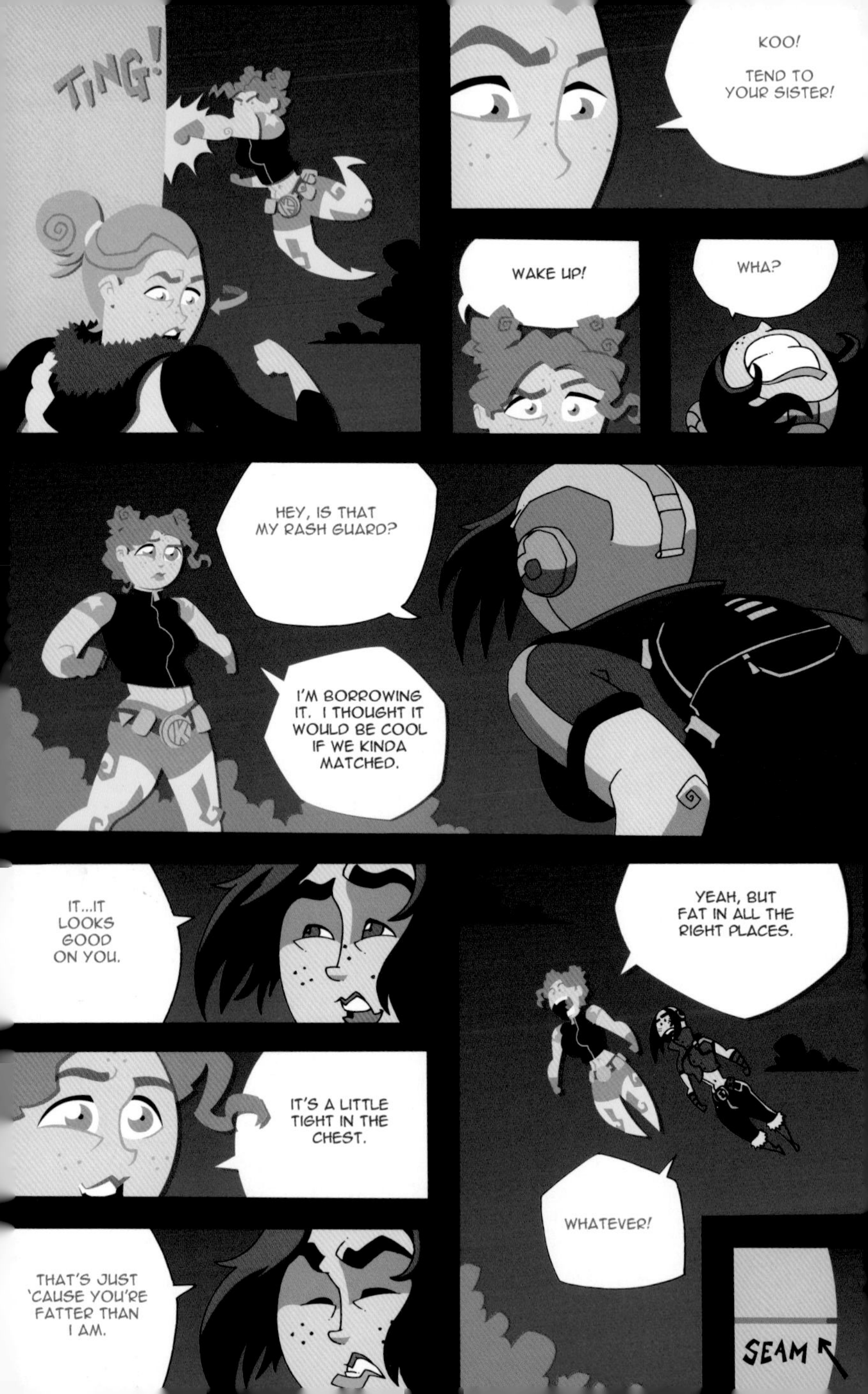
TING!
KOO! TEND TO YOUR SISTER!
WAKE UP!
WHA?
HEY, IS THAT MY RASH GUARD?
I'M BORROWING IT. I THOUGHT IT WOULD BE COOL IF WE KINDA MATCHED.
IT...IT LOOKS GOOD ON YOU.
IT'S A LITTLE TIGHT IN THE CHEST.
THAT'S JUST 'CAUSE YOU'RE FATTER THAN I AM.
YEAH, BUT FAT IN ALL THE RIGHT PLACES.
WHATEVER!
SEAM

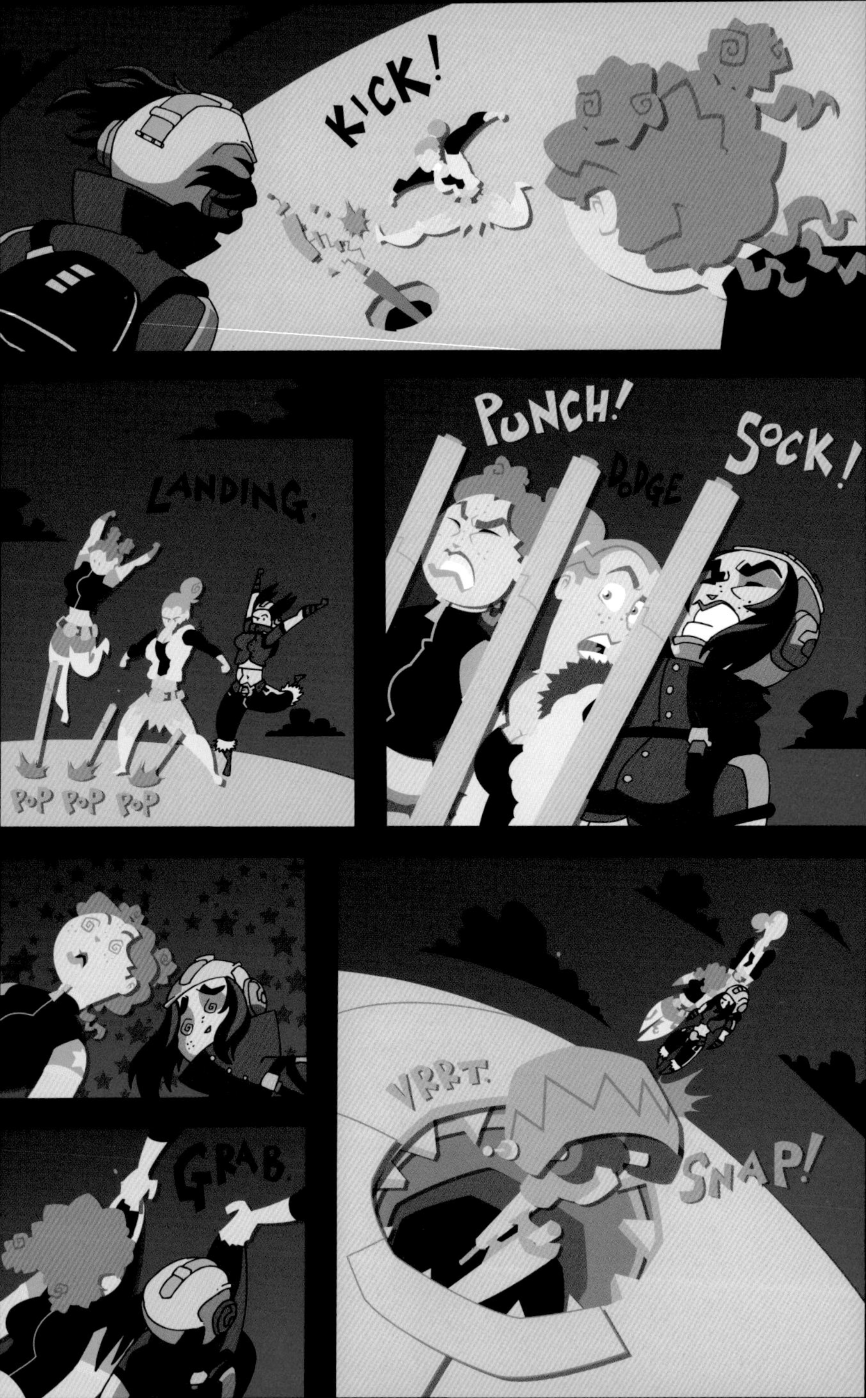
KICK!
LANDING.
POP POP POP
PUNCH!
DODGE
SOCK!
GRAB.
VRRT.
SNAP!

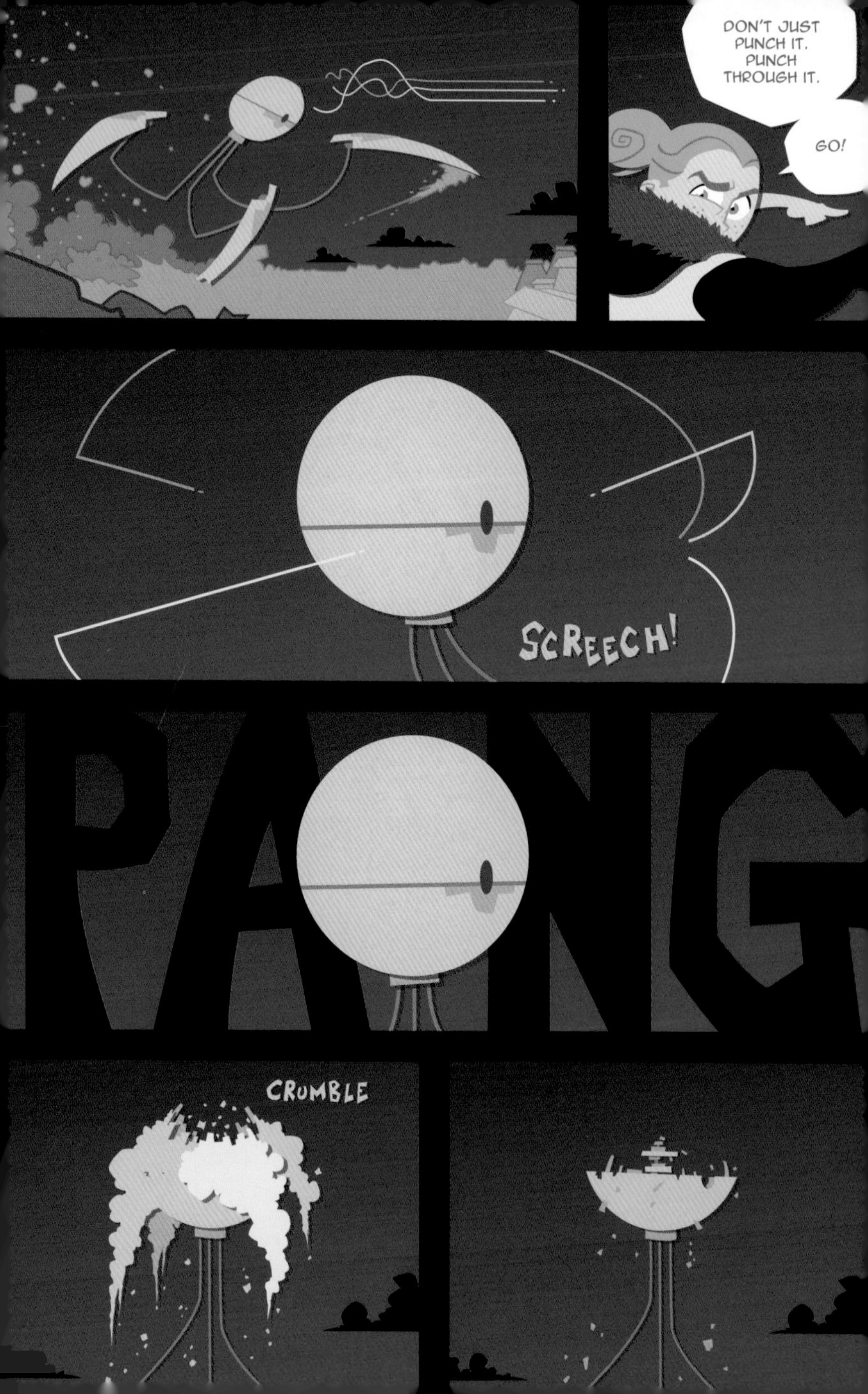
DON'T JUST PUNCH IT. PUNCH THROUGH IT.
GO!
SCREECH!
PANG
CRUMBLE

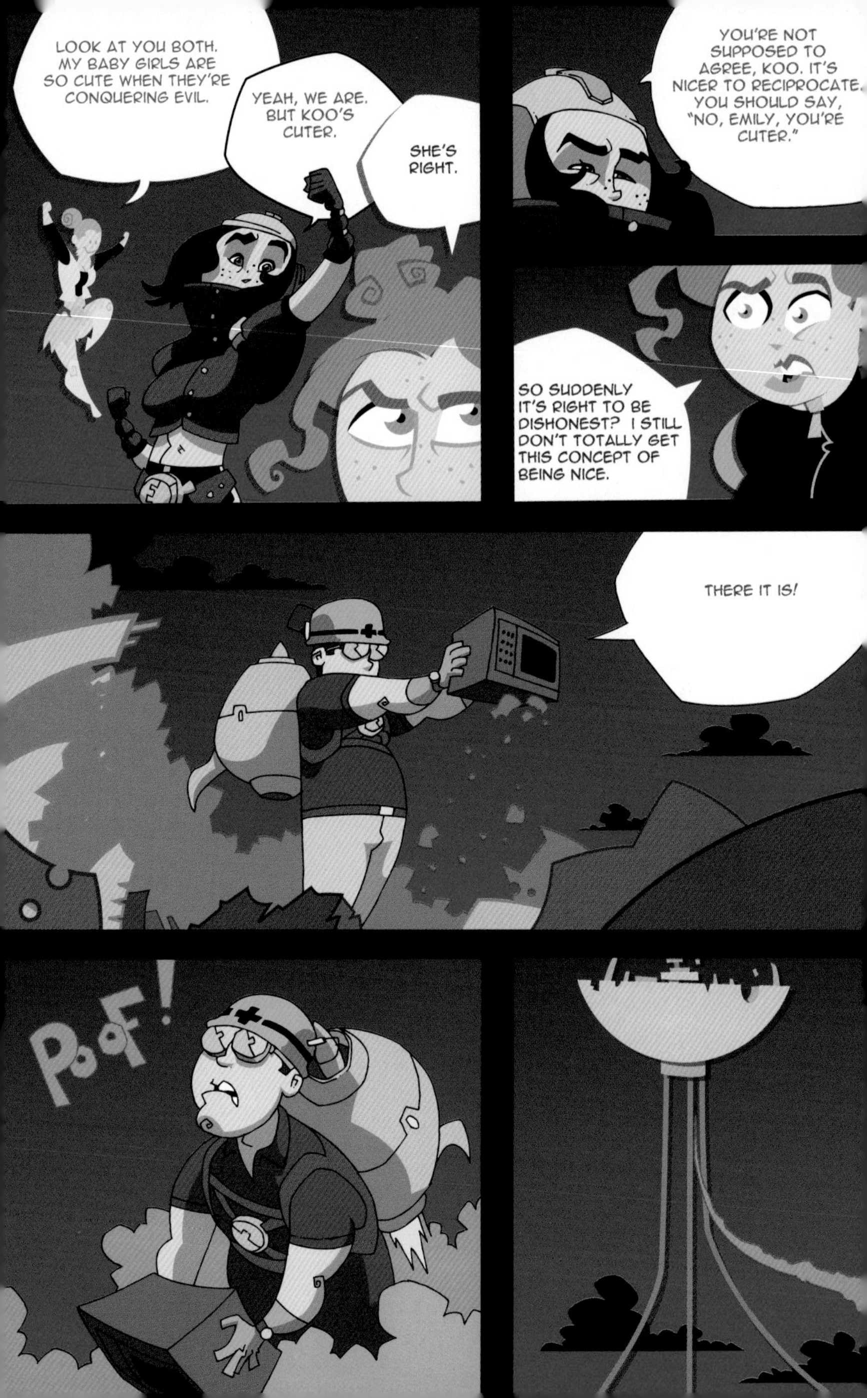
LOOK AT YOU BOTH. MY BABY GIRLS ARE SO CUTE WHEN THEY'RE CONQUERING EVIL.
YEAH, WE ARE. BUT KOO'S CUTER.
SHE'S RIGHT.
YOU'RE NOT SUPPOSED TO AGREE, KOO. IT'S NICER TO RECIPROCATE. YOU SHOULD SAY, "NO, EMILY, YOU'RE CUTER."
SO SUDDENLY IT'S RIGHT TO BE DISHONEST? I STILL DON'T TOTALLY GET THIS CONCEPT OF BEING NICE.
THERE IT IS!
POOF!

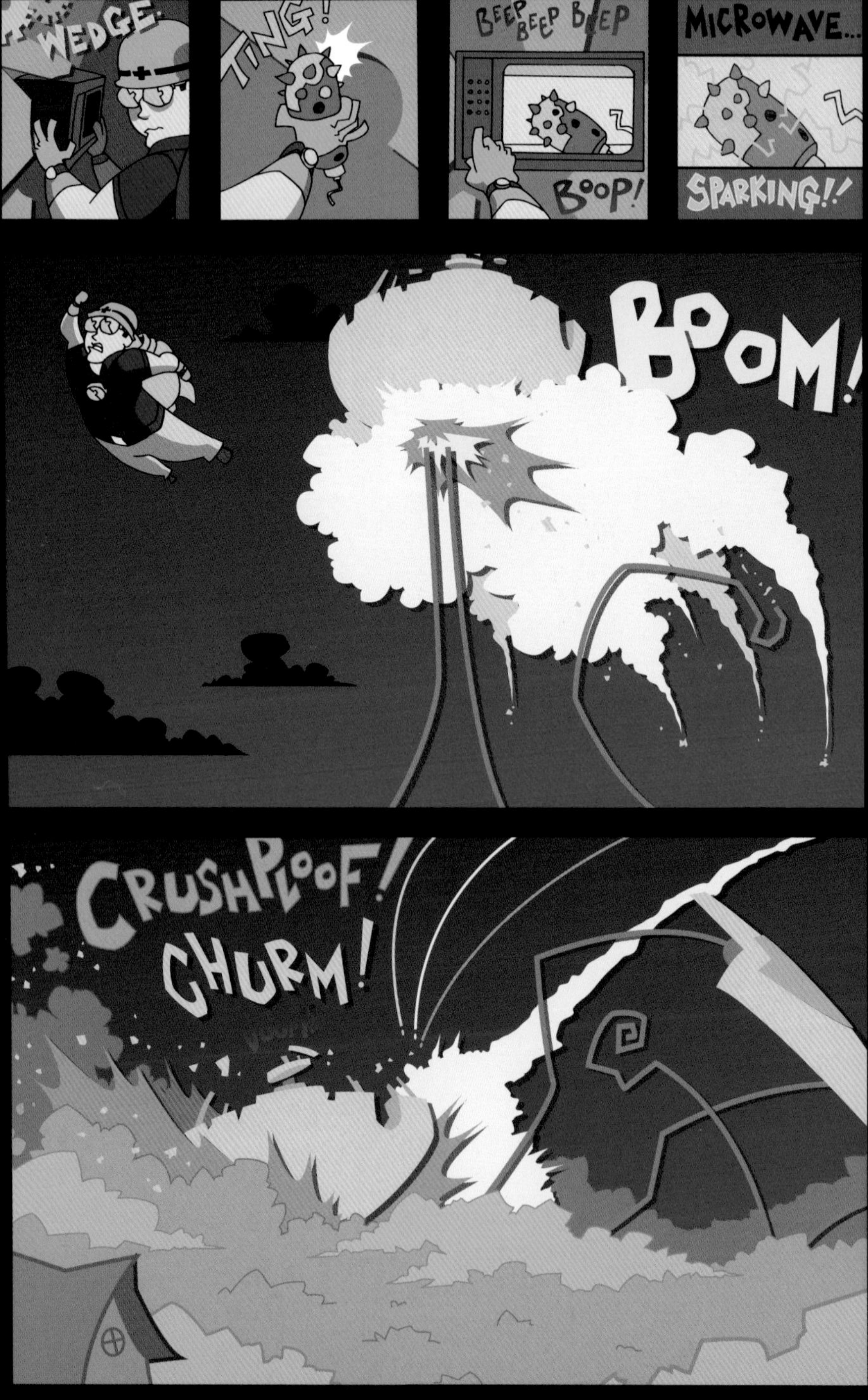
WEDGE.
TING!
BEEP BEEP BEEP
BOOP!
MICROWAVE...
SPARKING!!
BOOM!
CRUSHPLOOF!
CHURM!

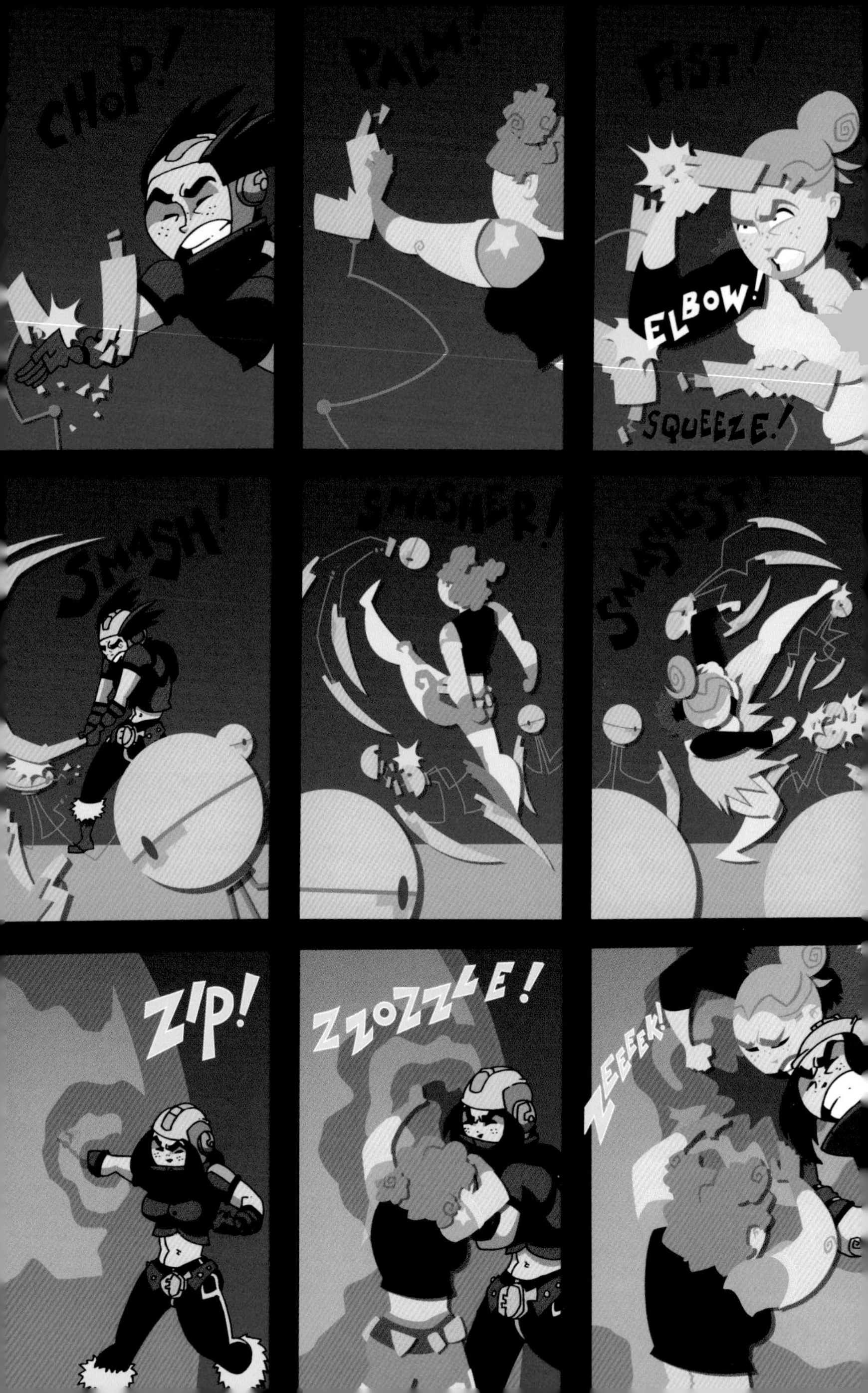
CHOP!
PALM!
FIST!
ELBOW!
SQUEEZE!
SMASH!
SMASHER!
SMASHEST!
ZIP!
ZZOZZLE!
ZEEEEK!

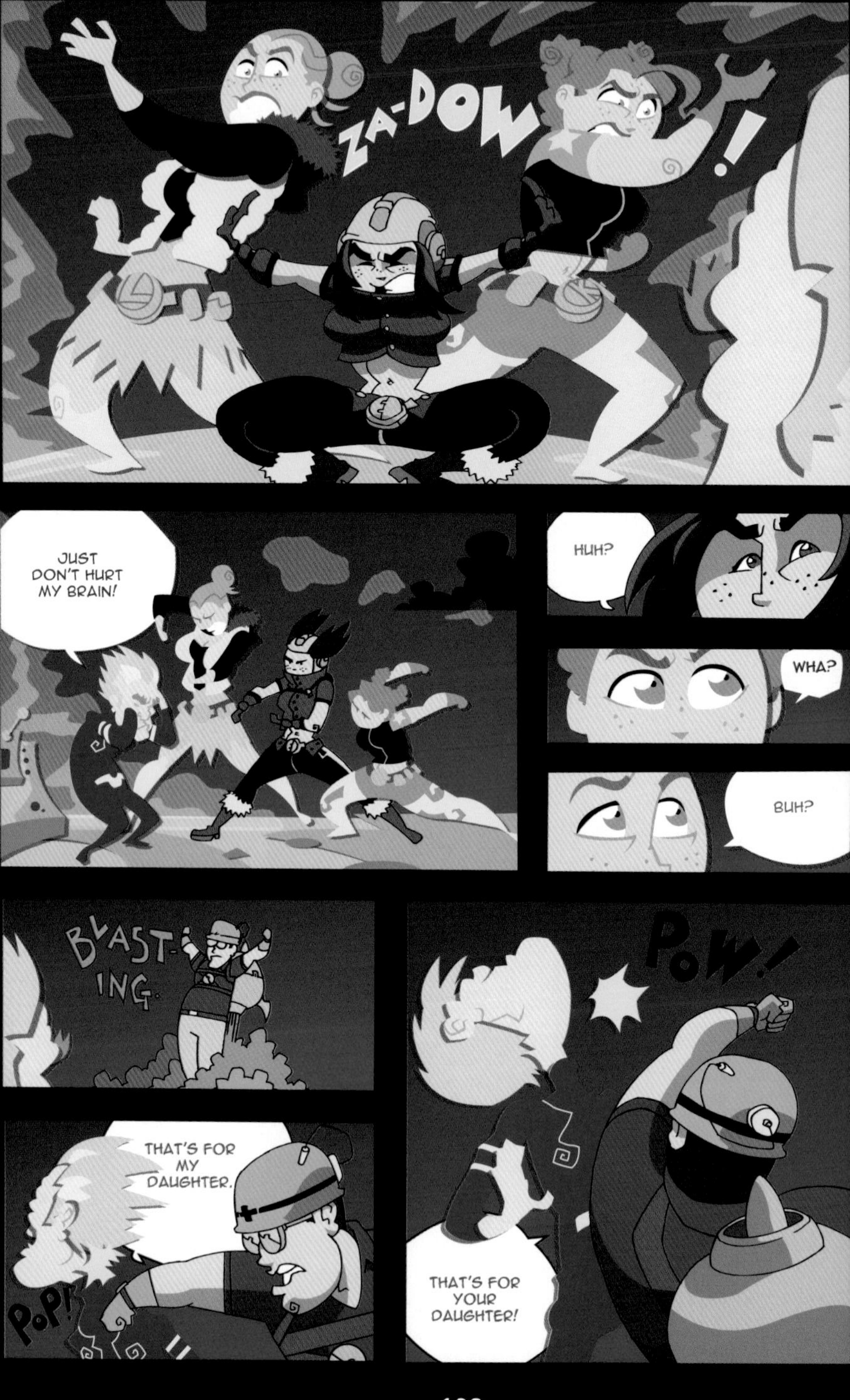
ZA-DOW!
JUST DON'T HURT MY BRAIN!
HUH?
WHA?
BUH?
BLAST-ING.
POW!
THAT'S FOR MY DAUGHTER.
POP!
THAT'S FOR YOUR DAUGHTER!

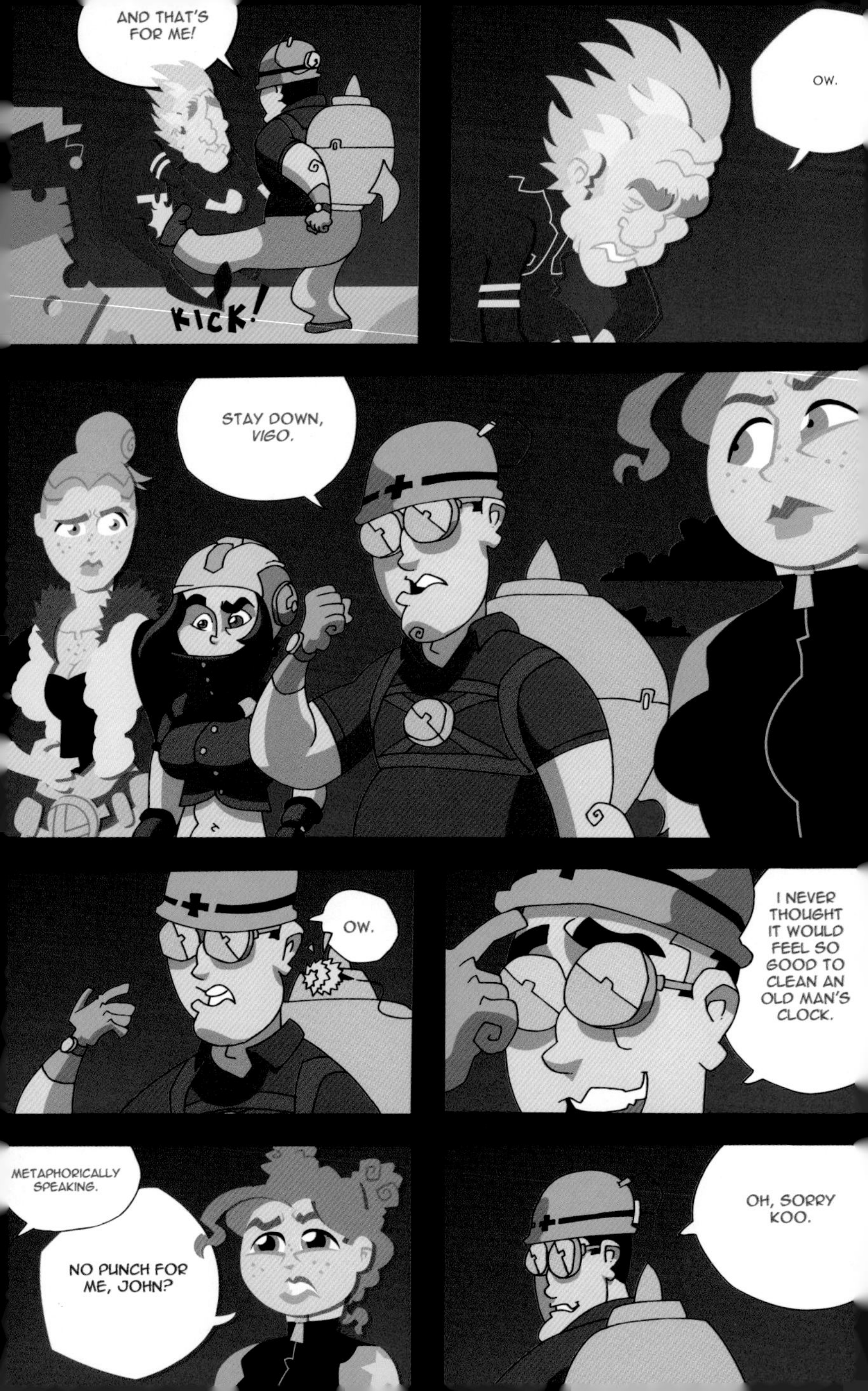
AND THAT'S FOR ME!
KICK!
OW.
STAY DOWN, VIGO.
OW.
I NEVER THOUGHT IT WOULD FEEL SO GOOD TO CLEAN AN OLD MAN'S CLOCK.
METAPHORICALLY SPEAKING.
NO PUNCH FOR ME, JOHN?
OH, SORRY KOO.

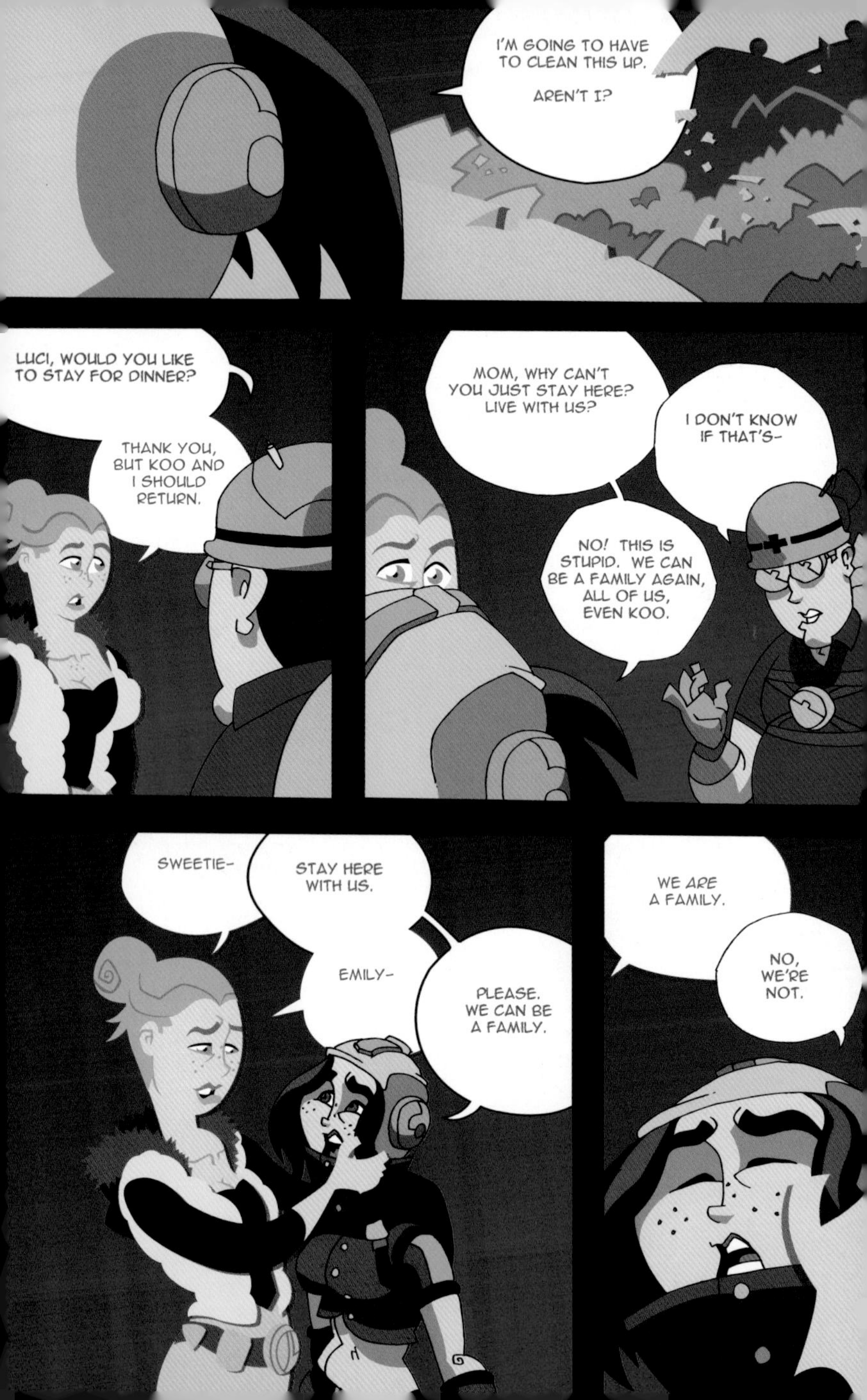
I'M GOING TO HAVE TO CLEAN THIS UP.
AREN'T I?
LUCI, WOULD YOU LIKE TO STAY FOR DINNER?
THANK YOU, BUT KOO AND I SHOULD RETURN.
MOM, WHY CAN'T YOU JUST STAY HERE? LIVE WITH US?
I DON'T KNOW IF THAT'S-
NO! THIS IS STUPID. WE CAN BE A FAMILY AGAIN, ALL OF US, EVEN KOO.
SWEETIE-
STAY HERE WITH US.
EMILY-
PLEASE. WE CAN BE A FAMILY.
WE ARE A FAMILY.
NO, WE'RE NOT.

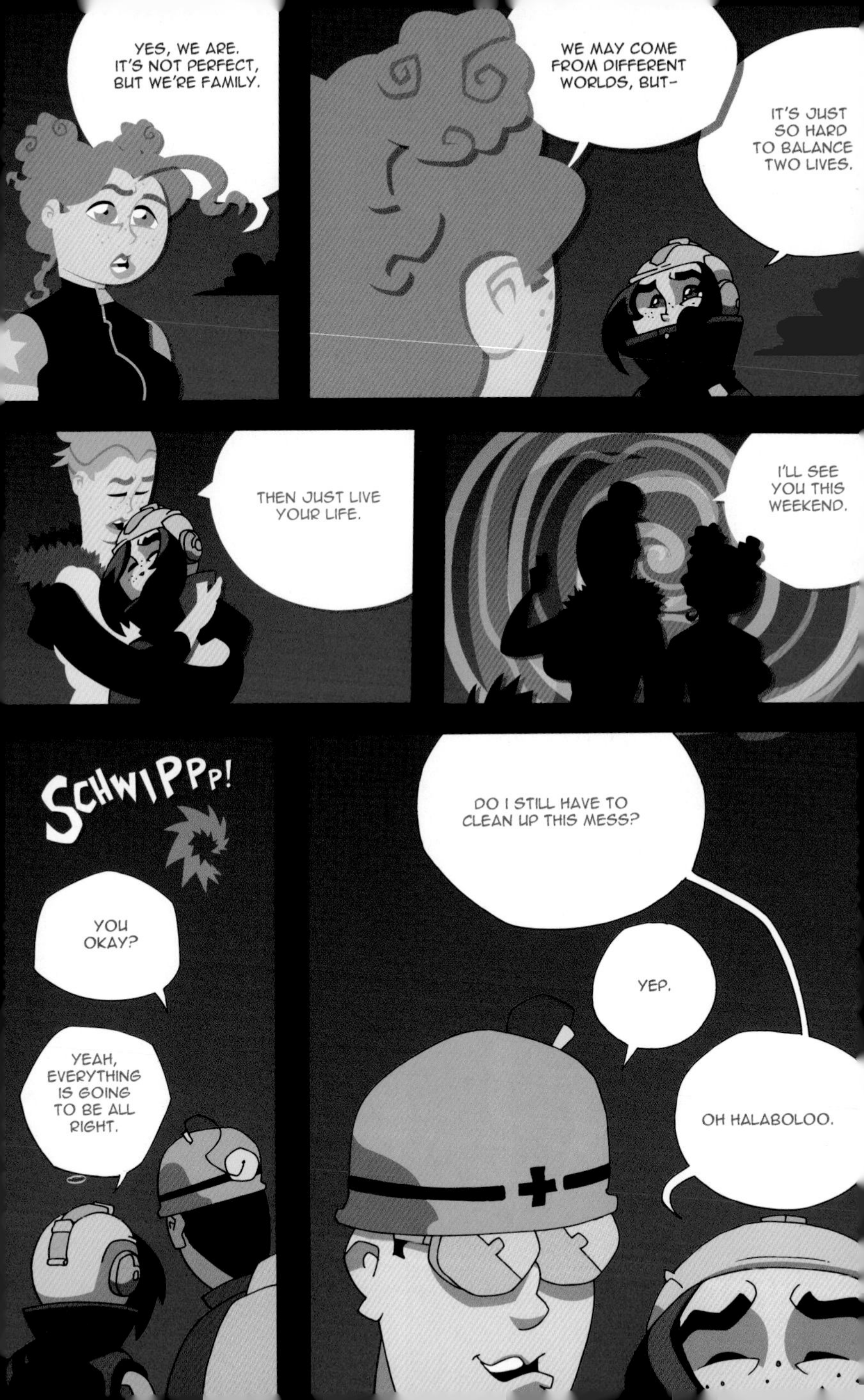
YES, WE ARE. IT'S NOT PERFECT, BUT WE'RE FAMILY.
WE MAY COME FROM DIFFERENT WORLDS, BUT-
IT'S JUST SO HARD TO BALANCE TWO LIVES.
THEN JUST LIVE YOUR LIFE.
I'LL SEE YOU THIS WEEKEND.
SCHWIPPP!
YOU OKAY?
YEAH, EVERYTHING IS GOING TO BE ALL RIGHT.
DO I STILL HAVE TO CLEAN UP THIS MESS?
YEP.
OH HALABOLOO.

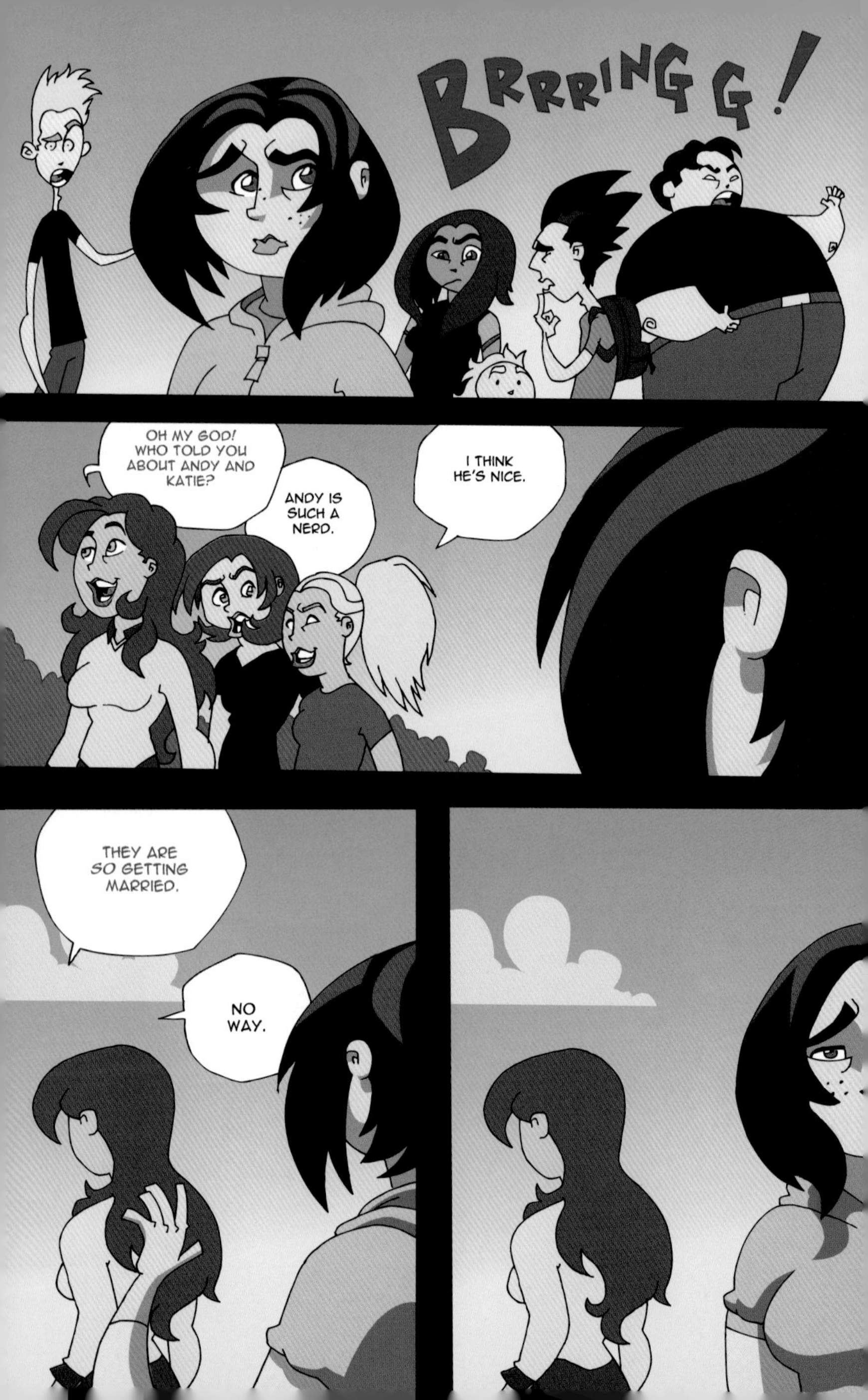
BRRRINGG!
OH MY GOD! WHO TOLD YOU ABOUT ANDY AND KATIE?
ANDY IS SUCH A NERD.
I THINK HE'S NICE.
THEY ARE SO GETTING MARRIED.
NO WAY.

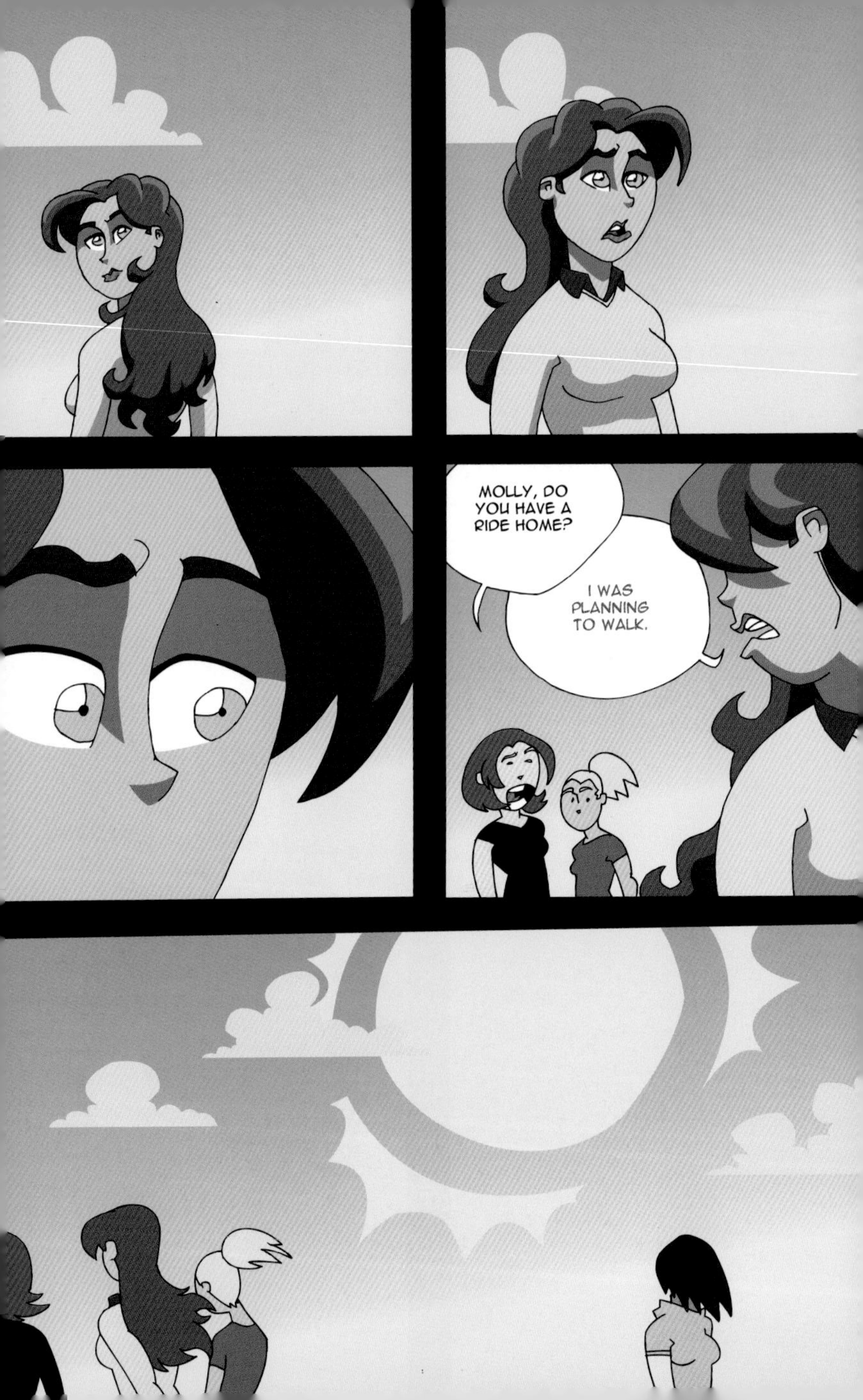
MOLLY, DO YOU HAVE A RIDE HOME?
I WAS PLANNING TO WALK.

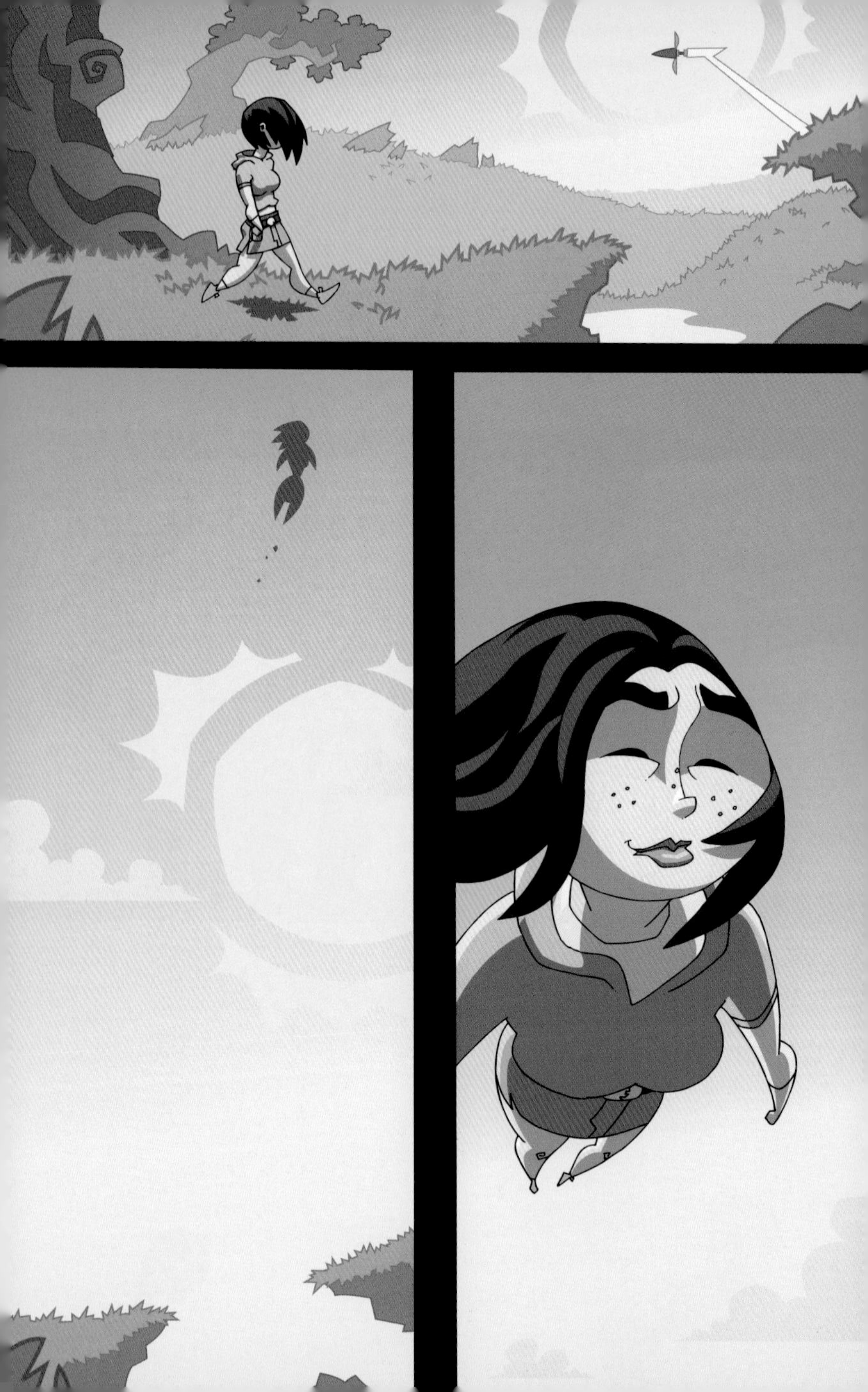

Special thanks to:
Jessie, Jim, and PJ at Viper Comics, Dave Crosland,
Jim Mahfood, Benjamin and Marlena Hall, Chad Hawks,
Ken Cursoe, Ryon Elliott, Augie Pagan, Scotty Law,
Chris Nicholas, Gary Bartos, Mark Walters, Richard Neal,
Brad Bankston, Jeremy Shorr, Keith Colvin, Mike Stover,
Sean Jackson, Steven New, Adan Gutierrez, Lisa Lanier,
Justin Rhody, Sarah Jane Semrad, and Roy Ivy

David would like to thank:
Scott Hinze and Fanboy Radio, Tom Kurzanski, Brent Schoonover,
Javier Grillo-Marxuach, Josh Howard, Wes Molebash,
Scott Zirkel, Cal Slayton, Jeff Elden, Matt Leong, Jim Lujan,
Greg Bowers, Devin Hyde, Oliver Tull, TJ Colligan, Justin Stewart,
Clay Harrison, Doug Hayes, Gian Cruz, Phillip Ginn, Derrick Fish,
Luke Hawkins, Joshua Fialkov, Les Weiler, Joe Riley, Bob Moser,
Travis Herrick, Ian Shaughnessy, Roxanne Bielskis,
Jamar Nicholas, Debbie Huey, Paul Kilpatrick, Wim Bens,
the Magnificent Seven, BenBella Books, Dallas chapter of the
Legion of Doom, my parents, my sister Lizz, and most importantly,
my beautiful wife Melissa—thank you for your support and love.

Brock would like to thank:
Mom, Dad, Jake, Sarah, Lyndy and "Brock 2" Rizy (the fambly).
Reagan Blank and the proverbial ¡Bike_Gang! The ol' Doodlebug
crew (including Kristy Millette, Mary Anne Avery and Travis
Kotzebue). Kevin Neece, Sean Estill, Jonothan Bourland,
Josh Martin, Cara, Heather, Lindsey, Jessica, Holly, and
Michelle Lee. Nick, Clayton, TJ, David and the Magnolia mob.
And most importantly, the man who first combined chocolate
and peanut butter.

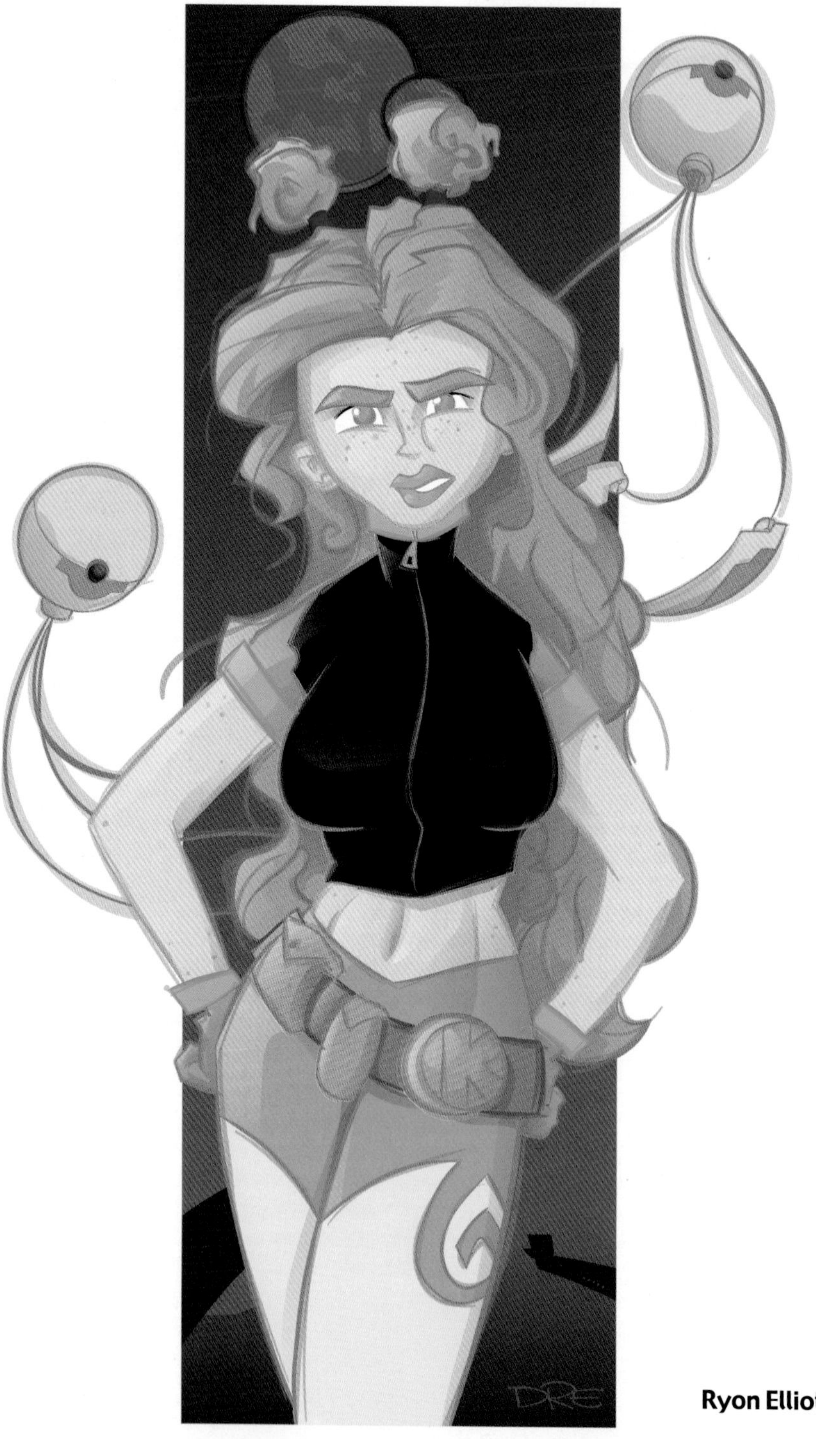
DRE

Ryon Elliott

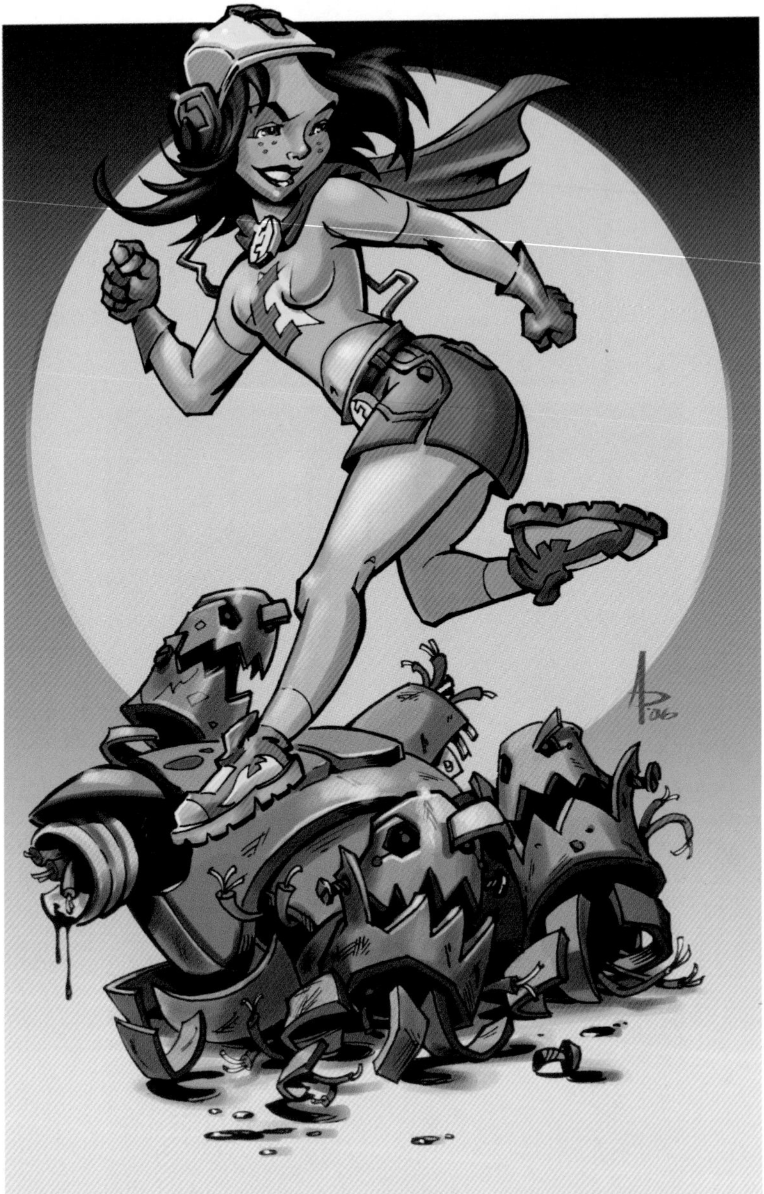

Augie Pagan

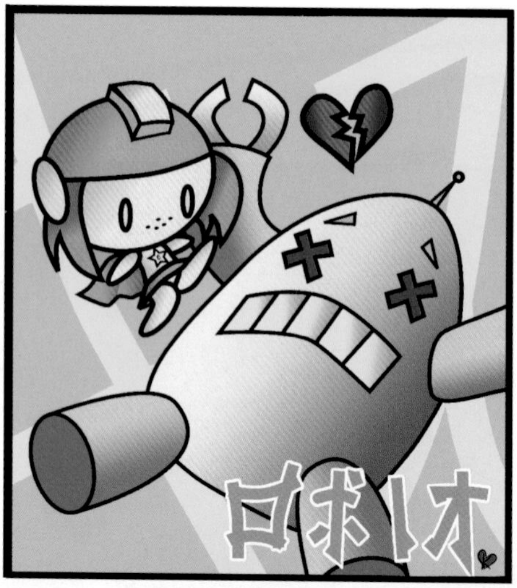
ロボト才

Ken Cursoe

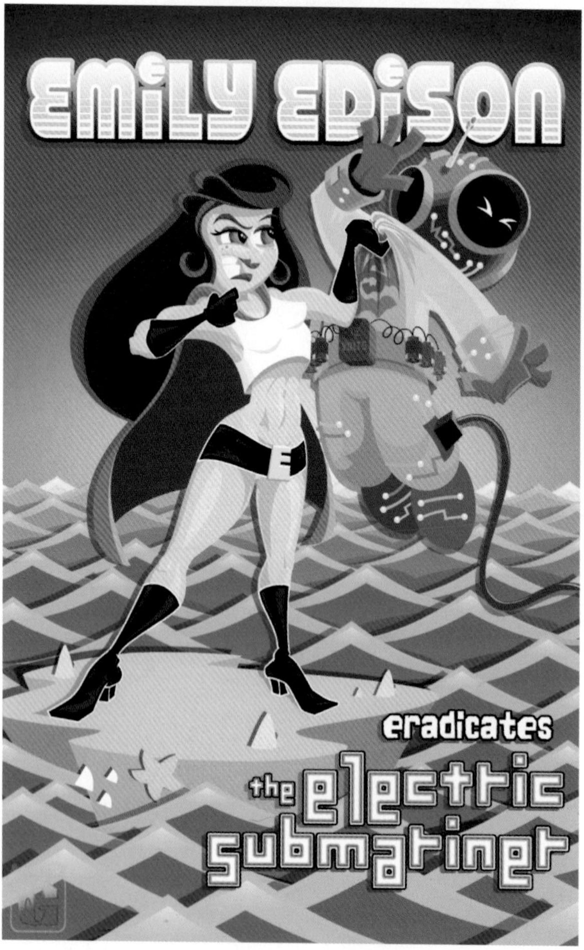
EMILY EDISON
eradicates
the electric
submariner

Chad Hawks

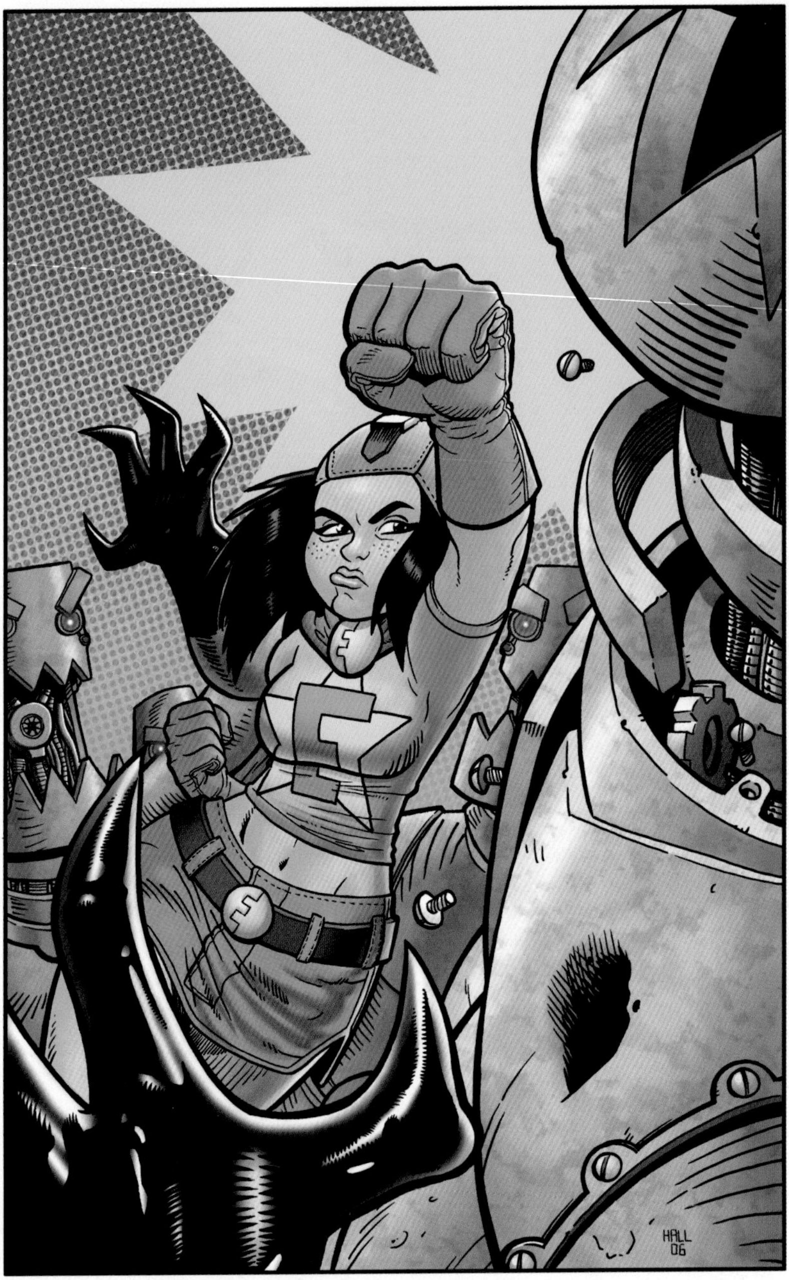
HALL
06

Benjamin Hall

David Hopkins is a comic book writer, essayist, and pop culture junkie. His first series Karma Incorporated is available from Viper Comics. David's written short stories for Dead@17: Rough Cut, Silent Forest Television Parody Special, Western Tales of Terror, and self-published a mini-comic "Some Other Day". He recently published an essay on Superman for BenBella Books. David lives in Arlington, Texas with his lovely wife and daughter. They all watch too much TV.

Brock Rizy is a cartoonist. He is known for redefining the word "chimichanga" and inventing the term "compupoo". Brock has animated, illustrated, and designed toys for sundry projects and companies. Co-author, concept designer, and storyboard artist of ¡Bike Gang!, the anthology of illustrated screenplays. Creator of Swamp Chicken and The Pyrotechnic Porno Babies. Emily Edison is Brock's first graphic novel. He "lives" in Dallas with his drawing table and Power Mac G5. Somebody better keep him away from the Oatmeal Creme Pies.

For more about Emily, visit emilyedison.com